MW01170051

ALSO BY MICHAEL MALICE

Dear Reader: The Unauthorized Autobiography of Kim Jong Il
The New Right: A Journey to the Fringe of American Politics

The
Anarchist
Handbook

The
Anarchist
Handbook

Organized by

MICHAEL MALICE

"What started the craze to kill was a lecture I heard some little time ago by Emma Goldman. She was in Cleveland and I and other Anarchists went to hear her. She set me on fire.

"Her doctrine that all rulers should be exterminated was what set me to thinking so that my head nearly split with the pain. Miss Goldman's words went right through me and when I left the lecture I had made up my mind that I would have to do something heroic for the cause I loved."

Leon Czolgosz

CONTENTS

For Eric D. Dixon

Who got there first

Chapter 1

HOCH DIE ANARCHIE!

When I was in college I took a bioethics course. Within the first couple of pages of our textbook there was an illustration charting the spectrum of relationships between morality and the law. One end was marked as legalism, the belief that the law defined what it is to be moral. The other end was labeled antinomianism, which was presented as the view that one's conscience is the arbiter of morality and that laws are of no moral relevance. I can't remember if it was the textbook or the professor, but our class discussion opened with, "Since no one believes in antinomianism, the answer is somewhere to the other side of the bar."

If an ideology had a name, the odds were quite high that someone did, in fact, believe in it. Antinomianism in ethics is anarchism in a sociopolitical context, the belief that the imposition of authority is illegitimate. In one sense, anarchism is nothing more than the declaration that "You do not speak for me." Everything else is just implementation.

It is impossible to have a radical philosophy without at first sounding like a lunatic or a moron. One of the reasons for this is that most radical philosophies are lunacy, and the rest for the most part are moronic. To proclaim earnestly that *This*, the status quo, doesn't just need tweaks or massive changes but a fundamental reorganization is an enormously high task to argue for. It's akin to discussing a friend and mentioning that he's very tall. One can perhaps push the envelope with an eight-foot-tall friend. But to claim someone is, say, twenty feet tall or apple feet tall simply wouldn't make any sense. The listener would have no frame of reference to even approximate what was meant to be said. This is what a society without the state sounds like to most people, for they have taken the legitimacy of government for granted all of their lives. An alternative is incomprehensible.

There are many common visceral arguments against anarchism: Anarchism is a bad idea because it would lead to a government. Anarchism would mean authoritarian warlords being in charge of the society. Anarchism is utopian and hasn't worked anywhere on earth—except when it has, in which case it doesn't count because a government exists somewhere and therefore made it work. Anarchism cannot work on a large scale, and anarchism cannot work on a small scale either because those areas would immediately be invaded. Inherent in this argument is that governments are, by their nature, invasive and predatory—this being the anarchist view of the nature of government.

There are already several countries on earth that don't have a military, and yes many rely on foreign governments to protect them against invasion. The argument is that these foreign governments are thereby the "real" government. But outsourcing the delivery of security is no different than outsourcing the delivery of food. If the security insurers were the "real" governments, they would be the ones giving and not taking orders. Yet all this misses the broader point: Anarchism is not a location. Anarchism is a relationship, one in which none of the parties has authority over the other.

Every nation is in an anarchist relationship with one another. If a Canadian kills an American in Mexico, there is some agreed-upon mechanism to adjudicate the situation without involving a higher authority—because there is no higher authority to invoke. The situation would be the same if one's "citizenship" were voluntary and as easy to switch as a cell-phone provider. Citizenship by geography is landline technology in a post-smartphone world.

At base level, all anarchism claims to do is to resolve one major problem in interpersonal relationships: the forceful interjection of the state. Curing cancer would make things a lot better for many people. Yes, there would be costs: oncologists would be out of work, and cancer researchers would need new subjects to explore. An anarchist world would still have murderers, and thieves, and evil men and women. It simply wouldn't put them in a position to enforce their evil on everyone else via getting elected and decreeing the law.

Curing cancer does not mean or imply curing diabetes. But neither does it mean or imply that curing cancer is "utopian" or a goal that should not be sought. As Randolph Bourne put it over a century ago, war is the health of the state—but plunder and societal conflict are not far behind when it comes to the government. It's quite easy to stump statists by asking if they would consider it anarchism if there was a system of taxes and state action in place without a police force. How would it work is beside the point. Whether this would be anarchism is the question.

If government was a useful mechanism for adjudicating disputes, lawsuits would be as common and as easily resolved as returning an item to the store or quitting one's job. If government was an effective mechanism at solving or preventing crime, crime would be as minor a political issue as fashion is. Everyone needs to feel safe in their person, just as everyone needs clothing. Yet only one is a political issue year in and year out.

So what is the alternative to the state? Private police—or none at all? The original version of anarchism, in the left-wing European tradition, is opposed to domination by one person over another and advocates for a society based on mutual aid and complete equality. The more recent version, the right-capitalists, define themselves by opposition to the state. The right-anarchists think the left-anarchists are naïve, and lack a fundamental understanding of economics. The left-anarchists think the right-anarchists aren't anarchists at all, but mere apologists for corporate control and predation. Anarchism has been both a vision of a peaceful, cooperative society—and an ideology of revolutionary terror. Since the term itself—*an*archism—is a negation, there is a great deal of disagreement on what the positive alternative would look like. The black flag comes in many colors.

On November 11, 1887, four men were hanged by the State of Illinois. They were accused of conspiring to murder because of their common bond in preaching their anarchist views, and they became martyrs for the cause. At the base of the monument erected in their memory are carved the last words of one of them, August Spies. "The day will come," he had proclaimed from the gallows, "when our silence will be more powerful than the voices you strangle today."

The Anarchist Handbook is an opportunity for all these many varied voices to speak for themselves, from across the decades. These were human beings who saw things differently from their fellow men. They fought and they loved. They lived and they died. They disagreed on much, but they all shared one vision: *Freedom*.

Chapter 2

WILLIAM GODWIN
from
Enquiry Concerning Political Justice and its Influence on Morals and Happiness
(1793)

Widely regarded as the first anarchist in modern times, the British William Godwin's Enquiry *was one of the most influential political tracts of his era. His devastating critique of social contract theory holds just as true today. As Godwin demonstrates, the social contract is one of those ideas that would come off as incoherent and deranged if one heard them for the first time as an adult. It is allegedly an unwritten "contract" that presumes both consent despite none having been given—even in the face of explicit lack of consent—and contains no specific terms (a key element of any contract). Though the social contract is often posited as the origin of a just government, no government in history has ever so much as pretended to have come about as the result of it.*

OF THE SOCIAL CONTRACT

Upon the first statement of the system of a social contract various difficulties present themselves. Who are the parties to this contract? For whom did they consent, for themselves only, or for others? For how long a time is this contract to be considered as binding? If the consent of every individual be necessary, in what manner is that consent to be given? Is it to be tacit, or declared in express terms?

Little will be gained for the cause of equality and justice if our ancestors, at the first institution of government, had a right indeed of choosing the system of regulations under which they thought proper to live, but at the same time could barter away the understandings and independence of all that came after them, to the latest posterity. But, if the contract must be renewed in each successive generation, what periods must be fixed on for that purpose? And if I be obliged to submit to the established government till my turn comes to assent to it, upon what principle is that obligation founded? Surely not upon the contract into which my father entered before I was born?

Secondly, what is the nature of the consent in consequence of which I am to be reckoned a party to the frame of any political constitution? It is usually said "that acquiescence is sufficient; and that this acquiescence is to be inferred from my living quietly under the protection of the laws." But if this be true, an end is as effectually put to all political science, all discrimination of better and worse, as by any system invented by the most slavish sycophant. Upon this hypothesis every government that is quietly submitted to is a lawful government, whether it be the usurpation of Cromwell, or the tyranny of Caligula. Acquiescence is frequently nothing more, than a choice on the part of the individual, of what he deems the least evil. In many cases it is not so much as this, since the peasant and the artisan, who form the bulk of a nation, however dissatisfied with the government of their country, seldom have it in their power to transport themselves to another. It is also to be observed upon the system of acquiescence, that it is in little agreement with the established opinions and practices of mankind. Thus what has been called the law of nations, lays least stress upon the allegiance of a foreigner settling among us, though his acquiescence is certainly most complete; while natives removing into an uninhabited region are claimed by the mother country, and removing into a neighbouring territory are punished by municipal law, if they take arms against the country in which they were born. But surely acquiescence can scarcely be construed into consent, while the individuals concerned are wholly unapprised of the authority intended to be rested upon it.[i]

Locke, the great champion of the doctrine of an original contract, has been aware of this difficulty, and therefore observes that "a tacit consent indeed obliges a man to obey the laws of any government, as long as he has any possessions, or enjoyment of any part of the dominions of that government; but nothing can make a man a member of the commonwealth, but his actually entering into it by positive engagement and express promise and compact."[iii] A singular distinction; implying upon the face of it that an acquiescence, such as has just been described is sufficient to render a man amenable to the penal regulations of society; but that his own consent is necessary to entitle him to the privileges of a citizen.

A third objection to the social contract will suggest itself, as soon as we attempt to ascertain the extent of the obligation, even supposing it to have been entered into in the most solemn manner by every member of the community. Allowing that I am called upon, at the period of my coming of age for example, to declare my assent or dissent to any system of opinions, or any code of practical institutes; for how long a period does this declaration bind me? Am I precluded from better information for the whole course of my life? And, if not for my whole life, why for a year, a week or even an hour? If my deliberate judgement, or my real sentiment, be of no avail in the case, in what sense can it be affirmed that all lawful government is founded in consent?

But the question of time is not the only difficulty. If you demand my assent to any proposition, it is necessary that the proposition should be stated simply and clearly. So numerous are the varieties of human understanding, in all cases where its independence and integrity are sufficiently preserved, that there is little chance of any two men coming to a precise agreement, about ten successive propositions that are in their own nature open to debate. What then can be more absurd, than to present to me the laws of England in fifty volumes folio, and call upon me to give an honest and uninfluenced vote upon their contents?

But the social contract, considered as the foundation of civil government, requires of me more than this. I am not only obliged to consent to all the laws that are actually upon record, but to all the laws that shall hereafter be made. It was under this view of the subject that Rousseau, in tracing the consequences of the social contract, was led to assert that "the great body of the people in whom the sovereign authority resides can neither delegate nor resign it. The essence of that authority," he adds, "is the general will; and will cannot be represented. It must either be the same or another; there is no alternative. The deputies of the people cannot be its representatives; they are merely its attorneys. The laws which the community does not ratify in person, are no laws, are nullities."[iii]

The difficulty here stated, has been endeavoured to be provided against by some late advocates for liberty, in the way of addresses of adhesion; addresses originating in the various districts and departments of a nation, and without which no regulation of constitutional importance is to be deemed valid. But this is a very superficial remedy. The addressers of course have seldom any other alternative, than that above alluded to, of indiscriminate admission or rejection. There is an infinite difference between the first deliberation, and the subsequent exercise of a negative. The former is a real power, the latter is seldom more than the shadow of a power. Not to add, that addresses are a most precarious and equivocal mode of collecting the sense of a nation. They are usually voted in a tumultuous and summary manner; they are carried along by the tide of party; and the signatures annexed to them are obtained by indirect and accidental methods, while multitudes of bystanders, unless upon some extraordinary occasion, remain ignorant of or indifferent to the transaction.

Lastly, if government be founded in the consent of the people, it can have no power over any individual by whom that consent is refused. If a tacit consent be not sufficient, still less can I be deemed to have consented to a measure upon which I put an express negative. This immediately follows from the observations of Rousseau. If the people, or the individuals of whom the people is constituted, cannot delegate their authority to a representative, neither can any individual delegate his authority to a majority, in an assembly of which he is himself a member. That must surely be a singular species of consent, the external indications of which are often to be found, in an unremitting opposition in the first instance, and compulsory subjection in the second.

---

[i] *Hume's Essays, Part II, Essay xii.*
[ii] *Treatise of Government, Book II, Chap. viii, § 119, 122.*
[iii] *'La souveraineté ne peut être représentée, par le même raison qu'elle ne peut être aliénée; elle consiste essentiellement dans la volonté générale, et la volonte ne se représente point: elle est la même, ou elle est autre; il n'y a point de milieu. Les députés du peuple ne sont donc point ses représentans, ils ne sont que ses commissaires; ils ne peuvent rien conclure définitivement. Toute loi que le peuple en personne n'a pas ratifiée, est nulle; ce n'est point une loi.' Du Contrat Social, Liv. III, Chap. XV.*

Chapter 3

MAX STIRNER
from
The Ego and His Own (1844)

Somewhat of a hipster precursor to Nietzsche—you probably haven't heard of him—Max Stirner's idiosyncratic book Der Einzige und sein Eigentum *was supposedly regarded as too crazy to bother censoring. Stirner died largely forgotten, with the only images left behind of him being a couple of drawings by Marx's comrade-in-arms Friedrich Engels. His unique, energetic text later inspired egoists and anarchists alike (though not Nietzsche, who apparently never read him), with the opening salvo of "All things are nothing to me" being a cry of proud rebellion. Stirner's reduction of purportedly morally binding concepts such as duty to mere "spooks" continues to resonate with anarchists today.*

MY POWER

Right is the *spirit of society*. If society has a *will*, this will is simply right: society exists only through right. But, as it endures only exercising a sovereignty over individuals, right is its SOVEREIGN WILL. Aristotle says justice is the advantage of society.

All existing right is—*foreign law*; some one makes me out to be in the right, "does right by me." But should I therefore be in the right if all the world made me out so? And yet what else is the right that I obtain in the State, in society, but a right of those *foreign* to me? When a blockhead makes me out in the right, I grow distrustful of my rightness; I don't like to receive it from him. But, even when a wise man makes me out in the right, I nevertheless am not in the right on that account. Whether I am in the right is completely independent of the fool's making out and of the wise man's.

All the same, we have coveted this right until now. We seek for right, and turn to the court for that purpose. To what? To a royal, a papal, a popular court, etc. Can a sultanic court declare another right than that which the sultan has ordained to be right? Can it make me out in the right if I seek for a right that does not agree with the sultan's law? Can it, for instance, concede to me high treason as a right, since it is assuredly not a right according to the sultan's mind? Can it as a court of censorship allow me the free utterance of opinion as a right, since the sultan will hear nothing of this my right? What am I seeking for in this court, then? I am seeking for sultanic right, not my right; I am seeking for—*foreign* right. As long as this foreign right harmonizes with mine, to be sure, I shall find in it the latter too.

The State does not permit pitching into each other man to man; it opposes the *duel*. Even every ordinary appeal to blows, notwithstanding that neither of the fighters calls the police to it, is punished; except when it is not an I whacking away at a you, but, say, the head of a family at the child. The family is entitled to this, and in its name the father; I as Ego am not.

The *Vossische Zeitung* presents to us the "commonwealth of right." There everything is to be decided by the judge and a *court*. It ranks the supreme court of censorship as a "court" where "right is declared." What sort of a right? The right of the censorship. To recognize the sentences of that court as right one must regard the censorship as right. But it is thought nevertheless that this court offers a protection. Yes, protection against an individual censor's error: it protects only the censorship-legislator against false interpretation of his will, at the same time making his statute, by the "sacred power of right," all the firmer against writers.

Whether I am in the right or not there is no judge but myself. Others can judge only whether they endorse my right, and whether it exists as right for them too.

12

In the meantime let us take the matter yet another way. I am to reverence sultanic law in the sultanate, popular law in republics, canon law in Catholic communities. To these laws I am to subordinate myself; I am to regard them as sacred. A "sense of right" and "law-abiding mind" of such a sort is so firmly planted in people's heads that the most revolutionary persons of our days want to subject us to a new "sacred law," the "law of society," the law of mankind, the "right of all," and the like. The right of "all" is to go before *my* right. As a right of all it would indeed be my right among the rest, since I, with the rest, am included in all; but that it is at the same time a right of others, or even of all others, does not move me to its upholding. Not as a *right of all* will I defend it, but as my right; and then every other may see to it how he shall likewise maintain it for himself. The right of all (for example, to eat) is a right of every individual. Let each keep this right unabridged for *himself*, then all exercise it spontaneously; let him not take care for all though—let him not grow zealous for it as for a right of all.

But the social reformers preach to us a "*law of society.*" There the individual becomes society's slave, and is in the right only when society *makes him out* in the right, when he lives according to society's *statutes* and so is—*loyal*. Whether I am loyal under a despotism or in a "society" *à la* Weitling, it is the same absence of right in so far as in both cases I have not my right but *foreign* right.

In consideration of right the question is always asked, "What or who gives me the right to it?" Answer: God, love, reason, nature, humanity, etc. No, only *your might*, *your* power gives you the right (your reason, therefore, may give it to you).

Communism, which assumes that men "have equal rights by nature," contradicts its own proposition until it comes to this, that men have no right at all by nature. For it is not willing to recognize, for instance, that parents have "by nature" rights as against their children, or the children as against the parents: it abolishes the family. Nature gives parents, brothers, and so on, no right at all. Altogether, this entire revolutionary or Babouvist principle rests on a religious, that is, false, view of things. Who can ask after "right" if he does not occupy the religious stand-point himself? Is not "right" a religious concept, something sacred? Why, "*equality of rights,*" as the Revolution propounded it, is only another name for "Christian equality," the "equality of the brethren," "of God's children," "of Christians"; in short, *fraternité*. Each and every inquiry after right deserves to be lashed with Schiller's words:

> Many a year I've used my nose
> To smell the onion and the rose;
> Is there any proof which shows
> That I've a right to that same nose?

When the Revolution stamped equality as a "right," it took flight into the religious domain, into the region of the sacred, of the ideal. Hence, since then, the fight for the "sacred, inalienable rights of man." Against the "eternal rights of man" the "well-earned rights of the established order" are quite naturally, and with equal right, brought to bear: right against right, where of course one is decried by the other as "wrong." This has been the *contest of rights* since the Revolution.

You want to be "in the right" as against the rest. That you cannot; as against them you remain forever "in the wrong"; for they surely would not be your opponents if they were not in "their right" too; they will always make you out "in the wrong." But, as against the right of the rest, yours is a higher, greater, *more powerful* right, is it not? No such thing! Your right is not more powerful if you are not more powerful. Have Chinese subjects a right to freedom? Just bestow it on them, and then look how far you have gone wrong in your attempt: because they do not know how to use freedom they have no right to it, or, in clearer terms, because they have not freedom they have not the right to it. Children have no right to the condition of majority because they are not of age, because they are children. Peoples that let themselves be kept in nonage have no rights to the condition of majority; if they ceased to be in nonage, then only would they have the right to be of age. This means nothing else than "What you have the *power* to be you have the *right* to." I derive all right and all warrant from *me*; I am *entitled* to everything that I have in my power. I am entitled to overthrow Zeus, Jehovah, God, if I *can*; if I cannot, then these gods will always remain in the right and in power as against me, and what I do will be to fear their right and their power in impotent "god-fearingness," to keep their commandments and believe that I do right in everything that I do according to *their* right, about as the Russian boundary-sentinels think themselves rightfully entitled to shoot dead the suspicious persons who are escaping, since they murder "by superior authority," "with right." But I am entitled by myself to murder if I myself do not forbid it to myself, if I myself do not fear murder as a "wrong." This view of things lies at the foundation of Chamisso's poem, "Das Mordtal," where the gray-haired Indian murderer compels reverence from the white man whose brethren he has murdered. The only thing I am not entitled to is what I do not do with a free cheer, that is, what I do not entitle myself to.

I decide whether it is the *right thing* in me; there is no right *outside* me. If it is right for me, it is right. Possibly this may not suffice to make it right for the rest; that is their care, not mine: let them defend themselves. And if for the whole world something were not right, but it were right for me, that is, I wanted it, then I would ask nothing about the whole world. So every one does who knows how to value *himself*, every one in the degree that he is an egoist; for might goes before right, and that—with perfect right.

Because I am "by nature" a man I have an equal right to the enjoyment of all goods, says Babeuf. Must he not also say: because I am "by nature" a first-born prince I have a right to the throne? The rights of man and the "well-earned rights" come to the same thing in the end, to wit, to *nature*, which *gives* me a right, that is, to *birth* (and, further, inheritance). "I am born as a man" is equal to "I am born as a king's son." The natural man has only a natural right (because he has only a natural power) and natural claims: he has right of birth and claims of birth. But *nature* cannot entitle me, give me capacity or might, to that to which only my act entitles me. That the king's child sets himself above other children, even this is his act, which secures to him the precedence; and that the other children approve and recognize this act is their act, which makes them worthy to be— subjects.

Whether nature gives me a right, or whether God, the people's choice, etc., does so, all of that is the same *foreign* right, a right that I do not give or take to myself.

Thus the Communists say, equal labor entitles man to equal enjoyment. Formerly the question was raised whether the "virtuous" man must not be "happy" on earth. The Jews actually drew this inference: "That it may go well with thee on earth." No, equal labor does not entitle you to it, but equal enjoyment alone entitles you to equal enjoyment. Enjoy, then you are entitled to enjoyment. But, if you have labored and let the enjoyment be taken from you, then—"it serves you right."

If you *take* the enjoyment, it is your right; if, on the contrary, you only pine for it without laying hands on it, it remains as before, a "well-earned right" of those who are privileged for enjoyment. It is *their* right, as by laying hands on it would become *your* right.

The conflict over the "right of property" wavers in vehement commotion. The Communists affirm that "the earth belongs rightfully to him who tills it, and its products to those who bring them out." I think it belongs to him who knows how to take it, or who does not let it be taken from him, does not let himself be deprived of it. If he appropriates it, then not only the earth, but the right to it too, belongs to him. This is *egoistic right*: it is right for me, therefore it is right.

Aside from this, right does have "a wax nose." The tiger that assails me is in the right, and I who strike him down am also in the right. I defend against him not my *right*, but *myself*.

As human right is always something given, it always in reality reduces to the right which men give, "concede," to each other. If the right to existence is conceded to new-born children, then they have the right; if it is not conceded to them, as was the case among the Spartans and ancient Romans, then they do not have it. For only society can give or concede it to them; they themselves cannot take it, or give it to themselves. It will be objected, the children had nevertheless "by nature" the right to exist; only the Spartans refused *recognition* to this right. But then they simply had no right to this recognition—no more than they had to recognition of their life by the wild beasts to which they were thrown.

> People talk so much about *birthright*, and complain:
> There is alas!—no mention of the rights
> That were born with us.

What sort of right, then, is there that was born with me? The right to receive an entailed estate, to inherit a throne, to enjoy a princely or noble education; or, again, because poor parents begot me, to—get free schooling, be clothed out of contributions of alms, and at last earn my bread and my herring in the coal-mines or at the loom? Are these not birthrights, rights that have come down to me from my parents through *birth*? You think—no; you think these are only rights improperly so called, it is just these rights that you aim to abolish through the *real birthright*. To give a basis for this you go back to the simplest thing and affirm that every one is by birth *equal* to another—to wit, a *man*. I will grant you that every one is born as man, hence the new-born are therein equal to each other. Why are they? Only because they do not yet show and exert themselves as anything but bare—*children of men*, naked little human beings. But thereby they are at once different from those who have already made something out of themselves, who thus are no longer bare "children of man," but—children of their own creation. The latter possesses more than bare birthrights: they have earned rights. What an antithesis, what a field of combat! The old combat of the birthrights of man and well-earned rights. Go right on appealing to your birthrights; people will not fail to oppose to you the well-earned. Both stand on the "ground of right"; for each of the two has a "right" against the other, the one the birthright of natural right, the other the earned or "well-earned" right.

If you remain on the ground of right, you remain in—*Rechthaberei*. The other cannot give you your right; he cannot "mete out right" to you. He who has might has—right; if you have not the former, neither have you the latter. Is this wisdom so hard to attain? Just look at the mighty and their doings! We are talking here only of China and Japan, of course. Just try it once, you Chinese and Japanese, to make them out in the wrong, and learn by experience how they throw you into jail. (Only do not confuse with this the "well-meaning counsels" which—in China and Japan—are permitted, because they do not hinder the mighty one, but possibly *help him on*.) For him who should want to make them out in the wrong there would stand open only one way thereto, that of might. If he deprives them of their might, then he has really made them out in the wrong, deprived them of their right; in any other case he can do nothing but clench his little fist in his pocket, or fall a victim as an obtrusive fool.

In short, if you Chinese or Japanese did not ask after right, and in particular if you did not ask after the rights "that were born with you," then you would not need to ask at all after the well-earned rights either.

You start back in fright before others, because you think you see beside them the *ghost of right*, which, as in the Homeric combats, seems to fight as a goddess at their side, helping them. What do you do? Do you throw the spear? No, you creep around to gain the spook over to yourselves, that it may fight on your side: you woo for the ghost's favor. Another would simply ask thus: Do I will what my opponent wills? "No!" Now then, there may fight for him a thousand devils or gods, I go at him all the same!

The "commonwealth of right," as the *Vossische Zeitung* among others stands for it, asks that office-holders be removable only by the *judge*, not by the *administration*. Vain illusion! If it were settled by law that an office-holder who is once seen drunken shall lose his office, then the judges would have to condemn him on the word of the witnesses. In short, the law-giver would only have to state precisely all the possible grounds which entail the loss of office, however laughable they might be (that is, he who laughs in his superiors' faces, who does not go to church every Sunday, who does not take the communion every four weeks, who runs in debt, who has disreputable associates, who shows no determination, etc., shall be removed. These things the law-giver might take it into his head to prescribe for a court of honour); then the judge would solely have to investigate whether the accused had "become guilty" of those "offences," and, on presentation of the proof, pronounce sentence of removal against him "in the name of the law."

The judge is lost when he ceases to be *mechanical*, when he "is forsaken by the rules of evidence." Then he no longer has anything but an opinion like everybody else; and, if he decides according to this *opinion*, his action is *no longer an official action*. As judge he must decide only according to the law. Commend me rather to the old French parliaments, which wanted to examine for themselves what was to be matters of right, and to register it only after their own approval. They at least judged according to a right of their own, and were not willing to give themselves up to be machines of the lawgiver, although as judges they must, to be sure, become their own machines.

It is said that punishment is the criminal's right. But impunity is just as much his right. If his undertaking succeeds, it serves him right, and, if it does not succeed, it likewise serves him right. You make your bed and lie in it. If some one goes foolhardily into dangers and perishes in them, we are apt to say, "It serves him right; he would have it so." But, if he conquered the dangers, if his *might* was victorious, then he would be in the *right* too. If a child plays with the knife and gets cut, it is served right; but, if it doesn't get cut, it is served right too. Hence right befalls the criminal, doubtless, when he suffers what he risked; why, what did he risk it for, since he knew the possible consequences? But the punishment that we decree against him is only our right, not his. Our right reacts against his, and he is—"in the wrong at last" because—we get the upper hand.

***

But what is right, what is matter of right in a society, is voiced too—in the *law*.

Whatever the law may be, it must be respected by the—loyal citizen. Thus the law-abiding mind of Old England is eulogized. To this that Euripidean sentiment (Orestes, 418) entirely corresponds: "We serve the gods, whatever the gods are." *Law as such, God as such*, thus far we are today.

People are at pains to distinguish *law* from arbitrary *orders*, from an ordinance: the former comes from a duly entitled authority. But a law over human action (ethical law, State law, etc.) is always a *declaration of will*, and so an order. Yes, even if I myself gave myself the law, it would yet be only my order, to which in the next moment I can refuse obedience. One may well enough declare what he will put up with, and so deprecate the opposite of the law, making known that in the contrary case he will treat the transgressor as his enemy; but no one has any business to command *my* actions, to say what course I shall pursue and set up a code to govern it. I must put up with it that he treats me as his *enemy*, but never that he makes free with me as his *creature*, and that he makes *his* reason, or even unreason, my plumb-line.

States last only so long as there is a ruling will and this *ruling will* is looked upon as tantamount to the own will. The lord's will is—law. What do your laws amount to if no one obeys them? What your orders, if nobody lets himself be ordered? The State cannot forbear the claim to determine the individual's will, to speculate and count on this. For the State it is indispensable that nobody have an *own will*; if one had, the State would have to exclude (lock up, banish, etc.) this one; if all had, they would do away with the State. The State is not thinkable without lordship and servitude (subjection); for the State must will to be the lord of all that it embraces, and this will is called the "will of the State."

He who, to hold his own, must count on the absence of will in others is a thing made by these others, as the master is a thing made by the servant. If submissiveness ceased, it would be over with all lordship.

The *own will* of Me is the State's destroyer; it is therefore branded by the State as "self-will." Own will and the State are powers in deadly hostility, between which no "eternal peace" is possible. As long as the State asserts itself, it represents own will, its ever-hostile opponent, as unreasonable, evil; and the latter lets itself be talked into believing this—indeed, it really is such, for no more reason than this, that it still lets itself be talked into such belief: it has not yet come to itself and to the consciousness of its dignity; hence it is still incomplete, still amenable to fine words.

Every State is a *despotism*, be the despot one or many, or (as one is likely to imagine about a republic) if all be lords, that is, despotize one over another. For this is the case when the law given at any time, the expressed volition of (it may be) a popular assembly, is thenceforth to be *law* for the individual, to which *obedience is due* from him or toward which he has the *duty* of obedience. If one were even to conceive the case that every individual in the people had expressed the same will, and hereby a complete "collective will" had come into being, the matter would still remain the same. Would I not be bound today and henceforth to my will of yesterday? My will would in this case be *frozen*. Wretched *stability*! My creature—to wit, a particular expression of will—would have become my commander. But I in my will, I the creator, should be hindered in my flow and my dissolution. Because I was a fool yesterday I must remain such my life long. So in the State-life I am at best—I might just as well say, at worst—a bondman of myself. Because I was a willer yesterday, I am today without will: yesterday voluntary, today involuntary.

How change it? Only be recognizing no *duty*, not *binding* myself nor letting myself be bound. If I have no duty, then I know no law either.

"But they will bind me!" My will nobody can bind, and my disinclination remains free.

"Why, everything must go topsy-turvy if every one could do what he would!" Well, who says that every one can do everything? What are you there for, pray, you who do not need to put up with everything? Defend yourself, and no one will do anything to you! He who would break your will has to do with you, and is your *enemy*. Deal with him as such. If there stand behind you for your protection some millions more, then you are an imposing power and will have an easy victory. But, even if as a power you overawe your opponent, still you are not on that account a hallowed authority to him, unless he be a simpleton. He does not owe you respect and regard, even though he will have to consider your might.

We are accustomed to classify States according to the different ways in which "the supreme might" is distributed. If an individual has it—monarchy; if all have it—democracy; etc. Supreme might then! Might against whom? Against the individual and his "self-will." The State practices "violence," the individual must not do so. The State's behavior is violence, and it calls its violence "law"; that of the individual, "crime." Crime, then—so the individual's violence is called; and only by crime does he overcome the State's violence when he thinks that the State is not above him, but he is above the State.

Now, if I wanted to act ridiculously, I might, as a well-meaning person, admonish you not to make laws which impair my self-development, self-activity, self-creation. I do not give this advice. For, if you should follow it, you would be unwise, and I should have been cheated of my entire profit. I request nothing at all from you; for, whatever I might demand, you would still be dictatorial law-givers, and must be so, because a raven cannot sing, nor a robber live without robbery. Rather do I ask those who would be egoists what they think the more egoistic—to let laws be given them by you, and to respect those that are given, or to practice *refractoriness*, yes, complete disobedience. Good-hearted people think the laws ought to prescribe only what is accepted in the people's feeling as right and proper. But what concern is it of mine what is accepted in the nation and by the nation? The nation will perhaps be against the blasphemer; therefore a law against blasphemy. Am I not to blaspheme on that account? Is this law to be more than an "order" to me? I put the question.

Solely from the principle that all *right* and all *authority* belong to the *collectivity of the people* do all forms of government arise. For none of them lacks this appeal to the collectivity, and the despot, as well as the president or any aristocracy, acts and commands "in the name of the State." They are in possession of the "authority of the State," and it is perfectly indifferent whether, were this possible, the people as a *collectivity* (all individuals) exercise this State–*authority*, or whether it is only the representatives of this collectivity, be there many of them as in aristocracies or one as in monarchies. Always the collectivity is above the individual, and has a power which is called *legitimate*, which is law.

Over against the sacredness of the State, the individual is only a vessel of dishonor, in which "exuberance, malevolence, mania for ridicule and slander, frivolity," are left as soon as he does not deem that object of veneration, the State, to be worthy of recognition. The spiritual *haughtiness* of the servants and subjects of the State has fine penalties against unspiritual "exuberance."

When the government designates as punishable all play of mind *against* the State, the moderate liberals come and opine that fun, satire, wit, humor, must have free play anyhow, and *genius* must enjoy freedom. So not the *individual man* indeed, but still *genius*, is to be free. Here the State, or in its name the government, says with perfect right: He who is not for me is against me. Fun, wit, etc.—in short, the turning of State affairs into a comedy—have undermined States from of old: they are not "innocent." And, further, what boundaries are to be drawn between guilty and innocent wit? At this question the moderates fall into great perplexity, and everything reduces itself to the prayer that the State (government) would please not be so *sensitive*, so *ticklish*; that it would not immediately scent malevolence in "harmless" things, and would in general be a little "more tolerant." Exaggerated sensitiveness is certainly a weakness, its avoidance may be praiseworthy virtue; but in time of war one cannot be sparing, and what may be allowed under peaceable circumstances ceases to be permitted as soon as a state of siege is declared. Because the well-meaning liberals feel this plainly, they hasten to declare that, considering "the devotion of the people," there is assuredly no danger to be feared. But the government will be wiser, and not let itself be talked into believing anything of that sort. It knows too well how people stuff one with fine words, and will not let itself be satisfied with the Barmecide dish.

But they are bound to have their play-ground, for they are children, you know, and cannot be so staid as old folks; boys will be boys. Only for this play-ground, only for a few hours of jolly running about, they bargain. They ask only that the State should not, like a splenetic papa, be too cross. It should permit some Processions of the Ass and plays of fools, as the church allowed them in the Middle Ages. But the times when it could grant this without danger are past. Children that now once come *into the open*, and live through an hour without the rod of discipline, are no longer willing to go into the *cell*. For the open is now no longer a *supplement* to the cell, no longer a refreshing *recreation*, but its opposite, an *aut—aut*. In short, the State must either no longer put up with anything, or put up with everything and perish; it must be either sensitive through and through, or, like a dead man, insensitive. Tolerance is done with. If the State but gives a finger, they take the whole hand at once. There can be no more "jesting," and all jest, such as fun, wit, humor, becomes bitter earnest.

The clamor of the Liberals for freedom of the press runs counter to their own principle, their proper *will*. They will what they *do not will*; they wish, they would like. Hence it is too that they fall away so easily when once so-called freedom of the press appears; then they would like censorship. Quite naturally. The State is sacred even to them; likewise morals. They behave toward it only as ill-bred brats, as tricky children who seek to utilize the weaknesses of their parents. Papa State is to permit them to say many things that do not please him, but papa has the right, by a stern look, to blue-pencil their impertinent gabble. If they recognize in him their papa, they must in his presence put up with the censorship of speech, like every child.

***

If you let yourself be made out in the right by another, you must no less let yourself be made out in the wrong by him; if justification and reward come to you from him, expect also his arraignment and punishment. Alongside right goes wrong, alongside legality *crime*. What are *you?*—*You* are a—*criminal!*

"The criminal is in the utmost degree the State's own crime!" says Bettina. One may let this sentiment pass, even if Bettina herself does not understand it exactly so. For in the State the unbridled I—I, as I belong to myself alone—cannot come to my fulfilment and realization. Every ego is from birth a criminal to begin with against the people, the State. Hence it is that it does really keep watch over all; it sees in each one an—egoist, and it is afraid of the egoist. It presumes the worst about each one, and takes care, police-care, that "no harm happens to the State," *ne quid respublica detrimenti capiat*. The unbridled ego—and this we originally are, and in our secret inward parts we remain so always—is the never-ceasing criminal in the State.

The man whom his boldness, his will, his inconsiderateness and fearlessness lead is surrounded with spies by the State, by the people. I say, by the people! The people (think it something wonderful, you good-hearted folks, what you have in the people)—the people is full of police sentiments through and through.—Only he who renounces his ego, who practices "self-renunciation," is acceptable to the people.

In the book cited Bettina is throughout good-natured enough to regard the State as only sick, and to hope for its recovery, a recovery which she would bring about through the "demagogues"; but it is not sick; rather is it in its full strength, when it puts from it the demagogues who want to acquire something for the individuals, for "all." In its believers it is provided with the best demagogues (leaders of the people). According to Bettina, the State is to "develop mankind's germ of freedom; otherwise it is a raven-mother and caring for raven-fodder!" It cannot do otherwise, for in its very caring for "mankind" (which, besides, would have to be the "humane" or "free" State to begin with) the "individual" is raven-fodder for it. How rightly speaks the burgomaster, on the other hand: "What? the State has no other duty than to be merely the attendant of incurable invalids?—That isn't to the point. From of old the healthy State has relieved itself of the diseased matter, and not mixed itself with it. It does not need to be so economical with its juices. Cut off the robber-branches without hesitation, that the others may bloom.—Do not shiver at the State's harshness; its morality, its policy and religion, point it to that. Accuse it of no want of feeling; its sympathy revolts against this, but its experience finds safety only in this severity! There are diseases in which only drastic remedies will help. The physician who recognizes the disease as such, but timidly turns to palliatives, will never remove the disease, but may well cause the patient to succumb after a shorter or longer sickness." Frau Rat's question, "If you apply death as a drastic remedy, how is the cure to be wrought then?" isn't to the point. Why, the State does not apply death against itself, but against an offensive member; it tears out an eye that offends it, etc."

"For the invalid State the only way of salvation is to make man flourish in it." If one here, like Bettina, understand by man the concept "Man," she is right; the "invalid" State will recover by the flourishing of "Man," for, the more infatuated the individuals are with "Man," the better it serves the State's turn. But, if one referred it to the individuals, to "all" (and the authoress half-does this too, because about "Man" she is still involved in vagueness), then it would sound somewhat like the following: For an invalid band of robbers the only way of salvation is to make the loyal citizen nourish in it! Why, thereby the band of robbers would simply go to ruin as a band of robbers; and, because it perceives this, it prefers to shoot every one who has a leaning toward becoming a "steady man."

In this book Bettina is a patriot, or, what is little more, a philanthropist, a worker for human happiness. She is discontented with the existing order in quite the same way as is the title-ghost of her book, along with all who would like to bring back the good old faith and what goes with it. Only she thinks, contrariwise, that the politicians, place-holders, and diplomats ruined the State, while those lay it at the door of the malevolent, the "seducers of the people."

What is the ordinary criminal but one who has committed the fatal mistake of endeavoring after what is the people's instead of seeking for what is his? He has sought despicable alien goods, has done what believers do who seek after what is God's. What does the priest who admonishes the criminal do? He sets before him the great wrong of having desecrated by his act what was hallowed by the State, its property (in which, of course, must be included even the life of those who belong to the State); instead of this, he might rather hold up to him the fact that he has befouled *himself* in not despising the alien thing, but thinking it worth stealing; he could, if he were not a parson. Talk with the so-called criminal as with an egoist, and he will be ashamed, not that he transgressed against your laws and goods, but that he considered your laws worth evading, your goods worth desiring; he will be ashamed that he did not—despise you and yours together, that he was too little an egoist. But you cannot talk egoistically with him, for you are not so great as a criminal, you—commit no crime! You do not know that an ego who is his own cannot desist from being a criminal, that crime is his life. And yet you should know it, since you believe that "we are all miserable sinners"; but you think surreptitiously to get beyond sin, you do not comprehend—for you are devil-fearing—that guilt is the value of a man. Oh, if you were guilty! But now you are "righteous." Well—just put every thing nicely to rights for your master!

When the Christian consciousness, or the Christian man, draws up a criminal code, what can the concept of crime be there but simply—

heartlessness? Each severing and wounding of a heart relation, each *heartless behavior* toward a sacred being, is crime. The more heartfelt the relation is supposed to be, the more scandalous is the deriding of it, and the more worthy of punishment the crime. Everyone who is subject to the lord should love him; to deny this love is a high treason worthy of death. Adultery is a heartlessness worthy of punishment; one has no heart, no enthusiasm, no pathetic feeling for the sacredness of marriage. So long as the heart or soul dictates laws, only the heartful or soulful man enjoys the protection of the laws. That the man of soul makes laws means properly that the moral man makes them: what contradicts these men's "moral feeling," this they penalize. How should disloyalty, secession, breach of oaths—in short, all *radical breaking off*, all tearing asunder of venerable ties—not be flagitious and criminal in their eyes? He who breaks with these demands of the soul has for enemies all the moral, all the men of soul. Only Krummacher and his mates are the right people to set up consistently a penal code of the heart, as a certain bill sufficiently proves. The consistent legislation of the Christian State must be placed wholly in the hands of the—parsons, and will not become pure and coherent so long as it is worked out only by—the *parson-ridden*, who are always only *half-parsons*. Only then will every lack of soulfulness, every heartlessness, be certified as an unpardonable crime, only then will every agitation of the soul become condemnable, every objection of criticism and doubt be anathematized; only then is the own man, before the Christian consciousness, a convicted–*criminal* to begin with.

The men of the Revolution often talked of the people's "just revenge" as its "right." Revenge and right coincide here. Is this an attitude of an ego to an ego? The people cries that the opposite party has committed "crimes" against it. Can I assume that one commits a crime against me, without assuming that he has to act as I see fit? And this action I call the right, the good, etc.; the divergent action, a crime. So I think that the others must aim at the *same* goal with me; I do not treat them as unique beings who bear their law in themselves and live according to it, but as beings who are to obey some "rational" law. I set up what "Man" is and what acting in a "truly human" way is, and I demand of every one that this law become norm and ideal to him; otherwise he will expose himself as a "sinner and criminal." But upon the "guilty" falls the "penalty of the law"!

One sees here how it is "Man" again who sets on foot even the concept of crime, of sin, and therewith that of right. A man in whom I do not recognize "man" is "sinner, a guilty one."

Only against a sacred thing are there criminals; you against me can never be a criminal, but only an opponent. But not to hate him who injures a sacred thing is in itself a crime, as St. Just cries out against Danton: "Are you not a criminal and responsible for not having hated the enemies of the fatherland?" —

If, as in the Revolution, what "Man" is is apprehended as "good citizen," then from this concept of "Man" we have the well-known "political offences and crimes."

In all this the individual, the individual man, is regarded as refuse, and on the other hand the general man, "Man," is honored. Now, according to how this ghost is named—as Christian, Jew, Mussulman, good citizen, loyal subject, freeman, patriot, etc.—just so do those who would like to carry through a divergent concept of man, as well as those who want to put *themselves* through, fall before victorious "Man."

And with what unction the butchery goes on here in the name of the law, of the sovereign people, of God, etc.!

Now, if the persecuted trickily conceal and protect themselves from the stern parsonical judges, people stigmatize them as St. Just does those whom he accuses in the speech against Danton. One is to be a fool, and deliver himself up to their Moloch.

Crimes spring from *fixed ideas*. The sacredness of marriage is a fixed idea. From the sacredness it follows that infidelity is a crime, and therefore a certain marriage law imposes upon it a shorter or longer *penalty*. But by those who proclaim "freedom as sacred" this penalty must be regarded as a crime against freedom, and only in this sense has public opinion in fact branded the marriage law.

Society would have *every one* come to his right indeed, but yet only to that which is sanctioned by society, to the society-right, not really to *his* right. But I give or take to myself the right out of my own plenitude of power, and against every superior power I am the most impenitent criminal. Owner and creator of my right, I recognize no other source of right than—me, neither God nor the State nor nature nor even man himself with his "eternal rights of man," neither divine nor human right.

Right "in and for itself." Without relation to me, therefore! "Absolute right." Separated from me, therefore! A thing that exists in and for itself! An absolute! An eternal right, like an eternal truth!

According to the liberal way of thinking, right is to be obligatory for me because it is thus established by *human reason*, against which *my reason* is "unreason." Formerly people inveighed in the name of divine reason against weak human reason; now, in the name of strong human reason, against egoistic reason, which is rejected as "unreason." And yet none is real but this very "unreason." Neither divine nor human reason, but only your and my reason existing at any given time, is real, as and because you and I are real.

The thought of right is originally my thought; or, it has its origin in me. But, when it has sprung from me, when the "Word" is out, then it has "become flesh," it is a *fixed idea*. Now I no longer get rid of the thought; however I turn, it stands before me. Thus men have not become masters again of the thought "right," which they themselves created; their creature is running away with them. This is absolute right, that which is absolved or unfastened from me. We, revering it as absolute, cannot devour it again, and it takes from us the creative power: the creature is more than the creator, it is "in and for itself."

Once you no longer let right run around free, once you draw it back into its origin, into you, it is your right; and that is right which suits you.

Right has had to suffer an attack within itself, from the standpoint of right; war being declared on the part of liberalism against "privilege."

Privileged and *endowed with equal rights*—on these two concepts turns a stubborn fight. Excluded or admitted—would mean the same. But where should there be a power—be it an imaginary one like God, law, or a real one like I, you—of which it should not be true that before it all are "endowed with equal rights," that is, no respect of persons holds? Every one is equally dear to God if he adores him, equally agreeable to the law if only he is a law-abiding person; whether the lover of God and the law is humpbacked and lame, whether poor or rich, and the like, that amounts to nothing for God and the law; just so, when you are at the point of drowning, you like a Negro as rescuer as well as the most excellent Caucasian—yes, in this situation you esteem a dog not less than a man. But to whom will not every one be also, contrariwise, a preferred or disregarded person? God punishes the wicked with his wrath, the law chastises the lawless, you let one visit you every moment and show the other the door.

The "equality of right" is a phantom just because right is nothing more and nothing less than admission, a matter of grace, which, be it said, one may also acquire by his desert; for desert and grace are not contradictory, since even grace wishes to be "deserved" and our gracious smile falls only to him who knows how to force it from us.

So people dream of "all citizens of the State having to stand side by side, with equal rights." As citizens of the State they are certainly all equal for the State. But it will divide them, and advance them or put them in the rear, according to its special ends, if on no other account; and still more must it distinguish them from one another as good and bad citizens.

Bruno Bauer disposes of the Jew question from the stand-point that "privilege" is not justified. Because Jew and Christian have each some point of advantage over the other, and in having this point of advantage are exclusive, therefore before the critic's gaze they crumble into nothingness. With them the State lies under the like blame, since it justifies their having advantages and stamps it as a "privilege." or prerogative, but thereby derogates from its calling to become a "free State."

But now every one has something of advantage over another—to wit, himself or his individuality; in this everybody remains exclusive.

And, again, before a third party every one makes his peculiarity count for as much as possible, and (if he wants to win him at all) tries to make it appear attractive before him.

Now, is the third party to be insensible to the difference of the one from the other? Do they ask that of the free State or of humanity? Then these would have to be absolutely without self-interest, and incapable of taking an interest in any one whatever. Neither God (who divides his own from the wicked) nor the State (which knows how to separate good citizens from bad) was thought of as so indifferent.

But they are looking for this very third party that bestows no more "privilege." Then it is called perhaps the free State, or humanity, or whatever else it may be.

As Christian and Jew are ranked low by Bruno Bauer on account of their asserting privileges, it must be that they could and should free themselves from their narrow stand-point by self-renunciation or unselfishness. If they threw off their "egoism," the mutual wrong would cease, and with it Christian and Jewish religiousness in general; it would be necessary only that neither of them should any longer want to be anything peculiar.

But, if they gave up this exclusiveness, with that the ground on which their hostilities were waged would in truth not yet be forsaken. In case of need they would indeed find a third thing on which they could unite, a "general religion," a "religion of humanity," and the like; in short, an equalization, which need not be better than that which would result if all Jews became Christians, by this likewise the "privilege" of one over the other would have an end. The tension would indeed be done away, but in this consisted not the essence of the two, but only their neighborhood. As being distinguished from each other they must necessarily be mutually resistant, and the disparity will always remain. Truly it is not a failing in you that you stiffen yourself against me and assert your distinctness or peculiarity: you need not give way or renounce yourself.

People conceive the significance of the opposition too *formally* and weakly when they want only to "dissolve" it in order to make room for a third thing that shall "unite." The opposition deserves rather to be *sharpened*. As Jew and Christian you are in too slight an opposition, and are contending only about religion, as it were about the emperor's beard, about a fiddle-stick's end. Enemies in religion indeed, *in the rest* you still remain good friends, and equal to each other, as men. Nevertheless the rest too is unlike in each; and the time when you no longer merely *dissemble* your opposition will be only when you entirely recognize it, and everybody asserts himself from top to toe as *unique*. Then the former opposition will assuredly be dissolved, but only because a stronger has taken it up into itself.

Our weakness consists not in this, that we are in opposition to others, but in this, that we are not completely so; that we are not entirely *severed* from them, or that we seek a "communion," a "bond," that in communion we have an ideal. One faith, one God, one idea, one hat, for all! If all were brought under one hat, certainly no one would any longer need to take off his hat before another.

The last and most decided opposition, that of unique against unique, is at bottom beyond what is called opposition, but without having sunk back into "unity" and unison. As unique you have nothing in common with the other any longer, and therefore nothing divisive or hostile either; you are not seeking to be in the right against him before a *third* party, and are standing with him neither "on the ground of right" nor on any other common ground. The opposition vanishes in complete—severance or singleness. This might indeed be regarded as the new point in common or a new parity, but here the parity consists precisely in the disparity, and is itself nothing but disparity, a par of disparity, and that only for him who institutes a "comparison."

The polemic against privilege forms a characteristic feature of liberalism, which fumes against "privilege" because it itself appeals to "right." Further than to fuming it cannot carry this; for privileges do not fall before right falls, as they are only forms of right. But right falls apart into its nothingness when it is swallowed up by might, when one understands what is meant by "Might goes before right." All right explains itself then as privilege, and privilege itself as power, as—*superior power*.

But must not the mighty combat against superior power show quite another face than the modest combat against privilege, which is to be fought out before a first judge, "Right," according to the judge's mind?

***

Now, in conclusion, I have still to take back the half-way form of expression of which I was willing to make use only so long as I was still rooting among the entrails of right, and letting the word at least stand. But, in fact, with the concept the word too loses its meaning. What I called "my right" is no longer "right" at all, because right can be bestowed only by a spirit, be it the spirit of nature or that of the species, of mankind, the Spirit of God or that of His Holiness or His Highness, etc. What I have without an entitling spirit I have without right; I have it solely and alone through my power.

I do not demand any right, therefore I need not recognize any either. What I can get by force I get by force, and what I do not get by force I have no right to, nor do I give myself airs, or consolation, with my imprescriptible right.

With absolute right, right itself passes away; the dominion of the "concept of right" is cancelled at the same time. For it is not to be forgotten that hitherto concepts, ideas, or principles ruled us, and that among these rulers the concept of right, or of justice, played one of the most important parts.

Entitled or unentitled—that does not concern me, if I am only *powerful*, I am of myself *empowered*, and need no other empowering or entitling.

Right—is a wheel in the head, put there by a spook; power—that am I myself, I am the powerful one and owner of power. Right is above me, is absolute, and exists in one higher, as whose grace it flows to me: right is a gift of grace from the judge; power and might exist only in me the powerful and mighty.

Chapter 4

PIERRE-JOSEPH PROUDHON
from
The Confessions of a Revolutionist (1850)

Proudhon can be regarded as the first modern intellectual to refer to himself as an anarchist, and he is the source for much of what followed philosophically. It was he who coined the expression "Property is theft!" Proudhon's brand of anarchism he chose to call "mutualism," which was regarded as a composite of sorts between anarchism and socialism. He would argue for a revolution that resulted in a socialist society where everyone worked voluntarily to the benefit of all.

THE NATURE AND DESTINATION OF GOVERNMENT

The Scriptures declare that "there must be *divisions* (*i. e.* parties) among men," and the priest exclaims, "terrible necessity," arising from the original sin! But a little reflection has shown us the origin and signification of parties; we have now to learn their object and final destiny.

All men are born free and equal;—society is therefore by nature self-governing, *i.e.* ungovernable; and he who lays his hand on me to govern me is a usurper and tyrant; my declared enemy. But this idea of equality did not appear in the earliest phases of society. When men met together the first thing they agreed to do was to appoint a ruler, *Constituamus super nos regem!* someone in authority. Such then was the first idea of human society, and the next was immediately to overthrow this society, each wishing to use it for his own liberty, against that of others. All parties have been eager for the possession of power, to work their own ends; hence the aphorism of the radicals, to which the absolutists would willingly subscribe. *Social revolution is the end, political revolution* (*i. e.* the transference of authority) *is the means;* which simply means;—give us power of life and death over your persons and property and we will make you free! what kings and priests have repeated for six thousand years.

So that government and party are reciprocally to each other cause, end and means, beginning middle and end; and, *thou shall not do this, thou shall not do that*, has been the sole education of man by governments from the time of Adam and Eve; but when mankind shall have arrived at years of discretion, parties and governments will disappear; thus liberty will grow out of authority, as we have seen Socialism result from absolutism. Philosophy therefore shows us that the establishment of authority over a people can be but a transition state, and must continually diminish until it is swallowed up in industrial organization; the aphorism, therefore, must be read inversely *Political revolution*, that is, the abolition of authority among men *is the end, social revolution is the means.* There can be no liberty for citizens, order for society, or union among producers, until there be

> *No more parties;*
> *No more authority;*
> *Absolute liberty of the individual and the citizen.*

In these three sentences I have made my profession of faith, political and social. M. de Girardin says, he is a revolutionist *par en haut* (from above) and never will be a revolutionist, *par en bas* (from below.) Now he thinks he has said something very original and profound in these expressions *par en haut, par en bas*, which are nothing more than the old idea of the demagogues. By the former he means evidently the government, and calls it revolutionizing by instruction, intelligence, progress and the extension of ideas; by the latter he means the people, and terms it revolutionizing by insurrection and despair: but the contrary is the truth. For let us examine which of the two is the most intelligent, progressive and peaceful, that by the government or that by the people. The former is manifestly revolutionizing according to the pleasure of the prince, the impulses of an assembly, the violence of a club, the whim of a dictator or a despot, Louis XIV., Napoleon, Charles X., and practiced it after this manner; and Guizot, Louis Blanc, Leon Faucher, wish to try the same mode.

The other way, however, by the people is revolutionizing by the common consent of all citizens, by the experience of the laborer, by the progress and diffusion of knowledge; it is the freedom of revolution, such as Condorcet, Turgot, and Robespierre desired.

The greatest revolutionist in France was St. Louis, when he was only the register of the public will.

The socialists have fallen into the same error as the radicals; St. Simon, Fourier, Owen, Cabet, Louis Blanc, are all for an organization of labor by means of the state, or by capital, or by some other form of authority! instead of teaching the people to organize themselves, and to appeal to their own reason and experience; they say "give us power." They are Utopians, like the despots.

Governments from their very nature never can be revolutionary. Society, the whole mass of the people elevated in intelligence, can alone revolutionize itself. Governments are the scourges of God to *discipline* the world; for them to create liberty would be to destroy themselves. Every revolution in the world, from the crowning of the first king down to the declaration of the rights of man, has been accomplished by the spontaneous will of the people. Did government possess the science of revolution and social progress they could not apply it; they must first transfer it to the people, and then gain their consent; which would be a contradiction, in terms, and a complete misconception of the meaning of power and authority.

Look at the countries that are the freest, are they not those where the power of the government is the most restricted—where the people generally take the initiative; the United States of America for instance? England, Switzerland, Holland; and those are the most enslaved—where the governing power is the best organized and the strongest; ourselves for example? and yet we are always complaining of not being governed, and asking for a stronger arm at the helm of state.

The Church, like an affectionate mother, came first; and said "everything *for* the people, but all *by* the prince."

Then came the monarchy, "everything *for* the people, but all *by* the prince."

Next the *doctrinaires* or liberals, "everything *for* the people, but all *by* the middle class."

The radicals, though changing the formula, have retained the principle, "everything *for* the people, but all *by* the government."

Always the same communism, the same governmentalism.

Who then will say? everything for the people, and everything by the people, even the government!

According to M. Lamartine, the government has to issue its commands, and the country only to yield its consent. Whereas all history tells us that that government is the best which comes nearest to making itself useless. Do we want parasites to labor or priests to speak to God? neither do we want representatives to govern us. It has been said by some one, that for man to speculate in his fellow-man is open robbery. And the government of man by man is slavery; so every religion founded upon any form whatever of papal infallibility is sheer idolatry, the worship of man by man.

And yet after all these fruits of the absolutist principle we have still,

The judgment of man by man.

The condemnation of man by man.

And to crown the list, the punishment of man by man.

All these, however, we must submit to, until in the progress of time they grow old, perish, and fall off like ripe fruits in their due season; they are the instruments of our apprenticeship. Philosophy repudiates these symbols of a barbarous age, and yet admits not the rights of any one to compel a people to be free, who wish to be governed.

It has no confidence in any social reforms that do not arise spontaneously from the people, and acknowledges no revolutions that do not receive the initiative from the masses.

Chapter 5

HERBERT SPENCER
from
Social Statics (1851)

Though largely forgotten today, Herbert Spencer was one of the preeminent British intellectuals of the latter half of the nineteenth century. It was he and not Darwin who coined the term "survival of the fittest," by which he meant that in any environment the fittest will survive, not necessarily that they "should." Decades later, Murray Rothbard reportedly called Social Statics *"the greatest single work of libertarian political philosophy ever written." Yet Spencer was no anarchist, and had the following chapter quietly removed from* Social Statics *when it was republished years later. Anarchists later found the excised chapter and republished it themselves after his death.*

THE RIGHT TO IGNORE THE STATE

§ 1. As a corollary to the proposition that all institutions must be subordinated to the law of equal freedom, we cannot choose but admit the right of the citizen to adopt a condition of voluntary outlawry. If every man has freedom to do all that he wills, provided he infringes not the equal freedom of any other man, then he is free to drop connection with the State,—to relinquish its protection and to refuse paying towards its support. It is self-evident that in so behaving he in no way trenches upon the liberty of others; for his position is a passive one, and, whilst passive, he cannot become an aggressor. It is equally self-evident that he cannot be compelled to continue one of a political corporation without a breach of the moral law, seeing that citizenship involves payment of taxes; and the taking away of a man's property against his will is an infringement of his rights. Government being simply an agent employed in common by a number of individuals to secure to them certain advantages, the very nature of the connection implies that it is for each to say whether he will employ such an agent or not. If any one of them determines to ignore this mutual-safety confederation, nothing can be said, except that he loses all claim to its good offices, and exposes himself to the danger of maltreatment,—a thing he is quite at liberty to do if he likes. He cannot be coerced into political combination without a breach of the law of equal freedom; he can withdraw from it without committing any such breach; and he has therefore a right so to withdraw.

§ 2. "No human laws are of any validity if contrary to the law of nature: and such of them as are valid derive all their force and all their authority mediately or immediately from this original." Thus writes Blackstone, to whom let all honour be given for having so far outseen the ideas of his time,—and, indeed, we may say of our time. A good antidote, this, for those political superstitions which so widely prevail. A good check upon that sentiment of power-worship which still misleads us by magnifying the prerogatives of constitutional governments as it once did those of monarchs. Let men learn that a legislature is *not* "our God upon earth," though, by the authority they ascribe to it and the things they expect from it, they would seem to think it is. Let them learn rather that it is an institution serving a purely temporary purpose, whose power, when not stolen, is, at the best, borrowed.

Nay, indeed, have we not seen that government is essentially immoral? Is it not the offspring of evil, bearing about it all the marks of its parentage? Does it not exist because crime exists? Is it not strong, or, as we say, despotic, when crime is great? Is there not more liberty—that is, less government—as crime diminishes? And must not government cease when crime ceases, for very lack of objects on which to perform its function? Not only does magisterial power exist *because* of evil, but it exists *by* evil. Violence is employed to maintain it; and all violence involves criminality. Soldiers, policemen, and gaolers; swords, batons, and fetters,—are instruments for inflicting pain; and all infliction of pain is, in the abstract, wrong. The State employs evil weapons to subjugate evil, and is alike contaminated by the objects with which it deals and the means by which it works. Morality cannot recognise it; for morality, being simply a statement of the perfect law, can give no countenance to anything growing out of, and living by, breaches of that law. Wherefore legislative authority can never be ethical—must always be conventional merely.

Hence there is a certain inconsistency in the attempt to determine the right position, structure, and conduct of a government by appeal to the first principles of rectitude. For, as just pointed out, the acts of an institution which is, in both nature and origin, imperfect cannot be made to square with the perfect law. All that we can do is to ascertain, firstly, in what attitude a legislature must stand to the community to avoid being by its mere existence an embodied wrong; secondly, in what manner it must be constituted so as to exhibit the least incongruity with the moral law; and, thirdly, to what sphere its actions must be limited to prevent it from multiplying those breaches of equity it is set up to prevent.

The first condition to be conformed to before a legislature can be established without violating the law of equal freedom is the acknowledgment of the right now under discussion—the right to ignore the State.

§ 3. Upholders of pure despotism may fitly believe State-control to be unlimited and unconditional. They who assert that men are made for governments and not governments for men may consistently hold that no one can remove himself beyond the pale of political organisation. But they who maintain that the people are the only legitimate source of power—that legislative authority is not original, but deputed—cannot deny the right to ignore the State without entangling themselves in an absurdity.

For, if legislative authority is deputed, it follows that those from whom it proceeds are the masters of those on whom it is conferred: it follows further that as masters they confer the said authority voluntarily: and this implies that they may give or withhold it as they please. To call that deputed which is wrenched from men whether they will or not is nonsense. But what is here true of all collectively is equally true of each separately. As a government can rightly act for the people only when empowered by them, so also can it rightly act for the individual only when empowered by him. If A, B, and C debate whether they shall employ an agent to perform for them a certain service, and if, whilst A and B agree to do so, C dissents, C cannot equitably be made a party to the agreement in spite of himself. And this must be equally true of thirty as of three: and, if of thirty, why not of three hundred, or three thousand, or three millions?

§ 4. Of the political superstitions lately alluded to, none is so universally diffused as the notion that majorities are omnipotent. Under the impression that the preservation of order will ever require power to be wielded by some party, the moral sense of our time feels that such power cannot rightly be conferred on any but the largest moiety of society. It interprets literally the saying that "the voice of the people is the voice of God," and, transferring to the one the sacredness attached to the other, it concludes that from the will of the people—that is, of the majority—there can be no appeal. Yet is this belief entirely erroneous.

Suppose, for the sake of argument, that, struck by some Malthusian panic, a legislature duly representing public opinion were to enact that all children born during the next ten years should be drowned. Does any one think such an enactment would be warrantable? If not, there is evidently a limit to the power of a majority. Suppose, again, that of two races living together—Celts and Saxons, for example—the most numerous determined to make the others their slaves. Would the authority of the greatest number be in such case valid? If not, there is something to which its authority must be subordinate. Suppose, once more, that all men having incomes under £50 a year were to resolve upon reducing every income above that amount to their own standard, and appropriating the excess for public purposes. Could their resolution be justified? If not, it must be a third time confessed that there is a law to which the popular voice must defer. What, then, is that law, if not the law of pure equity—the law of equal freedom? These restraints, which all would put to the will of the majority, are exactly the restraints set up by that law. We deny the right of a majority to murder, to enslave, or to rob, simply because murder, enslaving, and robbery are violations of that law—violations too gross to be overlooked. But, if great violations of it are wrong, so also are smaller ones. If the will of the many cannot supersede the first principle of morality in these cases, neither can it in any. So that, however insignificant the minority, and however trifling the proposed trespass against their rights, no such trespass is permissible.

When we have made our constitution purely democratic, thinks to himself the earnest reformer, we shall have brought government into harmony with absolute justice. Such a faith, though perhaps needful for the age, is a very erroneous one. By no process can coercion be made equitable. The freest form of government is only the least objectionable form. The rule of the many by the few we call tyranny: the rule of the few by the many is tyranny also, only of a less intense kind. "You shall do as we will, and not as you will," is in either case the declaration; and, if the hundred make it to ninety-nine, instead of the ninety-nine to the hundred, it is only a fraction less immoral. Of two such parties, whichever fulfils this declaration necessarily breaks the law of equal freedom: the only difference being that by the one it is broken in the persons of ninety-nine, whilst by the other it is broken in the persons of a hundred. And the merit of the democratic form of government consists solely in this,—that it trespasses against the smallest number.

The very existence of majorities and minorities is indicative of an immoral state. The man whose character harmonises with the moral law, we found to be one who can obtain complete happiness without diminishing the happiness of his fellows. But the enactment of public arrangements by vote implies a society consisting of men otherwise constituted—implies that the desires of some cannot be satisfied without sacrificing the desires of others—implies that in the pursuit of their happiness the majority inflict a certain amount of *un*happiness on the minority—implies, therefore, organic immorality. Thus, from another point of view, we again perceive that even in its most equitable form it is impossible for government to dissociate itself from evil; and further, that, unless the right to ignore the State is recognised, its acts must be essentially criminal.

§ 5. That a man is free to abandon the benefits and throw off the burdens of citizenship, may indeed be inferred from the admissions of existing authorities and of current opinion. Unprepared as they probably are for so extreme a doctrine as the one here maintained, the Radicals of our day yet unwittingly profess their belief in a maxim which obviously embodies this doctrine. Do we not continually hear them quote Blackstone's assertion that "no subject of England can be constrained to pay any aids or taxes even for the defence of the realm or the support of government, but such as are imposed by his own consent, or that of his representative in Parliament"? And what does this mean? It means, say they, that every man should have a vote. True: but it means much more. If there is any sense in words, it is a distinct enunciation of the very right now contended for. In affirming that a man may not be taxed unless he has directly or indirectly given his consent, it affirms that he may refuse to be so taxed; and to refuse to be taxed is to cut all connection with the State. Perhaps it will be said that this consent is not a specific, but a general, one, and that the citizen is understood to have assented to every thing his representative may do, when he voted for him. But suppose he did not vote for him; and on the contrary did all in his power to get elected some one holding opposite views—what then? The reply will probably be that by taking part in such an election, he tacitly agreed to abide by the decision of the majority. And how if he did not vote at all? Why then he cannot justly complain of any tax, seeing that he made no protest against its imposition. So, curiously enough, it seems that he gave his consent in whatever way he acted—whether he said "Yes," whether he said "No," or whether he remained neuter! A rather awkward doctrine, this. Here stands an unfortunate citizen who is asked if he will pay money for a certain proffered advantage; and, whether he employs the only means of expressing his refusal or does not employ it, we are told that he practically agrees, if only the number of others who agree is greater than the number of those who dissent. And thus we are introduced to the novel principle that A's consent to a thing is not determined by what A says, but by what B may happen to say!

It is for those who quote Blackstone to choose between this absurdity and the doctrine above set forth. Either his maxim implies the right to ignore the State, or it is sheer nonsense.

§ 6. There is a strange heterogeneity in our political faiths. Systems that have had their day, and are beginning here and there to let the daylight through, are patched with modern notions utterly unlike in quality and colour; and men gravely display these systems, wear them, and walk about in them, quite unconscious of their grotesqueness. This transition state of ours, partaking as it does equally of the past and the future, breeds hybrid theories exhibiting the oddest union of bygone despotism and coming freedom. Here are types of the old organisation curiously disguised by germs of the new—peculiarities showing adaptation to a preceding state modified by rudiments that prophesy of something to come—making altogether so chaotic a mixture of relationships that there is no saying to what class these births of the age should be referred.

As ideas must of necessity bear the stamp of the time, it is useless to lament the contentment with which these incongruous beliefs are held. Otherwise it would seem unfortunate that men do not pursue to the end the trains of reasoning which have led to these partial modifications. In the present case, for example, consistency would force them to admit that, on other points besides the one just noticed, they hold opinions and use arguments in which the right to ignore the State is involved.

For what is the meaning of Dissent? The time was when a man's faith and his mode of worship were as much determinable by law as his secular acts; and, according to provisions extant in our statute-book, are so still. Thanks to the growth of a Protestant spirit, however, we have ignored the State in this matter—wholly in theory, and partly in practice. But how have we done so? By assuming an attitude which, if consistently maintained, implies a right to ignore the State entirely. Observe the positions of the two parties. "This is your creed," says the legislator; "you must believe and openly profess what is here set down for you." "I shall not do anything of the kind," answers the Nonconformist; "I will go to prison rather." "Your religious ordinances," pursues the legislator, "shall be such as we have prescribed. You shall attend the churches we have endowed, and adopt the ceremonies used in them." "Nothing shall induce me to do so," is the reply; "I altogether deny your power to dictate to me in such matters, and mean to resist to the uttermost." "Lastly," adds the legislator, "we shall require you to pay such sums of money toward the support of these religious institutions as we may see fit to ask." "Not a farthing will you have from me," exclaims our sturdy Independent; "even did I believe in the doctrines of your church (which I do not), I should still rebel against your interference; and, if you take my property, it shall be by force and under protest."

What now does this proceeding amount to when regarded in the abstract? It amounts to an assertion by the individual of the right to exercise one of his faculties—the religious sentiment—without let or hindrance, and with no limit save that set up by the equal claims of others. And what is meant by ignoring the State? Simply an assertion of the right similarly to exercise *all* the faculties. The one is just an expansion of the other—rests on the same footing with the other—must stand or fall with the other. Men do indeed speak of civil and religious liberty as different things: but the distinction is quite arbitrary. They are parts of the same whole, and cannot philosophically be separated.

"Yes they can," interposes an objector; "assertion of the one is imperative as being a religious duty. The liberty to worship God in the way that seems to him right, is a liberty without which a man cannot fulfil what he believes to be divine commands, and therefore conscience requires him to maintain it." True enough; but how if the same can be asserted of all other liberty? How if maintenance of this also turns out to be a matter of conscience? Have we not seen that human happiness is the divine will—that only by exercising our faculties is this happiness obtainable—and that it is impossible to exercise them without freedom? And, if this freedom for the exercise of faculties is a condition without which the divine will cannot be fulfilled, the preservation of it is, by our objector's own showing, a duty. Or, in other words, it appears not only that the maintenance of liberty of action *may* be a point of conscience, but that it *ought* to be one. And thus we are clearly shown that the claims to ignore the State in religious and in secular matters are in essence identical.

The other reason commonly assigned for nonconformity admits of similar treatment. Besides resisting State dictation in the abstract, the Dissenter resists it from disapprobation of the doctrines taught. No legislative injunction will make him adopt what he considers an erroneous belief; and, bearing in mind his duty toward his fellow-men, he refuses to help through the medium of his purse in disseminating this erroneous belief. The position is perfectly intelligible. But it is one which either commits its adherents to civil nonconformity also, or leaves them in a dilemma. For why do they refuse to be instrumental in spreading error? Because error is adverse to human happiness. And on what ground is any piece of secular legislation disapproved? For the same reason—because thought adverse to human happiness. How then can it be shown that the State ought to be resisted in the one case and not in the other? Will any one deliberately assert that, if a government demands money from us to aid in *teaching* what we think will produce evil, we ought to refuse it, but that, if the money is for the purpose of *doing* what we think will produce evil, we ought not to refuse it? Yet such is the hopeful proposition which those have to maintain who recognise the right to ignore the State in religious matters, but deny it in civil matters.

§ 7. The substance of this chapter once more reminds us of the incongruity between a perfect law and an imperfect State. The practicability of the principle here laid down varies directly as social morality. In a thoroughly vicious community its admission would be productive of anarchy. In a completely virtuous one its admission will be both innocuous and inevitable. Progress toward a condition of social health—a condition, that is, in which the remedial measures of legislation will no longer be needed—is progress toward a condition in which those remedial measures will be cast aside, and the authority prescribing them disregarded. The two changes are of necessity co-ordinate. That moral sense whose supremacy will make society harmonious and government unnecessary is the same moral sense which will then make each man assert his freedom even to the extent of ignoring the State—is the same moral sense which, by deterring the majority from coercing the minority, will eventually render government impossible. And, as what are merely different manifestations of the same sentiment must bear a constant ratio to each other, the tendency to repudiate governments will increase only at the same rate that governments become needless.

Let not any be alarmed, therefore, at the promulgation of the foregoing doctrine. There are many changes yet to be passed through before it can begin to exercise much influence. Probably a long time will elapse before the right to ignore the State will be generally admitted, even in theory. It will be still longer before it receives legislative recognition. And even then there will be plenty of checks upon the premature exercise of it. A sharp experience will sufficiently instruct those who may too soon abandon legal protection. Whilst, in the majority of men, there is such a love of tried arrangements, and so great a dread of experiments, that they will probably not act upon this right until long after it is safe to do so.

Chapter 6

JOSIAH WARREN
from
True Civilization: An Immediate Necessity, and the Last Ground of Hope for Mankind (1863)

America in the nineteenth century was a truly odd place, with many varied social experiments occurring throughout the vast, quickly growing nation. Among them was Josiah Warren's Utopian community Modern Times on New York's Long Island. Warren took the labor theory of value seriously and advocated for an economics under his slogan of "cost the limit of price." He decreed the price of an item should not be set by the market but by how much work went into producing it, and even issued currency based on hours-worked to his followers. As America was ripping itself in half, brother slaughtering brother in the Civil War, Warren was denouncing the state's authority in his book True Civilization.

GOVERNMENT AND ITS TRUE FUNCTION

1. With all due deference to other judgments I venture to assert that our present deplorable condition, like that of many other parts of the world, is in consequence of the people in general never having perceived, or else having lost sight of, the legitimate object of all governments as displayed or implied in the American "Declaration of Independence."

2. Every individual of mankind has an "INALIENABLE right to Life, Liberty, and the pursuit of Happiness;" "and it is solely to *protect* and *secure* the enjoyment of these rights unmolested that governments can properly be instituted among men." In other terms, SELF-SOVEREIGNTY is an instinct of every living organism; and it being an *instinct,* cannot be alienated or separated from that organism. It is the instinct of Self-Preservation; the votes of ten thousand men cannot alienate it from a single individual, nor could the bayonets of twenty thousand men neutralize it in any one person any more than they could put a stop to the instinctive desire for food in a hungry man.

3. The action of this instinct being INVOLUNTARY, every one has the same absolute right to its exercise that he has to his complexion or the forms of his features, to any extent, not disturbing another; and it is solely to prevent or restrain such disturbances or encroachments, that governments are properly instituted. In still shorter terms, the legitimate and appropriate mission of governments is the defence and protection of the inalienable right of *Sovereignty* in every individual within his or her own sphere.

But what is it that constitutes encroachment?

4. Suppose my house to be on fire, and I seize a pail of water in the hands of a passer-by, without waiting to explain or ask leave—this would be one degree of encroachment, but perhaps the owner would excuse it on the ground of its necessity. Suppose a man walks into my house without waiting for leave—it may or may not disturb or offend me, or constitute a degree of encroachment. If I find that he has no excusable errand, and require him to retire and he refuses, this would be a degree of encroachment which I might meet with a few words, and might need no government to assist me. If he proceeds to rob the house, I may have reason to think that he is driven to desperation by having a starving family, and I may not resort to violence; or I may perceive that he is a wanton and reckless robber or fillibuster, and that this is an *unnecessary* encroachment, which, in defence of my own rights, as well as the same rights in others, I am justifiable in resisting; and if I have not sufficient power to do so without endangering myself or property, I will call for help:—this help, whether in the form of police or an army, is government, and its function is to use force, to prevent him from using force against me and mine; it interferes, with my consent, to

prevent interference with my sovereign right to control my own:—its mission is "intervention for the sake of non-intervention."

5. If he has already got possession of my purse, I should want him to be compelled, without any unnecessary violence, to give it up; and, perhaps, to compensate the police; and, till I had learned better, I might have approved of his being confined in prison till he had done this, and compensated me for being disturbed: but there are objections to proceeding to these complicated measures. There is no principle *(generally)* known, by which to determine what constitutes compensation!—He could not get properly compensated for his work, which might be a greater injustice to him than he had done to me; and it would inflict on his innocent father, mother, brothers, and sisters, his wife and children, and all his friends, incalculable injustice and suffering, and this would be no compensation to me: besides, *I* (as a citizen of the same world) am a partner in the crime by not having *prevented the temptation to it.*

6. With all these considerations against pursuing him farther, I think it the best present *expedient* to put up with the restoration of my purse, as he gains nothing to tempt the continuance of the business. The word *expedient* may look loose and unsatisfactory: but, among all the works of mankind there is nothing higher than expedients.

7. The instinct of self-preservation or self-sovereignty is not the work of man; but to keep it constantly in mind as a sacred right in all human intercourse is highly expedient.

8. Perceiving that we can invent nothing higher than expedients, we necessarily set aside all imperative or absolute authorities, all sanguinary and unbending codes, creeds, and theories, and leave every one *Free* to choose among expedients: or, in other words, we place all action upon the *voluntary* basis. Do not be alarmed, we shall see this to be the highest expedient whenever it is possible.

9. It is only when the voluntary is wantonly encroached upon, that the employment of force is expedient or justifiable.

10. It appears, however, that no rule or law can be laid down to determine beforehand, what will constitute an offensive encroachment—what one will resist another will excuse, and the subtle diversities of different persons and cases, growing out of the inherent individualities of each, have defied all attempts at perfect formulizing excepting this of the *Sovereignty of every individual over his or her own;* and even this must be violated in resisting its violation!

11. The legitimate sphere of every individual has never been publicly determined; but until it is clearly defined, we can never tell what constitutes encroachment—what may be safely excused, or what may be profitably resisted.

12. We will attempt then to define the sphere within which every individual may legitimately, rightly exercise *supreme* power or absolute authority. This sphere would include his or her person, time, property, and responsibilities.

13. By the word right is meant simply that which necessarily tends towards the end in view—the end in view here is permanent and universal peace, and security of person and property.

14. I have said (in effect) that the present confusion and wide-spread violence and destruction result from a want of appreciation of this great right of Individual Sovereignty, and its defence by government.

15. I now proceed to illustrate and prove this by considering what would be the natural consequences of bearing these two ideas all the time in mind as the regulators of political and moral movements, and holding them, as it were, as substitutes for all previous laws customs, precedents, and theories.

16. First, then, while admitting this right of Sovereignty in every one, I shall not be guilty of the ill manners of attempting to *offensively* enforce any of my theoretical speculations, which has been the common error of all governments! This itself would be an attempted encroachment that would justify resistance.

17. The whole mission of coercive government being the defence of persons and property against offensive encroachments, it must have force enough for the purpose. This force necessarily resolves itself into the military, for the advantages of drill and systematic cooperation: and this being perhaps the best form that *government* can assume, while a coercive force is needed, I make no issue with it but only with the misapplications of its immense power.

18. Adhering closely to the idea of *restraining violence* as the mission of government or military power, if this *sole* purpose was instilled into the general mind as an element of education or discipline, no force could be raised to invade any persons or property whatever, and no defence would be necessary.

19. If the Declaration of Independence, or this sacred right of Individual Sovereignty, had been commonly appreciated a year ago in

the "United States," they would not now be disunited. None of the destruction of persons and property which has blackened the past year would have occurred, nor would twelve hundred thousand citizens now be bent on destroying each other and their families and homes in these States!

20. Every individual would have been *"Free"* to entertain any theory of government whatever for himself or herself, and to test it by experiment within equitable limits; an issue would be raised only where this sacred right was denied, or against any who should have undertaken to *enforce* any theory of government whatever upon any individual against his or her *"consent."* The frank and honest admission of this "inalienable" right would even now change the issue of this present war, and carry relief and protection to the invaded or oppressed, and war or resistance to the oppressor only, whether he were found on one side or the other of a geographical line. Mere theorists say that "the laws of nations decide that a state of war (between two nations) puts all the members of each, in hostility to each other:" and that "the laws of nations justify us in doing all the harm we can to our enemies." We need no death-warrant from "authority" against these barbarian theories—the very statement of them becomes their execution.

21. *Every* person being entitled to *sovereignty* within his own sphere, there can be, consistently, no limits or exceptions to the title to protection in the legitimate exercise of this sacred right, whether on this side or the other side of the Atlantic, and whether "in a state of war" or not: and, as soon as we take position for this universal right for all the world, we shall have all the world *for us* and *with us* and no enemies to contend with. Did military men ever think of this? Did governments ever think of it?

22. The whole proper business of government is the restraining offensive encroachments, or unnecessary violence to persons and property, or enforcing compensation therefor: but if, in the exercise of this power, we commit any unnecessary violence to *any person whatever or to any property,* we, ourselves, have become the aggressors, and should be resisted.

23. But who is to decide *how much* violence is *necessary* in any given case? We here arrive at the pivot upon which all power now turns for good or evil; this pivot, under formal, exacting, aggressive institutions or *constitutions,* is the person who decides as to their meaning. If one

decides for all, then all but that one are, perhaps, enslaved; if each one's title to Sovereignty is admitted, there will be different interpretations, and this *freedom to differ* will ensure emancipation, safety, repose, even in a political atmosphere! and all the co-operation we ought to expect will come from the coincidence of motives according to the merits of each case as estimated by different minds. Where there is evidence of aggression palpable to all minds, all might co-operate to resist it: and where the case is not clearly made out, there will be more or less hesitation: Two great nations will not then be so *very* ready to jump at each other's throats when the most cunning lawyers are puzzled to decide which is wrong!

24. Theorize as we may about the interpretation of "the Constitution," every individual *does* unavoidably measure it and all other words by his own peculiar understanding or conceits, whether he understands himself or not, and should, like General Jackson, recognize the fact, "take the responsibility of it," and qualify himself to meet its consequences. The full appreciation of this simple but almost unknown fact will neutralize the war element in all verbal controversies, and the binding power of all indefinite words, and place conformity thereto on the voluntary basis! Did any institution-makers (except the signers of the "Declaration") ever think of this?

25. It will be asked, what could be accomplished by a military organization, if every subordinate were allowed to judge of the propriety of an order before he obeyed it? I answer that nothing could be accomplished that did not commend itself to men educated to understand, and trained to respect the rights of persons and property as set forth in the "Declaration of Independence;" and that here, and *here only,* will be found the long-needed check to the barbarian wantonness that lays towns in ashes and desolates homes and hearts for brutal revenge, or to act office or a little vulgar newspaper notoriety.

26. But what shall ensure propriety of judgment or uniformity or coincidence between the subordinates and the officers? I answer, Drill, Discipline,—of *mind* as well as of arms and legs,—teaching *all* to realize their true mission. The true object of all their power being clearly defined and made familiar, there would at once be a coincidence unknown before, and but slight chance of dissent when there was good ground for co-operation.

27. No subordination can be more perfect than that of an Orchestra; but it is all *voluntary*.

28. When we are ready to protect *any* person or property without regard to locality or party, there can be no hostile parties or nations!—Nothing to betray by treason!—Nothing to rebel against!—No party to desert to! Then, whose fault is it that there are persons called "Traitors," "Rebels," and "Deserters"?

29. If it be true that the sole proper function of coercive force is to restrain or repair all unnecessary violence, then the conclusion is inevitable that all penal laws (for *punishing* a crime or an act after it is committed except so far as they work to compensate the injured party *Equitably)* are themselves criminal! The excuse is that punishment is "a terror to evildoers;" but those who punish instead of *preventing* crime are themselves evildoers; and according to their own theory they should be punished and terrified; but the theory is false: consistently carried out, it would depopulate the world. Such are the fogs in which we get astray when we trust ourselves away from first premises and substitute speculative theories in their stead. Had our military been properly educated to know its true function and purpose, Ellsworth would not have been shot for taking down a flag; the shooting of him did not restrain him, nor did the shooting of Mr. Jackson compensate Ellsworth: but it caused Mrs. Jackson to become insane with grief, and has spread a hostile spirit to an incalculable extent among millions, which will descend to future generations; all of which originated in the denial to Mr. Jackson of his "inalienable right" to choose his own government, which the "Declaration" guarantees in explicit terms to every one.

30. To take down Mr. Jackson's flag was one degree of encroachment, but it was not necessary to shoot Ellsworth for bad manners; failing to educate him or to prevent him, one party was as much in fault as the other. The barbarian habit of shedding blood for irreparable offences ("as a terror to evil-doers") was acted upon in this case—carried fully out, mutual slaughter would have continued till there would not be a man, woman, or child, living upon the earth.

31. Are not these statements perfectly in accordance with the Declaration of Independence as well as with the teachings of the wisest and best of our species? I invite thought on the subject. I make the assertions not because they are implied in that

"Declaration," but because they are just such as are demanded at this hour as the only possible means of salvation from barbarism.

32. If the solutions herein presented should appear to require more steady manliness and consistent thought than such as commonly prevail, then Instruction, Drill, Discipline, are as necessary for the *minds* as for the bodies of our military forces: but even in this discipline, the principal labor will consist in keeping the mind's eye steadily upon two ideas so simple as the right of Sovereignty in every person and its judicious defence.

33. Experience drifts us, against all theories of combination, to refer everything to *Individual* decision and action: and we cannot, therefore safely dispense with an ever-watchful DISCRIMINATION and a strong *Self-government* in every person in proportion to the magnitude of his or her sphere of action. Practical experience in this country in less than one year has driven us, against the hopeful theory of Democratic government, under the dreaded government of military despotisms, which is merely placing the deciding power in a few persons, and the persons and property of all the people at their disposal; while the Declaration of Independence and the instinct of Self-preservation assert the absolute and "inalienable right" of every one to control his own! Man-made powers are arrayed against NATURE'S LAW! Here we have the fatal issue! What can be done? Are we again at the eve of a long night of desolation, or is there some untried element in modern thought which can reconcile the seeming contradiction between instinct and experience?

34. Can it be possible that one simple thought found in our own charter of rights, if introduced into military discipline, would solve, not this great problem only, but others of even greater magnitude?

35. A man cannot alienate his *"inalienable right"* of self-preservation or Sovereignty by joining the military or any other combination—the assumption that this is possible has produced all our political confusion and violence, and will continue to produce just such fruits to the end of time, if the childish blunder is not exposed and corrected.

36. Admitting this indestructible right of Sovereignty in *every Individual, at all times and in all conditions,* one will not attempt to *govern* (but only guide or lead) another; but we shall trust to principle or *purpose* for a general and voluntary coincidence and co-operation. Military officers will then become directors or leaders,—*not*

"commanders,"—obedience will be all the more prompt because it is rendered for *an object*—the greatest that can inspire human action, RESISTANCE TO ALL ATTEMPTS AT OFFENSIVE AND UNNECESSARY GOVERNING OR ENCROACHMENTS upon ANY persons or property whatsoever, as the great guarantee for the security of each and every individual. Then every Man, Woman, and Child in the world is interested in acting for and with such a government!

37. Our problem is theoretically solved! But its brightness dazzles us, and its sublime magnitude bewilders—Let us take time!

38. Having one man as general over thousands, arises from the natural necessity for *Individuality* in the directing mind when numbers wish to move together; but it does not necessarily imply any superiority of judgment or motive in the director of a movement beyond those of the subordinates, any more shall the driver of an omnibus is presumed to know the road better than the passengers; they may all know the road equally well, but if they all undertake to drive the horses, none of their purposes will be answered; and it would be equally ridiculous for the driver, under the plea of upholding subordination, to insist on carrying his passengers where they did not want to go, or refuse to let them get out when they wanted to "secede."

39. The necessity for the prompt execution of the directions of the one lead, or director, where numbers are acting together to attain an object in view, is so self-evident, or can be so easily explained, that where there is a walls of this promptness, it implies that the fault is in having a bad cause, or unfit associates in a good one.

40. The most intelligent people always make the best subordinates in a good cause, and in our *modern military* it will require more true manhood to make a good subordinate than it will to be a leader; for the leader may very easily give orders, but they take the responsibility of that *only,* while the subordinate takes the responsibility of executing them; and it will require the greatest and highest degree of manhood, of self-government, presence of mind, and real heroism to *discriminate* on the instant and to stand up individually before all the corps and future criticisms, and assume, alone, the responsibility of dissent or disobedience. His only support and strength would be in his consciousness of being more true to his professed mission than the order was, and in the assurance that he would be sustained by

public opinion and sympathy as far as that mission was understood.

41. Subordinates have many times refused to fire on their fellow-citizens in obedience to the mere wantonness of authority, or of the ferocity of a crude discipline, and have thus, like William Tell, entitled themselves to the lasting gratitude and affection of generations.

42. Men may *lead* and men must execute, but intelligence, principle, must *regulate:* and that principle must be THE PREVENTION OR REPAIR OF ALL UNNECESSARY VIOLENCE, OR WANTON DISTURBANCE OF PERSONS OR PROPERTY, if we are ever to have order or peace on earth.

43. Even Children, when drilled and trained with this idea (which is simply the true Democratic idea), would become an ever-ready police to protect each other and the gardens, fruits, and other property around them, instead of being, as they often are, the Imps of disturbance and destruction. The height of their ambition being to play "soger," and fight somebody or destroy something.

44. This is our fault. The Democratic idea, theoretically at the base of American institutions, has never been introduced into our military discipline, nor into our courts, nor into our laws, and only in a caricatured and distorted shape into our political system, our commerce, our education, and public opinion.

45. Let this element be practically and consistently introduced, especially in the military department, and our country is saved:— Otherwise, it is LOST.

46. When a high degree of intelligence, great manhood, self-government, close discrimination, *real* heroism, and gentle humanity are known to be necessary to membership in our military corps (or government), these qualities will come into fashion, and become the characteristics of the people; and to be thought destitute of them, and unworthy of membership in the military would cause the greatest mortification: while to be known as a member in good standing would be an object sought as the highest honor.

47. Is all this in exact and scientific accordance with our first premises in the "Declaration of Independence," or is it all a romantic dream?

48. If we have been correct in our reasonings, then we have found the clue to the true mission and form of Government—To the most perfect, yet harmless subordination—The reconciliation of obedience with FREEDOM—To the cessation of all hostilities

between parties and Nations—To universal co-operation for universal preservation and security of persons and property. We have found a government, literally *in* the people, *of* the people, *for* the people—a government that *is* the people: for Men, Women, and Children can take some direct or indirect part in it—a ready police or army adapted to all demands for either—a self-protecting *"Party of the whole."*

49. A "Union" not only on paper, but rooted in the heart—whose members, trained in the constant reverence for the "inalienable right" of Sovereignty in every person, would be habituated to forbearance towards even wrong opinions and different educations and tastes, to patient endurance of irremediable injuries, and a self-governing deportment and gentleness of manner, and a prompt but careful resistance to wanton aggression wherever found, which would meet with a ready and an affectionate welcome in any part of the world.

50. Every intelligent person would wish to be a member or to contribute, in some manlier, to the great common cause.

51. No coercive system of taxation could be necessary to such a government! A government so simple that children will be first to comprehend it, and which even they can see it for their interests to assist: and then would as readily play "soger" to prevent mischief, as to *do* mischief.

52. With our mind's eye steadily fixed on this great Democratic principle and object, let us immediately commence the agitation of the idea of forming companies of home-guards on this principle.

53. Let any one who feels so disposed, take the first steps and invite the co-operation of persons sufficiently intelligent to comprehend the object to form a nucleus. (The known habitual regard to the "inalienable rights" of persons and property would be the best title to membership). Then, commence Drill and Discipline, keeping in mind all the time the *kind* of discipline required, which would be partly in the form of lectures; taking as texts, the details of the destruction of persons an I property going on all around us, and showing with how much less violence the same or better objects could have been accomplished: and in the drill, giving some orders to do some unnecessary harm, *on purpose to be disobeyed* in order to accustom the subordinates to "look before they leap" or strike!

54. Such a Military force would be *within* but not under discipline. In other words, its "sabbath would be made for man—not man for

its sabbath." To be *under* instead of *within* discipline is a mistake as fatal as that of getting *under* water in stead of *within* water.

55. If the true mission of the military or enforcing power is kept constantly in view, and made, as it were, the guiding star, scarcely anything can go seriously amiss; and NVC need no other guide for the use of a governing force: nor will it answer to allow any theories or *"precedents"* to override this one supreme consideration.

56. Companies thus formed would do well to communicate with each other, which would be all the general *organization* required for a world-wide co-operation.

57. Here would be a government to preserve, and not to destroy—to protect and not to invade; a government that can include the whole strength of the world—when might would be *for* the right, and no enemies to contend with!

58. The charms of music, of mutual sympathy, the beauties of order, and of unity of dress and of movement in military displays, now so seductive to purposes of destruction and degradation, would entice to the highest and noblest objects of human ambition, which would never need a field of activity as long as wanton oppression (even of a single individual) has footing on the earth.

59. Thus far we have considered the true function of government, and find that it has to deal only with offensive encroachments upon persons or property: like a volunteer guard on a wrecked vessel in the confusion of disaster, the frenzy of hlunger, and the fear of starvation, to prevent unnecessary destruction of life or property,— an expedient choice of evils where there is nothing but evils to choose from.

60. Society has thus far been only a "series of failures," and is at this day a mere assemblage of wrecks thrown against each other on a tempestuous sea without pilots, charts, rudders, or compass.

61. The first ship has not yet been constructed that is not liable to be wrecked by the very element that moves it on a successful voyage; and the first form of general society is yet to be developed that would not be liable to destruction from the instinctive "pursuit of happiness," without which no society would exist.

62. Government, strictly and scientifically speaking is a *coercive force;* a man, while governed with his own consent, is not *governed* at all.

63. Deliberative bodies, such as Legislatures, Congresses, Conventions, Courts, etc., are not, scientifically speaking, are not

government, which is simply *coercive force.* But, inasmuch as that force should never be employed without a deliberate reference to its legitimate object, and upon which all available wisdom should be brought to bear, a *Deliberative Council,* acting before or with the government, seems highly expedient if not indispensable.

64. Moreover there are subjects now before us, and continually arising, on which, by timely forethought, violent issues may be *prevented* from arising, and many most important subjects may be adjusted by counsel alone, without any appeal to force.

65. Such Counsellors should not be tempted by unearned salaries and honors, nor by compensation measured by the necessities or weakness and defencelessness of their clients; nor should they consist of those who, like editors of news, can make more money by wars and other calamities than they can by peace and general prosperity, but let the Counsellors be those who are willing to wait, like tillers of the soil, for compensation according to the quantity and quality of their work. Let compensation or honors come in the form of *voluntary* contributions AFTER but not before benefits have been realized.

66. It is therefore suggested that any person, of either sex, who may coincide with this proposition, and who feels competent to give Counsel in any department of human affairs, publicly announce the fact, as lawyers and physicians now do, or permit their names and functions to be made accessible to the public in some manner, so that whoever may need honest counsel on any subject may know where to find it. If a meeting of such Counsellors is thought desirable by any interested party, he or she can invite such as are thought to be most competent for the occasion, according to the subject to be considered.

67. These Counsellors, while in session, would constitute a deliberative assembly, or advisory tribunal. It might consist of both sexes or either sex, according to the nature of the subject to be deliberated upon.

68. After deliberation, or whenever any interested party feels ready to make up an opinion, let him or her write it down with the reasons for it, and present it to the Counsellors and the audience, for their signatures, and let the document go forth to the public or to the interested parties. If there are several such documents, those having the signatures of counsellors or persons most known to be reliable

would have the most weight; but, in order to ensure any influence or benefit from either, let compensation come to the Counsellors like that to Rowland Hill, in voluntary contributions *after* the benefits of the opinions have, to some extent, been realized.

69. After having thus brought the best experience and well-balanced counsels to bear upon any subject without satisfying all parties, every person has a Sovereign right to differ from all the opinions of the tribunal while not invading or disturbing other persons or property.

70. When an issue has already been raised, and no one of these decisions is acceptable to both parties, the decisions may be laid before the military (or government) to act at its discretion; selecting that course which promises the least violence or disturbance. If any member declines to act, his "inalienable right" to do so, being sacredly respected, would tend to confirm and illustrate the only principle that can regulate, at the very moment that it should regulate, the action of the others!

71. To ensure the best order in such a deliberative assembly, no *other subject than the one for which it is called* should be introduced without unanimous consent; as each and *every* one has a *sovereign* right to appropriate his own time and to choose the subjects that shall occupy his attention: and a constant regard to the same right, fully appreciated by all, will suggest the careful avoidance of all unnecessary disturbance which might prevent any one from hearing whatever he or she prefers to listen to. This sentiment becoming familiar to all as a monitor, but little disturbance would occur—when it did occur, the principle itself would immediately prompt its appreciators to stop it with as little violence as possible.

72. Here, again, we need no other regulator for the most perfect order than this great Democratic principle!

73. With such Counsellors ready to act, we should be immediately exempted from the necessity for any disagreeable personal disputations on subjects which so often lead to violence or lasting enmity between individuals and Nations! All of the doubtful and unsettled can at once be referred to the highest tribunal, with the assurance of obtaining the best decision that present attainments within our reach can furnish.

74. A subject of great or universal interest may be laid before all such tribunals in the world, and their decisions brought to every city,

village, and neighborhood, and to every door; and the relief from all disturbing controversies would be felt at every fireside.

75. The sanction of such tribunals, to any enterprise for public benefit, would place its author or inventor fairly before the public for their patronage, instead of being left to starve for want of attention; while the absence or want of such sanction would put a sudden stop to the swarms of impostures and fallacies that now wear out the attention to no purpose, and render valueless the announcements of even valuable things: while with such a sanction, the public might fool; at advertisements with some prospect of benefit therefrom.

76. This absolute right of *Sovereignty* in every individual, over his or her *person, time, and property* is the only rule or principle known to this writer that is not subject to exceptions and failures as a regulator of human intercourse. It is very often, however, impossible in our complicated entanglements, for one or some to exercise this right without violating the same right in others. We will ask our Counsellors to examine DISINTEGRATION as tile remedy!

77. We will ask them what constitutes legitimate property? We will ask them for the least violent mode of securing land to the homeless and starving. Also, what would constitute the just reward of LABOR? We shall invite them to consider what ought to be the circulating medium, or Money? How it happens that the producers and makers of everything have comparatively nothing? And we shall ask them for some mode of Adapting Supplies to Demands—For a better Postal system—For a more Equitable system of buying and selling—For a programme of Education in accordance with the Democratic principle.

78. And we will ask them, What will be the use of Congresses, Legislatures, and Courts of Law.

79. These are some of the subjects that must immediately employ the best minds, if the "American Experiment" is not to prove a total failure. Not to say that the best minds have not been employed upon them, but that the required solutions were impossible without the aid of very recent, though very simple, developments.

80. A Conservatory and Library will naturally spring up, where the records of the tribunal decisions and other contributions to public welfare will be preserved for reference and diffusion; and the world will begin to know its benefactors.

81. This Modern Military, as a Government, will be necessary only in the transitionary stage of society from confusion and wanton violence to true order and mature civilization.

82. When the simply wise shall sit in calm deliberation, patiently tracing out the complicated and entangled CAUSES of avarice, of robberies, of murders, of wars, of poverty, of desperation, of suicides, of Slaveries and fraud, violence and suffering of all kinds, and shall have found appropriate and practical means of PREVENTING instead of punishing them, then the Military will be the fitting messengers of relief and harbingers of security and of peace, of order and unspeakable benefits wherever their footsteps are found; and, instead of being the desolators of the world, they will be hailed from far and near as the blessed benefactors of mankind.

83. Those who may dissent from these views are, in that act, *exercising* the "inalienable right" which has no exceptions; and they may perceive that they are thus assisting in the scientific inauguration of EQUITABLE FREEDOM.

84. In deference to the pressing exigencies of the time, I have endeavored to put forth, in the fewest possible words, thoughts which seem to promise the relief required by all classes, parties, and Nations, and have not dwelt upon existing errors and wrongs they being, sufficiently evident by contrast with tile right, any prolonged attack upon them is unnecessary.

85. I have endeavored to show the sublime powers and dazzling beauties of an Absolute *Principle* of right, as a guiding star to our path, along with expedients entirely consistent therewith. If this search after the narrow path has been more fortunate than that of our predecessors, it is owing to circumstances so peculiar that they may be excused for being less successful. If we are self-deluded, with all our best energies devoted to general benefit, we shall need all the forbearance that we exercise towards them.

86. It will be seen, by some at least, that each individual assuming his or her share of the deciding power or government as proposed, the great "American idea" may be practically realized; and that the ever-disturbing problem of the "balance of political power" becomes solved, and security for person and property (the great proposed object of all governments) prospectively attained.

87. If others see in this only the 'inauguration of Anarchy," let no attempt be made to urge them into conformity, but let them *freely and securely* await the results of demonstration.

Chapter 7

MIKHAIL BAKUNIN
from
The State and Marxism (1867) and *God and the State* (1870)

Contemporary right-anarchists frequently proclaim that left-anarchists are secret authoritarians, statists at heart. Historically, however, Marx's foremost ideological rival was Mikhail Bakunin. At the time there was an enormous debate on the left as to whether communism should achieved through the state—the Marxist position—or Bakunin's view that anarchism was the way. Fifty years before the Soviet Union was founded, Bakunin was anticipating and denouncing what the theory of Marxism would mean in practice.

All work to be performed in the employ and pay of the State—such is the fundamental principle of Authoritarian Communism, of State Socialism. The State having become sole proprietor—at the end of a certain period of transition which will be necessary to let society pass without too great political and economic shocks from the present organization of bourgeois privilege to the future organization of the official equality of all—the State will be also the only Capitalist, banker, money-lender, organizer, director of all national labor and distributor of its products. Such is the ideal, the fundamental principle of modern Communism.

Enunciated for the first time by Babeuf, towards the close of the Great French Revolution, with all the array of antique civism and revolutionary violence, which constituted the character of the epoch, it was recast and reproduced in miniature, about forty-five years later by Louis Blanc in his tiny pamphlet on *The Organization of Labor*, in which that estimable citizen, much less revolutionary, and much more indulgent towards bourgeois weaknesses than was Babeuf, tried to gild and sweeten the pill so that the bourgeois could swallow it without suspecting that they were taking a poison which would kill them. But the bourgeois were not deceived, and returning brutality for politeness, they expelled Louis Blanc from France. In spite of that, with a constancy which one must admire, he remained alone in faithfulness to his economic system and continued to believe that the whole future was contained in his little pamphlet on the organization of Labor.

The Communist idea later passed into more serious hands. Karl Marx, the undisputed chief of the Socialist Party in Germany—a great intellect armed with a profound knowledge, whose entire life, one can say it without flattering, has been devoted exclusively to the greatest cause which exists to-day, the emancipation of labor and of the toilers—Karl Marx who is indisputably also, if not the only, at least one of the principal founders of the International Workingmen's Association, made the development of the Communist idea the object of a serious work. His great work, *Capital*, is not in the least a fantasy, an "a priori" conception, hatched out in a single day in the head of a young man more or less ignorant of economic conditions and of the actual system of production. It is founded on a very extensive, very detailed knowledge and a very profound analysis of this system and of its conditions. Karl Marx is a man of immense statistical and economic knowledge. His work on Capital, though unfortunately bristling with formulas and metaphysical subtleties which render it unapproachable for the great mass of readers, is in the highest degree a scientific or realist work: in the sense that it absolutely excludes any other logic than that of the facts.

Living for very nearly thirty years, almost exclusively among German workers, refugees like himself and surrounded by more or less intelligent friends and disciples belonging by birth and relationship to the bourgeois world, Marx naturally has managed to form a Communist school, or a sort of little Communist Church, composed of fervent adepts and spread all over Germany. This Church, restricted though it may be on the score of numbers, is skillfully organized, and thanks to its numerous connections with working-class organizations in all the principal places in Germany, it has already become a power. Karl Marx naturally enjoys an almost supreme authority in this Church, and to do him justice, it must be admitted that he knows how to govern this little army of fanatical adherents in such a way as always to enhance his prestige and power over the imagination of the workers of Germany.

Marx is not only a learned Socialist, he is also a very clever Politician and an ardent patriot. Like Bismarck, though by somewhat different means, and like many other of his compatriots, Socialists or not, he wants the establishment of a great Germanic State for the glory of the German people and for the happiness and the voluntary, or enforced civilization of the world.

The policy of Bismarck is that of the present; the policy of Marx, who considers himself at least as his successor, and his continuator, is that of the future. And when I say that Marx considers himself the continuator of Bismarck, I am far from calumniating Marx. If he did not consider himself as such, he would not have permitted Engels, the confidant of all his thoughts, to write that Bismarck serves the cause of Social Revolution. He serves it now in his own way; Marx will serve it later, in another manner. That is the sense in which he will be later, the continuator, as to-day he is the admirer of the policy of Bismarck.

Now let us examine the particular character of Marx's policy, let us ascertain the essential points on which it is to be separated from the Bismarckian policy. The principal point, and, one might say, the only one, is this: Marx is a democrat, an Authoritarian Socialist, and a Republican; Bismarck is an out and out Pomeranian, aristocratic, monarchical Junker. The difference is therefore very great, very serious, and both sides are sincere in this difference. On this point, there is no possible understanding or reconciliation possible between Bismarck and Marx. Even apart from the numerous irrevocable pledges that Marx throughout his life, has given to the cause of Socialist democracy, his very position and his ambitions give a positive guarantee on this issue. In a monarchy, however Liberal it might be, or even cannot be any place, any role for Marx, and so much the more so in the Prussian Germanic Empire founded by Bismarck, with a bugbear of an Emperor, militarist and bigoted, as chief and with all the barons and bureaucrats of Germany for guardians. Before he can arrive at power, Marx will have to sweep all that away.

Therefore he is forced to be Revolutionary. That is what separates Marx from Bismarck—the form and the conditions of Government. One is an out and out aristocrat and monarchist; and in a Conservative Republic like that of France under Thiers, there the other is an out and out democrat and republican, and, into the bargain, a Socialist democrat and a Socialist republican.

Let us see now what unites them. *It is the out and out cult of the State.* I have no need to prove it in the case of Bismarck, the proofs are there. From head to foot he is a State's man and nothing but a State's man. But neither do I believe that I shall have need of too great efforts to prove that it is the same with Marx. He loves government to such a degree that he even wanted to institute one in the International Workingmen's Association; and he worships power so much that he wanted to impose and still means to-day to impose his dictatorship on us. It seems to me that that is sufficient to characterize his personal attitude. But his Socialist and political program is a very faithful expression of it. The supreme objective of all his efforts, as is proclaimed to us by the fundamental statutes of his party in Germany, is the establishment of the great People's State.

But whoever says State, necessarily says a particular limited State, doubtless comprising, if it is very large, many different peoples and countries, but excluding still more. For unless he is dreaming of the Universal State as did Napoleon and the Emperor Charles the Fifth, or as the Papacy dreamed of the Universal Church, Marx, in spite of all the international ambition which devours him to-day, will have, when the hour of the realization of his dreams has sounded for him—if it ever does sound—he will have to content himself with governing a single State and not several States at once. Consequently, who ever says State says, *a* State, and whoever says *a* State affirms by that the existence of several States, and whoever says *several* States, immediately says: competition, jealousy, truceless and endless war. The simplest logic as well as all history bear witness to it.

Any State, under pain of perishing and seeing itself devoured by neighboring States, must tend towards complete power, and, having become powerful, it must embark on a career of conquest, so that it shall not be itself conquered; for two powers similar and at the same time foreign to each other could not co-exist without trying to destroy each other. Whoever says conquest, says conquered peoples, enslaved and in bondage, under whatever form or name it may be.

It is in the nature of the State to break the solidarity of the human race and, as it were, to deny humanity. The State cannot preserve itself as such in its integrity and in all its strength except it sets itself up as supreme and absolute be-all and end-all, at least for its own citizens, or to speak more frankly, for its own subjects, not being able to impose itself as such on the citizens of other States unconquered by it. From that there inevitably results a break with human, considered as universal, morality and with universal reason, by the birth of State morality and reasons of State. The principle of political or State morality is very simple. The State, being the supreme objective, everything that is favorable to the development of its power is good; all that is contrary to it, even if it were the most humane thing in the world, is bad. This morality is called *Patriotism*. The International is the negation of patriotism and consequently the negation of the State. If therefore Marx and his friends of the German Socialist Democratic Party should succeed in introducing the State principle into our program, they would kill the International.

The State, for its own preservation, must necessarily be powerful as regards foreign affairs; but if it is so as regards foreign affairs, it will infallibly be so as regards home affairs. Every State, having to let itself be inspired and directed by some particular morality, conformable to the particular conditions of its existence, by a morality which is a restriction and consequently a negation of human and universal morality, must keep watch that all its subjects, in their thoughts and above all in their acts, are inspired also only by the principles of this patriotic or particular morality, and that they remain deaf to the teachings of pure or universally human morality. From that there results the necessity for a State censorship; too great liberty of thought and opinions being, as Marx considers, very reasonably too from his eminently political point of view, incompatible with that unanimity of adherence demanded by the security of the State. That that in reality is Marx's opinion is sufficiently proved by the attempts which he made to introduce censorship into the International, under plausible pretexts, and covering it with a mask.

But however vigilant this censorship may be, even if the State were to take into its own hands exclusively education and all the instruction of the people, as Mazzini wished to do, and as Marx wishes to do to-day the State can never be sure that prohibited and dangerous thoughts may not slip in and be smuggled somehow into the consciousness of the population that it governs. Forbidden fruit has such an attraction for men, and the demon of revolt, that eternal enemy of the State, awakens so easily in their hearts when they are not sufficiently stupified, that neither this education nor this instruction, nor even the censorship, sufficiently guarantee the tranquility of the State. It must still have a police, devoted agents who watch over and direct, secretly and unobtrusively, the current of the peoples' opinions and passions. We have seen that Marx himself is so convinced of this necessity, that he believed he should fill with his secret agents all the regions of the International and above all, Italy, France, and Spain. Finally, however perfect may be, from the point of view of the preservation of the State, the organisation of education and instruction for the people, of censorship and the police, the State cannot be secure in its existence while it does not have, to defend it against its *enemies at home*, an armed force. The State is government from above downward of an immense number of men, very different from the point of view of the degree of their culture, the nature of the countries or localities that they inhabit, the occupation they follow, the interests and the aspirations directing them—the State is the government of all these by some or other minority; this minority, even if it were a thousand times elected by universal suffrage and controlled in its acts by popular institutions, unless it were endowed with the omniscience, omnipresence and the omnipotence which the theologians attribute to God, it is impossible that it could know and foresee the needs, or satisfy with an even justice the most legitimate and pressing interests in the world. There will always be discontented people because there will always be some who are sacrificed.

Besides, the State, like the Church, by its very nature is a great sacrificer of living beings. It is an arbitrary being, in whose heart all the positive, living, individual, and local interests of the population meet, clash, destroy each other, become absorbed in that abstraction called the common interest, the *public good*, the *public safety*, and where all real wills cancel each other in that other abstraction which hears the name of the *will of the people*. It results from this, that this so-called will of the people is never anything else than the sacrifice and the negation of all the real wills of the population; just as this so-called public good is nothing else than the sacrifice of their interests. But so that this omnivorous abstraction could impose itself on millions of men, it must be represented and supported by some real being, by living force or other. Well, this being, this force, has always existed. In the Church it is called the clergy, and in the State—the ruling or governing class.

And, in fact, what do we find throughout history? The State has always been the patrimony of some privileged class or other; a priestly class, an aristocratic class, a bourgeois class, and finally a bureaucratic class, when, all the other classes having become exhausted, the State falls or rises, as you will, to the condition of a machine; but it is absolutely necessary for the salvation of the State that there should be some privileged class or other which is interested in its existence. And it is precisely the united interest of this privileged class which is called Patriotism.

By excluding the immense majority of the human race from its bosom, by casting it beyond the pale of the engagements and reciprocal duties of morality, justice and right, the State denies humanity, and with that big word, "Patriotism", imposes injustice and cruelty on all its subjects, as a supreme duty. It restrains, it mutilates, it kills humanity in them, so that, ceasing to be men, they are no longer anything but citizens—or rather, more correctly considered in relation to the historic succession of facts—so that they shall never raise themselves beyond the level of the citizen to the level of a man.

If we accept the fiction of a free State derived from a social contract, then discerning, just, prudent people ought not to have any longer any need of government or of State. Such a people can need only to live, leaving a free course to all their instincts: justice and public order will naturally and of their accord proceed from the life of the people, and the State, ceasing to be the providence, guide, educator, and regulator of society, renouncing all its repressive power, and failing to the subaltern role which Proudhon assigns it, will no longer anything else but a simple business office, a sort of central clearing house at the service of society.

Doubtless, such a political organization, or rather, such a reduction of political action in favor of liberty in social life, would be a great benefit for society, but it would not at all please the devoted adherents of the State. They absolutely must have a State-Providence, a State directing social life, dispensing justice, and administering public order. That is to say, whether they admit it or not, and even when they call themselves Republicans, democrats, or even Socialists, they always must have a people who are more or less ignorant, minor, incapable, or to call things by their right names, riff-raff, to govern; in order, of course, that doing violence to their own disinterestedness and modesty, they can keep the best places for themselves, in order always to have the opportunity to devote themselves to the common good, and that, strong in their virtuous devotion and their exclusive intelligence, privileged guardians of the human flock, whilst urging it on for its own good and leading it to security, they may also fleece it a little.

Every logical and sincere theory of the State is essentially founded on the principle of *authority*—that is to say on the eminently theological, metaphysical and political idea that the masses, *always* incapable of governing themselves, must submit at all times to the benevolent yoke of a wisdom and a justice, which in one way or another, is imposed on them from above. But imposed in the name of what and by whom? Authority recognized and respected as such by the masses can have only three possible sources—force, religion, or the action of a superior intelligence; and this supreme intelligence is always represented by minorities.

Slavery can Change its form and its name—its basis remains the same. This basis is expressed by the words: being a slave is being forced to work for other people—as being a master is to live on the labor of other people. In ancient times, as to-day in Asia and Africa, slaves were simply called slaves. In the Middle Ages, they took the name of "serfs", to-day they are called "wage-earners". The position of these latter is much more honorable and less hard than that of slaves, but they are none the less forced by hunger as well as by the political and social institutions, to maintain by very hard work the absolute or relative idleness of others. Consequently, they are slaves. And, in general, no State, either ancient or modern, has ever been able, or ever will be able to do without the forced labor of the masses, whether wage-earners or slaves, as a principal and absolutely necessary basis of the liberty and culture of the political class: the citizens.

Even the United States is no exception to this rule. Its marvelous prosperity and enviable progress are due in great part and above all to one important advantage—the great territorial wealth of North America. The immense quantity of uncultivated and fertile lands, together with a political liberty that exists nowhere else attracts every year hundreds of thousands of energetic, industrious and intelligent colonists. This wealth, at the same time keeps off pauperism and delays the moment when the social question will have to be put. A worker who does not find work or who is dissatisfied with the wages offered by the capitalist can always, if need be, emigrate to the far West to clear there some wild and unoccupied land.

This possibility always remaining open as a last resort to all American workers, naturally keeps wages at a level, and gives to every individual an independence, unknown in Europe. Such is the advantage, but here is the disadvantage. As cheapness of the products of industry is achieved in great part by cheapness of labor, the American manufacturers for most of the time are not in a condition to compete against the manufacturers of Europe—from which there results, for the industry of the Northern States, the necessity for a protectionist tariff. But that has a result, firstly to create a host of artificial industries and above all to oppress and ruin the non-manufacturing Southern States and make them want secession; finally to crowd together into cities like New York, Philadelphia, Boston and many others, proletarian working masses who, little by little, are beginning to find themselves already in a situation analogous to that of the workers in the great manufacturing States of Europe. And we see, in effect the social question already being posed in the Northern States, just as it was posed long before in our countries.

And there too, the self-government of the masses, in spite of all the display of the people's omnipotence, remains most of the time in a state of fiction. In reality, it is minorities which govern. The so-called Democratic Party, up to the time of the Civil War to emancipate the slaves, were the out and out partizans of slavery and of the ferocious oligarchy of the planters, demagogues without faith or conscience, capable of sacrificing everything to their greed and evil-minded ambition, and who, by their detestable influence and actions, exercised almost unhindered, for nearly fifty years continuously, have greatly contributed to deprave the political morality of North America.

The Republican Party, though really intelligent and generous, is still and always a minority, and whatever the sincerity of this party of liberation, however great and generous the principles it professes, do not let us hope that, in power, it will renounce this exclusive position of a governing minority to merge into the mass of the nation so that the self-government of the people shall finally become a reality. For that there will be necessary a revolution far more profound than all those which hitherto have shaken the Old and New Worlds.

In Switzerland, in spite of all the democratic revolutions that have taken place there, it is still always the class in comfortable circumstances, the bourgeoisie, that is to say, the class privileged by wealth, leisure, and education, which governs. The sovereignty of the people—a word which, anyway, we detest because in our eyes, all sovereignty is detestable—the government of the people by themselves is likewise a fiction. The people is sovereign in law, not in fact, for necessarily absorbed by their daily labor, which leaves them no leisure, and if not completely ignorant, at least very inferior in education to the bourgeoisie, they are forced to place in the hands of the latter their supposed sovereignty. The sole advantage which they get out of it in Switzerland, as in the United States, is that ambitious minorities, the political classes, cannot arrive at power otherwise than by paying court to the people, flattering their fleeting passions, which may sometimes be very bad, and most often deceiving them.

It is true that the most imperfect republic is a thousand times better than the most enlightened monarchy, for at least in the republic there are moments when, though always exploited, the people are not oppressed, while in monarchies they are never anything else. And then the democratic regime trains the masses little by little in public life, which the monarchy never does. But whilst giving the preference to the republic we are nevertheless forced to recognize and proclaim that whatever may be the form of government, whilst human society remains divided into different classes because of the hereditary inequality of occupations, wealth, education, and privileges, there will always be minority government and the inevitable exploitation of the majority by that minority.

The State is nothing else but this domination and exploitation regularized and systematized. We shall attempt to demonstrate it by examining the consequence of the government of the masses of the people by a minority, at first as intelligent and as devoted as you like, in an ideal State, founded on a free contract.

Suppose the government to be confined only to the best citizens. At first these citizens are privileged not by right, but by fact. They have been elected by the people because they are the most intelligent, clever, wise, and courageous and devoted. Taken from the mass of the citizens, who are regarded as all equal, they do not yet form a class apart, but a group of men privileged only by nature and for that very reason singled out for election by the people. Their number is necessarily very limited, for in all times and countries the number of men endowed with qualities so remarkable that they automatically command the unanimous respect of a nation is, as experience teaches us, very small. Therefore, under pain of making a bad choice, the people will be always forced to choose its rulers from among them.

Here, then, is society divided into two categories, if not yet to say two classes, of which one, composed of the immense majority of the citizens, submits freely to the government of its elected leaders, the other, formed of a small number of privileged natures, recognized and accepted as such by the people, and charged by them to govern them. Dependent on popular election, they are at first distinguished from the mass of the citizens only by the very qualities which recommended them to their choice and are naturally, the most devoted and useful of all. They do not yet assume to themselves any privilege, any particular right, except that of exercising, insofar as the people wish it, the special functions with which they have been charged. For the rest, by their manner of life, by the conditions and means of their existence, they do not separate themselves in any way from all the others, so that a perfect equality continues to reign among all. Can this equality be long maintained? We claim that it cannot and nothing is easier to prove it.

Nothing is more dangerous for man's private morality than the habit of command. The best man, the most intelligent, disinterested, generous, pure, will infallibly and always be spoiled at this trade. Two sentiments inherent in power never fail to produce this demoralization; they are: contempt for the masses and the overestimation of one's own merits.

"The masses," a man says to himself, "recognizing their incapacity to govern on their own account, have elected me their chief. By that act they have publicly proclaimed their inferiority and my superiority. Among this crowd of men, recognizing hardly any equals of myself, I am alone capable of directing public affairs. The people have need of me; they cannot do without my services, while I, on the contrary, can get along all right by myself: they, therefore, must obey me for their own security, and in condescending to command them, I am doing them a good turn."

Is not there something in all that to make a man lose his head and his heart as well, and become mad with pride? It is thus that power and the habit of command become for even the most intelligent and virtuous men, a source of aberration, both intellectual and moral.

But in the People's State of Marx, there will be, we are told, no privileged class at all. All will be equal, not only from the juridical and political point of view, but from the economic point of view. At least that is what is promised, though I doubt very much, considering the manner in which it is being tackled and the course it is desired to follow, whether that promise could ever be kept. There will therefore be no longer any privileged class, but there will be a government and, note this well, an extremely complex government, which will not content itself with governing and administering the masses politically, as all governments do to-day, but which will also administer them economically, concentrating in its own hands the production and the just division of wealth, the cultivation of land, the establishment and development of factories, the organization and direction of commerce, finally the application of capital to production by the only banker, the State. All that will demand an immense knowledge and many "heads overflowing with brains" in this government. It will be the reign of *scientific intelligence*, the most aristocratic, despotic, arrogant and contemptuous of all regimes. There will be a new class, a new hierarchy of real and pretended scientists and scholars, and the world will be divided into a minority ruling in the name of knowledge and an immense ignorant majority. And then, woe betide the mass of ignorant ones!

Such a regime will not fail to arouse very considerable discontent in this mass and in order to keep it in check the enlightenment and liberating government of Marx will have need of a not less considerable armed force. For the government must be strong, says

Engels, to maintain order among these millions of illiterates whose brutal uprising would be capable of destroying and overthrowing everything, even a government directed by heads overflowing with brains.

You can see quite well that behind all the democratic and socialistic phrases and promises of Marx's program, there is to be found in his State all that constitutes the true despotic and brutal nature of all States, whatever may be the form of their government and that in the final reckoning, the People's State so strongly commended by Marx, and the aristocratic-monarchic State, maintained with as much cleverness as power by Bismarck, are completely identical by the nature of their objective at home as well as in foreign affairs. In foreign affairs it is the same deployment of military force, that is to say, conquest; and in home affairs it is the same employment of this armed force, the last argument of all threatened political powers against the masses, who, tired of believing, hoping, submitting and obeying always, rise in revolt.

Marx's Communist idea comes to light in all his writings; it is also manifest in the motions put forward by the General Council of the International Workingmen's Association, situated in London, at the Congress of Basel in 1869, as well as by the proposals which he had intended to present to the Congress which was to take place in September, 1870, but which had to be suspended because of the Franco-German War. As a member of the General Council in London and as corresponding Secretary for Germany, Marx enjoys in this Council, as is well known, a great and it must be admitted, legitimate influence, so that it can be taken for certain that of the motions put to the Congress by the Council, several are principally derived from the system and the collaboration of Marx. It was in this way that the English citizen Lucraft, a member of the General Council, put forward at the Congress of Basel the idea that all the land in a country should become the property of the State, and that the cultivation of this land should be directed and administered by State officials, "Which," he added, "will only be possible in a democratic and Socialist State, in which the people will have to watch carefully over the good administration of the national land by the State."

This cult of the State is, in general, the principal characteristic of German Socialism. Lassalle, the greatest Socialist agitator and the true founder of the practical Socialist movement in Germany was steeped in it. He saw no salvation for the workers except in the power of the State; of which the workers should possess themselves, according to him, by means of universal suffrage.

WHAT IS AUTHORITY?

What is authority? Is it the inevitable power of the natural laws which manifest themselves in the necessary linking and succession of phenomena in the physical and social worlds? Indeed, against these laws revolt is not only forbidden—it is even impossible. We may misunderstand them or not know them at all, but we cannot disobey them; because they constitute the basis and the fundamental conditions of our existence; they envelop us, penetrate us, regulate all our movements. thoughts and acts; even when we believe that we disobey them, we only show their omnipotence.

Yes, we are absolutely the slaves of these laws. But in such slavery there is no humiliation, or, rather, it is not slavery at all. For slavery supposes an external master, a legislator outside of him whom he commands, while these laws are not outside of us; they are inherent in us; they constitute our being, our whole being, physically, intellectually, and morally; we live, we breathe, we act, we think, we wish only through these laws. Without them we are nothing, we are not. Whence, then, could we derive the power and the wish to rebel against them?

In his relation to natural laws but one liberty is possible to man— that of recognizing and applying them on an ever-extending scale of conformity with the object of collective and individual emancipation of humanization which he pursues. These laws, once recognized, exercise an authority which is never disputed by the mass of men. One must, for instance, be at bottom either a fool or a theologician or at least a metaphysician, jurist or bourgeois economist to rebel against the law by which twice two make four. One must have faith to imagine that fire will not burn nor water drown, except, indeed, recourse be had to some subterfuge founded in its turn on some other natural law. But these revolts, or rather, these attempts at or foolish fancies of an impossible revolt, are decidedly the exception: for, in general, it may be said that the mass of men, in their daily lives, acknowledge the government of common sense—that is, of the sum of the general laws generally recognized—in an almost absolute fashion.

The great misfortune is that a large number of natural laws, already established as such by science, remain unknown to the masses, thanks to the watchfulness of those tutelary governments that exist, as we know, only for the good of the people. There is another difficulty—namely, that the major portion of the natural laws connected with the development of human society, which are quite as necessary, invariable, fatal, as the laws that govern the physical world, have not been duly established and recognized by science itself.

Once they shall have been recognized by science, and then from science, by means of an extensive system of popular education and instruction, shall have passed into the consciousness of all, the question of liberty will be entirely solved. The most stubborn authorities must admit that then there will be no need either of political organization or direction or legislation, three things which, whether they emanate from the will of the sovereign or from the vote of a parliament elected by universal suffrage, and even should they conform to the system of natural laws—which has never been the case and never will be the case—are always equally fatal and hostile to the liberty of the masses from the very fact that they impose on them a system of external and therefore despotic laws.

The Liberty of man consists solely in this: that he obeys natural laws because he has himself recognized them as such, and not because they have been externally imposed upon him by any extrinsic will whatsoever, divine or human, collective or individual.

Suppose a learned academy, composed of the most illustrious representatives of science; suppose this academy charged with legislation for and the organization of society, and that, inspired only by the purest love of truth, it frames none but the laws but the laws in absolute harmony with the latest discoveries of science. Well, I maintain, for my part, that such legislation and such organization would be a monstrosity, and that, and that for two reasons: first, that human science is always and necessarily imperfect, and that, comparing what it has discovered with what remains to be discovered, we may say that it is still in its cradle. So that were we to try to force the practical life of men, collective as well as individual, into strict and exclusive conformity with the latest data of science, we should condemn society as well as individuals to suffer martyrdom on a bed of Procrustes, which would soon end by dislocating and stifling them, life ever remaining an infinitely greater thing than science.

The second reason is this: a society which should obey legislation emanating from a scientific academy, not because it understood itself the rational character of this legislation (in which case the existence of the academy would become useless), but because this legislation, emanating from the academy, was imposed in the name of a science which it venerated without comprehending—such a society would be a society, not of men, but of brutes. It would be a second edition of those missions in Paraguay which submitted so long to the government of the Jesuits. It would surely and rapidly descend to the lowest stage of idiocy.

But there is still a third reason which would render such a government impossible—namely that a scientific academy invested with a sovereignty, so to speak, absolute, even if it were composed of the most illustrious men, would infallibly and soon end in its own moral and intellectual corruption. Even today, with the few privileges allowed them, such is the history of all academies. The greatest scientific genius, from the moment that he becomes an academian, an officially liscenced savant, inevitably lapses into sluggishness. He loses his spontaneity, his revolutionary hardihood, and that troublesome and savage energy characteristic of the grandest geniuses, ever called to destroy old tottering worlds and lay the foundations of new. He undoubtedly gains in politeness, in utilitarian and practical wisdom, what he loses in power of thought. In a word, he becomes corrupted.

It is the characteristic of privilege and of every privileged position to kill the mind and heart of men. The privileged man, whether practically or economically, is a man depraved in mind and heart. That is a social law which admits of no exception, and is as applicable to entire nations as to classes, corporations and individuals. It is the law of equality, the supreme condition of liberty and humanity. The principle object of this treatise is precisely to demonstrate this truth in all the manifestations of social life.

A scientific body to which had been confided the government of society would soon end by devoting itself no longer to science at all, but to quite another affair; and that affair, as in the case of all established powers, would be its own eternal perpetuation by rendering the society confided to its care ever more stupid and consequently more in need of its government and direction.

But that which is true of scientific academies is also true of all constituent and legislative assemblies, even those chosen by universal suffrage. In the latter case they may renew their composition, it is true, but this does not prevent the formation in a few years' time of a body of politicians, privileged in fact though not in law, who, devoting themselves exclusively to the direction of the public affairs of a country, finally form a sort of political aristocracy or oligarchy. Witness the United States of America and Switzerland.

Consequently, no external legislation and no authority—one, for that matter, being inseparable from the other, and both tending to the servitude of society and the degradation of the legislators themselves.

Does it follow that I reject all authority? Far from me such a thought. In the matter of boots, I refer to the authority of the bootmaker; concerning houses, canals, or railroads, I consult that of the architect or the engineer. For such or such special knowledge I apply to such or such a savant. But I allow neither the bootmaker nor the architect nor savant to impose his authority upon me. I listen to them freely and with all the respect merited by their intelligence, their character, their knowledge, reserving always my incontestable right of criticism and censure. I do not content myself with consulting a single authority in any special branch; I consult several; I compare their opinions, and choose that which seems to me the soundest. But I recognize no infallible authority, even in special questions; consequently, whatever respect I may have for the honesty and the sincerity of such or such individual, I have no absolute faith in any person. Such a faith would be fatal to my reason, to my liberty, and even to the success of my undertakings; it would immediately transform me into a stupid slave, an instrument of the will and interests of others.

If I bow before the authority of the specialists and avow my readiness to follow, to a certain extent and as long as may seem to me necessary, their indications and even their directions, it is because their authority is imposed on me by no one, neither by men nor by God. Otherwise I would repel them with horror, and bid the devil take their counsels, their directions, and their services, certain that they would make me pay, by the loss of my liberty and self-respect, for such scraps of truth, wrapped in a multitude of lies, as they might give me.

I bow before the authority of special men because it is imposed on me by my own reason. I am conscious of my own inability to grasp, in all its detail, and positive development, any very large portion of human knowledge. The greatest intelligence would not be equal to a comprehension of the whole. Thence results, for science as well as for industry, the necessity of the division and association of labor. I receive and I give—such is human life. Each directs and is directed in his turn. Therefore there is no fixed and constant authority, but a continual exchange of mutual, temporary, and, above all, voluntary authority and subordination.

This same reason forbids me, then, to recognize a fixed, constant and universal authority, because there is no universal man, no man capable of grasping in all that wealth of detail, without which the application of science to life is impossible, all the sciences, all the branches of social life. And if such universality could ever be realized in a single man, and if he wished to take advantage thereof to impose his authority upon us, it would be necessary to drive this man out of society, because his authority would inevitably reduce all the others to slavery and imbecility. I do not think that society ought to maltreat men of genius as it has done hitherto: but neither do I think it should indulge them too far, still less accord them any privileges or exclusive rights whatsoever; and that for three reasons: first, because it would often mistake a charlatan for a man of genius; second, because, through such a system of privileges, it might transform into a charlatan even a real man of genius, demoralize him, and degrade him; and, finally, because it would establish a master over itself.

Chapter 8

LYSANDER SPOONER
No Treason, No. VI: The Constitution of No Authority (1870)

Abolitionist and attorney Lysander Spooner's essay "No Treason" consisted of three parts. It is the third part—oddly numbered as VI—that holds the most sway today. The Constitution is like a "No Guns Zone" sign for conservatives, in that the only people it would bind are those who are already generally honest and peaceable. The ones who would lie or commit harm would simply look at the piece of paper and scoff. With unrelenting logic, Spooner dissects the sanctity of the Constitution and demonstrates that it cannot be said to have moral authority over anyone.

I

The Constitution has no inherent authority or obligation. It has no authority or obligation at all, unless as a contract between man and man. And it does not so much as even purport to be a contract between persons now existing. It purports, at most, to be only a contract between persons living eighty years ago. And it can be supposed to have been a contract then only between persons who had already come to years of discretion, so as to be competent to make reasonable and obligatory contracts. Furthermore, we know, historically, that only a small portion even of the people then existing were consulted on the subject, or asked, or permitted to express either their consent or dissent in any formal manner. Those persons, if any, who did give their consent formally, are all dead now. Most of them have been dead forty, fifty, sixty, or seventy years. *And the Constitution, so far as it was their contract, died with them.* They had no natural power or right to make it obligatory upon their children. It is not only plainly impossible, in the nature of things, that they *could* bind their posterity, but they did not even attempt to bind them. That is to say, the instrument does not purport to be an agreement between any body but "the people" *then* existing; nor does it, either expressly or impliedly, assert any right, power, or disposition, on their part, to bind anybody but themselves. Let us see. Its language is:

> We, the people of the United States (that is, the people *then existing* in the United States), in order to form a more perfect union, insure domestic tranquility, provide for the common defense, promote the general welfare, and secure the blessings of liberty to ourselves *and our posterity*, do ordain and establish this Constitution for the United States of America.

It is plain, in the first place, that this language, *as an agreement*, purports to be only what it at most really was, viz., a contract between the people then existing; and, of necessity, binding, as a contract, only upon those then existing. In the second place, the language neither expresses nor implies that they had any intention or desire, nor that they imagined they had any right or power, to bind their "posterity" to live under it. It does not say that their "posterity" will, shall, or must live under it. It only says, in effect, that their hopes and motives in adopting it were that it might prove useful to their posterity, as well as to themselves, by promoting their union, safety, tranquility, liberty, etc.

Suppose an agreement were entered into, in this form:

We, the people of Boston, agree to maintain a fort on Governor's Island, to protect ourselves and our posterity against invasion.

This agreement, as an agreement, would clearly bind nobody but the people then existing. Secondly, it would assert no right, power, or disposition, on their part, to compel their "posterity" to maintain such a fort. It would only indicate that the supposed welfare of their posterity was one of the motives that induced the original parties to enter into the agreement.

84

When a man says he is building a house for himself and his posterity, he does not mean to be understood as saying that he has any thought of binding them, nor is it to be inferred that he is so foolish as to imagine that he has any right or power to bind them, to live in it. So far as they are concerned, he only means to be understood as saying that his hopes and motives, in building it, are that they, or at least some of them, may find it for their happiness to live in it.

So when a man says he is planting a tree for himself and his posterity, he does not mean to be understood as saying that he has any thought of compelling them, nor is it to be inferred that he is such a simpleton as to imagine that he has any right or power to compel them, to eat the fruit. So far as they are concerned, he only means to say that his hopes and motives, in planting the tree, are that its fruit may be agreeable to them.

So it was with those who originally adopted the Constitution. Whatever may have been their personal intentions, the legal meaning of their language, so far as their "posterity" was concerned, simply was, that their hopes and motives, in entering into the agreement, were that it might prove useful and acceptable to their posterity; that it might promote their union, safety, tranquility, and welfare; and that it might tend "to secure to them the blessings of liberty." The language does not assert nor at all imply, any right, power, or disposition, on the part of the original parties to the agreement, to compel their "posterity" to live under it. If they had intended to bind their posterity to live under it, they should have said that their object was, not "to secure to them the blessings of liberty," but to make slaves of them; for if their "posterity" are bound to live under it, they are nothing less than the slaves of their foolish, tyrannical, and dead grandfathers.

It cannot be said that the Constitution formed "the people of the United States," for all time, into a corporation. It does not speak of "the people" as a corporation, but as individuals. A corporation does not describe itself as "we," nor as "people," nor as "ourselves." Nor does a corporation, in legal language, have any "posterity." It supposes itself to have, and speaks of itself as having, perpetual existence, as a single individuality.

Moreover, no body of men, existing at any one time, have the power to create a perpetual corporation. A corporation can become practically perpetual only by the voluntary accession of new members, as the old ones die off. But for this voluntary accession of new members, the corporation necessarily dies with the death of those who originally composed it.

Legally speaking, therefore, there is, in the Constitution, nothing that professes or attempts to bind the "posterity" of those who established it.

If, then, those who established the Constitution, had no power to bind, and did not attempt to bind, their posterity, the question arises, whether their posterity have bound themselves. If they have done so, they can have done so in only one or both of these two ways, viz., by voting, and paying taxes.

II

Let us consider these two matters, voting and tax paying, separately. And first of voting.

All the voting that has ever taken place under the Constitution, has been of such a kind that it not only did not pledge the whole people to support the Constitution, but it did not even pledge any one of them to do so, as the following considerations show.

1. In the very nature of things, the act of voting could bind nobody but the actual voters. But owing to the property qualifications required, it is probable that, during the first twenty or thirty years under the Constitution, not more than one-tenth, fifteenth, or perhaps twentieth of the whole population (black and white, men, women, and minors) were permitted to vote. Consequently, so far as voting was concerned, not more than one-tenth, fifteenth, or twentieth of those then existing, could have incurred any obligation to support the Constitution.

At the present time, it is probable that not more than one-sixth of the whole population are permitted to vote. Consequently, so far as voting is concerned, the other five-sixths can have given no pledge that they will support the Constitution.

2. Of the one-sixth that are permitted to vote, probably not more than two-thirds (about one-ninth of the whole population) have usually voted. Many never vote at all. Many vote only once in two, three, five, or ten years, in periods of great excitement.

No one, by voting, can be said to pledge himself for any longer period than that for which he votes. If, for example, I vote for an officer who is to hold his office for only a year, I cannot be said to have thereby pledged myself to support the government beyond that term. Therefore, on the ground of actual voting, it probably cannot be said that more than one-ninth or one-eighth, of the whole population are usually under any pledge to support the Constitution.

3. It cannot be said that, by voting, a man pledges himself to support the Constitution, unless the act of voting be a perfectly voluntary one on his part. Yet the act of voting cannot properly be called a voluntary one on the part of any very large number of those who do vote. It is rather a measure of necessity imposed upon them by others, than one of their own choice. On this point I repeat what was said in a former number,[i] viz.:

"In truth, in the case of individuals, their actual voting is not to be taken as proof of consent, *even for the time being*. On the contrary, it is to be considered that, without his consent having even been asked a man finds himself environed by a government that he cannot resist; a government that forces him to pay money, render service, and forego the exercise of many of his natural rights, under peril of weighty punishments. He sees, too, that other men practice this tyranny over him by the use of the ballot. He sees further, that, if he will but use the ballot himself, he has some chance of relieving himself from this tyranny of others, by subjecting them to his own. In short, he finds himself, without his consent, so situated that, if he use the ballot, he may become a master; if he does not use it, he must become a slave. And he has no other alternative than these two. In self-defence, he attempts the former. His case is analogous to that of a man who has been forced into battle, where he must either kill others, or be killed himself. Because, to save his own life in battle, a man attempts to take the lives of his opponents, it is not to be inferred that the battle is one of his own choosing. Neither in contests with the ballot—which is a mere substitute for a bullet—because, as his only chance of self-preservation, a man uses a ballot, is it to be inferred that the contest is one into which he voluntarily entered; that he voluntarily set up all his own natural rights, as a stake against those of others, to be lost or won by the mere power of numbers. On the contrary, it is to be considered that, in an exigency into which he had been forced by others, and in which no other means of self-defence offered, he, as a matter of necessity, used the only one that was left to him.

"Doubtless the most miserable of men, under the most oppressive government in the world, if allowed the ballot, would use it, if they could see any chance of thereby meliorating their condition. But it would not, therefore, be a legitimate inference that the government itself, that crushes them, was one which they had voluntarily set up, or even consented to.

"Therefore, a man's voting under the Constitution of the United States, is not to be taken as evidence that he ever freely assented to the Constitution, *even for the time being*. Consequently we have no proof that any very large portion, even of the actual voters of the United States, ever really and voluntarily consented to the Constitution, *even for the time being*. Nor can we ever have such proof, until every man is left perfectly free to consent, or not, without thereby subjecting himself or his property to be disturbed or injured by others."

As we can have no legal knowledge as to who votes from choice, and who from the necessity thus forced upon him, we can have no legal knowledge, as to any particular individual, that he voted from choice; or, consequently, that by voting, he consented, or pledged himself, to support the government. Legally speaking, therefore, the act of voting utterly fails to pledge *any one* to support the government. It utterly fails to prove that the government rests upon the voluntary support of anybody. On general principles of law and reason, it cannot be said that the government has any voluntary supporters at all, until it can be distinctly shown who its voluntary supporters are.

4. As taxation is made compulsory on all, whether they vote or not, a large proportion of those who vote, no doubt do so to prevent their own money being used against themselves; when, in fact, they would have gladly abstained from voting, if they could thereby have saved themselves from taxation alone, to say nothing of being saved from all the other usurpations and tyrannies of the government. To take a man's property without his consent, and then to infer his consent because he attempts, by voting, to prevent that property from being used to his injury, is a very insufficient proof of his consent to support the Constitution. It is, in fact, no proof at all. And as we can have no legal knowledge as to who the particular individuals are, if there are any, who are willing to be taxed for the sake of voting, we can have no legal knowledge that any particular

individual consents to be taxed for the sake of voting; or, consequently, consents to support the Constitution.

5. At nearly all elections, votes are given for various candidates for the same office. Those who vote for the unsuccessful candidates cannot properly be said to have voted to sustain the Constitution. They may, with more reason, be supposed to have voted, not to support the Constitution, but specially to prevent the tyranny which they anticipate the successful candidate intends to practice upon them under color of the Constitution; and therefore may reasonably be supposed to have voted against the Constitution itself. This supposition is the more reasonable, inasmuch as such voting is the only mode allowed to them of expressing their dissent to the Constitution.

6. Many votes are usually given for candidates who have no prospect of success. Those who give such votes may reasonably be supposed to have voted as they did, with a special intention, not to support, but to obstruct the execution of, the Constitution; and, therefore, against the Constitution itself.

7. As all the different votes are given secretly (by secret ballot), there is no legal means of knowing, from the votes themselves, who votes for, and who against, the Constitution. Therefore, voting affords no legal evidence that any particular individual supports the Constitution. And where there can be no legal evidence that any particular individual supports the Constitution, it cannot legally be said that anybody supports it. It is clearly impossible to have any legal proof of the intentions of large numbers of men, where there can be no legal proof of the intentions of any particular one of them.

8. There being no legal proof of any man's intentions, in voting, we can only conjecture them. As a conjecture, it is probable, that a very large proportion of those who vote, do so on this principle, viz., that if, by voting, they could but get the government into their own hands (or that of their friends), and use its powers against their opponents, they would then willingly support the Constitution; but if their opponents are to have the power, and use it against them, then they would *not* willingly support the Constitution.

In short, men's voluntary support of the Constitution is doubtless, in most cases, wholly contingent upon the question whether, by means of the Constitution, they can make themselves masters, or are to be made slaves.

Such contingent consent as that is, in law and reason, no consent at all.

9. As everybody who supports the Constitution by voting (if there are any such) does so secretly (by secret ballot), and in a way to avoid all personal responsibility for the act of his agents or representatives, it cannot legally or reasonably be said that anybody at all supports the Constitution by voting. No man can reasonably or legally be said to do such a thing as to assent to, or support, the Constitution, *unless he does it openly, and in a way to make himself personally responsible for the acts of his agents, so long as they act within the limits of the power he delegates to them.*

10. As all voting is secret (by secret ballot), and as all secret governments are necessarily only secret bands of robbers, tyrants, and murderers, the general fact that our government is practically carried on by means of such voting, only proves that there is among us a secret band of robbers, tyrants and murderers, whose purpose is to rob, enslave, and, so far as necessary to accomplish their purposes, murder, the rest of the people. The simple fact of the existence of such a band does nothing towards proving that "the people of the United States," or any one of them, voluntarily supports the Constitution.

For all the reasons that have now been given, voting furnishes no legal evidence as to who the particular individuals are (if there are any), who voluntarily support the Constitution. It therefore furnishes no legal evidence that anybody supports it voluntarily.

So far, therefore, as voting is concerned, the Constitution, legally speaking, has no supporters at all.

And, as matter of fact, there is not the slightest probability that the Constitution has a single bona fide supporter in the country. That is to say, there is not the slightest probability that there is a single man in the country, who both understands what the Constitution really is, *and sincerely supports it for what it really is.*

The ostensible supporters of the Constitution, like the ostensible supporters of most other governments, are made up of three classes, viz.: 1. Knaves, a numerous and active class, who see in the government an instrument which they can use for their own aggrandizement or wealth. 2. Dupes—a large class, no doubt—each of whom, because he is allowed one voice out of millions in deciding what he may do with his own person and his own property, and because he is permitted to have the same voice in robbing, enslaving, and murdering others, that others have in robbing, enslaving, and murdering himself, is stupid enough to imagine that he is a "free man," a "sovereign"; that this is "a free government"; "a government of equal rights," "the best government on earth,"[ii] and such like absurdities. 3. A class who have some appreciation of the evils of government, but either do not see how to get rid of them, or do not choose to so far sacrifice their private interests as to give themselves seriously and earnestly to the work of making a change.

III

The payment of taxes, being compulsory, of course furnishes no evidence that any one voluntarily supports the Constitution.

1. It is true that the *theory* of our Constitution is, that all taxes are paid voluntarily; that our government is a mutual insurance company, voluntarily entered into by the people with each other; that each man makes a free and purely voluntary contract with all others who are parties to the Constitution, to pay so much money for so much protection, the same as he does with any other insurance company; and that he is just as free not to be protected, and not to pay tax, as he is to pay a tax, and be protected.

But this theory of our government is wholly different from the practical fact. The fact is that the government, like a highwayman, says to a man: "Your money, or your life." And many, if not most, taxes are paid under the compulsion of that threat.

The government does not, indeed, waylay a man in a lonely place, spring upon him from the roadside, and, holding a pistol to his head, proceed to rifle his pockets. But the robbery is none the less a robbery on that account; and it is far more dastardly and shameful.

The highwayman takes solely upon himself the responsibility, danger, and crime of his own act. He does not pretend that he has any rightful claim to your money, or that he intends to use it for your own benefit. He does not pretend to be anything but a robber. He has not acquired impudence enough to profess to be merely a "protector," and that he takes men's money against their will, merely to enable him to "protect" those infatuated travellers, who feel perfectly able to protect themselves, or do not appreciate his peculiar system of protection. He is too sensible a man to make such professions as these. Furthermore, having taken your money, he leaves you, as you wish him to do. He does not persist in following you on the road, against your will; assuming to be your rightful "sovereign," on account of the "protection" he affords you. He does not keep "protecting" you, by commanding you to bow down and serve him; by requiring you to do this, and forbidding you to do that; by robbing you of more money as often as he finds it for his interest or pleasure to do so; and by branding you as a rebel, a traitor, and an enemy to your country, and shooting you down without mercy, if you dispute his authority, or resist his demands. He is too much of a gentleman to be guilty of such impostures, and insults, and villainies as these. In short, he does not, in addition to robbing you, attempt to make you either his dupe or his slave.

The proceedings of those robbers and murderers, who call themselves "the government," are directly the opposite of these of the single highwayman.

In the first place, they do not, like him, make themselves individually known; or, consequently, take upon themselves personally the responsibility of their acts. On the contrary, they secretly (by secret ballot) designate some one of their number to commit the robbery in their behalf, while they keep themselves practically concealed. They say to the person thus designated:

Go to A—— B——, and say to him that "the government" has need of money to meet the expenses of protecting him and his property. If he presumes to say that he has never contracted with us to protect him, and that he wants none of our protection, say to him that that is our business, and not his; that we *choose* to protect him, whether he desires us to do so or not; and that we demand pay, too, for protecting him. If he dares to inquire who the individuals are, who have thus taken upon themselves the title of "the government," and who assume to protect him, and demand payment of him, without his having ever made any contract with them, say to him that that, too, is our business, and not his; that we do not *choose* to make ourselves *individually* known to him; that we have secretly (by secret ballot) appointed you our agent to give him notice of our demands, and, if he complies with them, to give him, in our name, a receipt that will protect him against any similar demand for the present year. If he refuses to comply, seize and sell enough of his property to pay not only our demands, but all your own expenses and trouble beside. If he resists the seizure of his property, call upon the bystanders to help you (doubtless some of them will prove to be members of our band). If, in defending his property, he should kill any of our band who are assisting you, capture him at all hazards; charge him (in one of our courts) with murder; convict him, and hang him. If he should call upon his neighbors, or any others who, like him, may be disposed to resist our demands, and they should come in large numbers to his assistance, cry out that they are all rebels and traitors; that "our country" is in danger; call upon the commander of our hired murderers; tell him to quell the rebellion and "save the country," cost what it may. Tell him to kill all who resist, though they should be hundreds of thousands; and thus strike terror into all others similarly disposed. See that the work of murder is thoroughly done; that we may have no further trouble of this kind hereafter. When these traitors shall have thus been taught our strength and our determination, they will be good loyal citizens for many years, and pay their taxes without a why or a wherefore.

It is under such compulsion as this that taxes, so called, are paid. And how much proof the payment of taxes affords, that the people consent to support "the government," it needs no further argument to show.

2. Still another reason why the payment of taxes implies no consent, or pledge, to support the government, is that the taxpayer does not know, and has no means of knowing, who the particular individuals are who compose "the government." To him "the government" is a myth, an abstraction, an incorporeality, with which he can make no contract, and to which he can give no consent, and make no pledge. He knows it only through its pretended agents. "The government" itself he never sees. He knows indeed, by common report, that certain persons, of a certain age, are permitted to vote; and thus to make themselves parts of, or (if they choose) opponents of, the government, for the time being. But who of them do thus vote, and especially how each one votes (whether so as to aid or oppose the government), he does not know; the voting being all done secretly (by secret ballot). Who, therefore, practically compose "the government," for the time being, he has no means of knowing. Of course he can make no contract with them, give them no consent, and make them no pledge. Of necessity, therefore, his paying taxes to them implies, on his part, no contract, consent, or pledge to support them—that is, to support "the government," or the Constitution.

3. Not knowing who the particular individuals are, who call themselves "the government," the taxpayer does not know whom he pays his taxes to. All he knows is that a man comes to him, representing himself to be the agent of "the government"—that is, the agent of a secret band of robbers and murderers, who have taken to themselves the title of "the government," and have determined to kill everybody who refuses to give them whatever money they demand. To save his life, he gives up his money to this agent. But as this agent does not make his principals individually known to the taxpayer, the latter, after he has given up his money, knows no more who are "the government"—that is, who were the robbers—than he did before. To say, therefore, that by giving up his money to their agent, he entered into a voluntary contract with them, that he pledges himself to obey them, to support them, and to give them whatever money they should demand of him in the future, is simply ridiculous.

4. All political power, as it is called, rests practically upon this matter of money. Any number of scoundrels, having money enough to start with, can establish themselves as a "government"; because, with money, they can hire soldiers, and with soldiers extort more money; and also compel general obedience to their will. It is with government, as Caesar said it was in war, that money and soldiers mutually supported each other; that with money he could hire soldiers, and with soldiers extort money. So these villains, who call themselves governments, well understand that their power rests primarily upon money. With money they can hire soldiers, and with soldiers extort money. And, when their authority is denied, the first use they always make of money, is to hire soldiers to kill or subdue all who refuse them more money.

For this reason, whoever desires liberty, should understand these vital facts, viz.: 1. That every man who puts money into the hands of a "government" (so called), puts into its hands a sword which will be used against himself, to extort more money from him, and also to keep him in subjection to its arbitrary will. 2. That those who will take his money, without his consent, in the first place, will use it for his further robbery and enslavement, if he presumes to resist their demands in the future. 3. That it is a perfect absurdity to suppose that any body of men would ever take a man's money without his consent, for any such object as they profess to take it for, viz., that of protecting him; for why should they wish to protect him, if he does not wish them to do so? To suppose that they would do so, is just as absurd as it would be to suppose that they would take his money without his consent, for the purpose of buying food or clothing for him, when he did not want it. 4. If a man wants "protection," he is competent to make his own bargains for it; and nobody has any occasion to rob him, in order to "protect" him against his will. 5. That the only security men can have for their political liberty, consists in their keeping their money in their own pockets, until they have assurances, perfectly satisfactory to themselves, that it will be used as they wish it to be used, for their benefit, and not for their injury. 6. That no government, so called, can reasonably be trusted for a moment, or reasonably be supposed to have honest purposes in view, any longer than it depends wholly upon voluntary support.

These facts are all so vital and so self-evident, that it cannot reasonably be supposed that any one will voluntarily pay money to a "government," for the purpose of securing its protection, unless he first makes an explicit and purely voluntary contract with it for that purpose.

It is perfectly evident, therefore, that neither such voting, nor such payment of taxes, as actually takes place, proves anybody's consent, or obligation, to support the Constitution. Consequently we have no evidence at all that the Constitution is binding upon anybody, or that anybody is under any contract or obligation whatever to support it. And nobody is under any obligation to support it.

IV

The Constitution not only binds nobody now, but it never did bind anybody. It never bound anybody, because it was never agreed to by anybody in such a manner as to make it, on general principles of law and reason, binding upon him.

It is a general principle of law and reason, that a *written* instrument binds no one until he has signed it. This principle is so inflexible a one, that even though a man is unable to write his name, he must still "make his mark," before he is bound by a written contract. This custom was established ages ago, when few men could write their names; when a clerk—that is, a man who could write—was so rare and valuable a person, that even if he were guilty of high crimes, he was entitled to pardon, on the ground that the public could not afford to lose his services. Even at that time, a written contract must be signed; and men who could not write, either "made their mark," or signed their contracts by stamping their seals upon wax affixed to the parchment on which their contracts were written. Hence the custom of affixing seals, that has continued to this time.

The law holds, and reason declares, that if a written instrument is not signed, the presumption must be that the party to be bound by it, did not choose to sign it, or to bind himself by it. And law and reason both give him until the last moment, in which to decide whether he will sign it, or not. Neither law nor reason requires or expects a man to agree to an instrument, *until it is written*; for until it is written, he cannot know its precise legal meaning. And when it is written, and he has had the opportunity to satisfy himself of its precise legal meaning, he is then expected to decide, and not before, whether he will agree to it or not. And if he does not *then* sign it, his reason is supposed to be, that he does not choose to enter into such a contract. The fact that the instrument was written for him to sign, or with the hope that he would sign it, goes for nothing.

Where would be the end of fraud and litigation, if one party could bring into court a written instrument, without any signature, and claim to have it enforced, upon the ground that it was written for another man to sign? that this other man had promised to sign it? that he ought to have signed it? that he had had the opportunity to sign it, if he would? but that he had refused or neglected to do so? Yet that is the most that could ever be said of the Constitution.[iii] The very judges, who profess to derive all their authority from the Constitution—from an instrument that nobody ever signed—would spurn any other instrument, not signed, that should be brought before them for adjudication.

Moreover, a written instrument must, in law and reason, not only be signed, but must also be delivered to the party (or to some one for him), in whose favor it is made, before it can bind the party making it. The signing is of no effect, unless the instrument be also delivered. And a party is at perfect liberty to refuse to deliver a written instrument, after he has signed it. He is as free to refuse to deliver it, as he is to refuse to sign it. The Constitution was not only never signed by anybody, but it was never delivered by anybody, or to anybody's agent or attorney. It can therefore be of no more validity as a contract, than can any other instrument, that was never signed or delivered.

V

As further evidence of the general sense of mankind, as to the practical necessity there is that all men's *important* contracts, especially those of a permanent nature, should be both written and signed, the following facts are pertinent.

For nearly two hundred years—that is, since 1677—there has been on the statute book of England, and the same, in substance, if not precisely in letter, has been re-enacted, and is now in force, in nearly or quite all the States of this Union, a statute, the general object of which is to declare that no action shall be brought to enforce contracts of the more important class, *unless they are put in writing, and signed by the parties to be held chargeable upon them.*[iv]

The principle of the statute, be it observed, is, not merely that written contracts shall be signed, but also that all contracts, except those specially exempted—generally those that are for small amounts, and are to remain in force but for a short time—*shall be both written and signed*.

The reason of the statute, on this point, is, that it is now so easy a thing for men to put their contracts in writing, and sign them, and their failure to do so opens the door to so much doubt, fraud, and litigation, that men who neglect to have their contracts—of any considerable importance—written and signed, ought not to have the benefit of courts of justice to enforce them. And this reason is a wise one; and that experience has confirmed its wisdom and necessity, is demonstrated by the fact that it has been acted upon in England for nearly two hundred years, and has been so nearly universally adopted in this country, and that nobody thinks of repealing it.

We all know, too, how careful most men are to have their contracts written and signed, even when this statute does not require it. For example, most men, if they have money due them, of no larger amount than five or ten dollars, are careful to take a note for it. If they buy even a small bill of goods, paying for it at the time of delivery, they take a receipted bill for it. If they pay a small balance of a book account, or any other small debt previously contracted, they take a written receipt for it.

Furthermore, the law everywhere (probably) in our country, as well as in England, requires that a large class of contracts, such as wills, deeds, etc., shall not only be written and signed, but also sealed, witnessed, and acknowledged. And in the case of married women conveying their rights in real estate, the law, in many States, requires that the women shall be examined separate and apart from their husbands, and declare that they sign their contracts free of any fear or compulsion of their husbands.

Such are some of the precautions which the laws require, and which individuals—from motives of common prudence, even in cases not required by law—take, to put their contracts in writing, and have them signed, and, to guard against all uncertainties and controversies in regard to their meaning and validity. And yet we have what purports, or professes, or is claimed, to be a contract—the Constitution—made eighty years ago, by men who are now all dead, and who never had any power to bind *us*, but which (it is claimed) has nevertheless bound three generations of men, consisting of many millions, and which (it is claimed) will be binding upon all the millions that are to come; but which nobody ever signed, sealed, delivered, witnessed, or acknowledged; and which few persons, compared with the whole number that are claimed to be bound by it, have ever read, or even seen, or ever will read, or see. And of those who ever have read it, or ever will read it, scarcely any two, perhaps no two, have ever agreed, or ever will agree, as to what it means.

Moreover, this supposed contract, which would not be received in any court of justice sitting under its authority, if offered to prove a debt of five dollars, owing by one man to another, is one by which— *as it is generally interpreted by those who pretend to administer it*—all men, women and children throughout the country, and through all time, surrender not only all their property, but also their liberties, and even lives, into the hands of men who by this supposed contract, are expressly made wholly irresponsible for their disposal of them. And we are so insane, or so wicked, as to destroy property and lives without limit, in fighting to compel men to fulfill a supposed contract, which, inasmuch as it has never been signed by anybody, is, on general principles of law and reason—such principles as we are all governed by in regard to other contracts—the merest waste paper, binding upon nobody, fit only to be thrown into the fire; or, if preserved, preserved only to serve as a witness and a warning of the folly and wickedness of mankind.

VI

It is no exaggeration, but a literal truth, to say that, by the Constitution—*not as I interpret it, but as it is interpreted by those who pretend to administer it*—the properties, liberties, and lives of the entire people of the United States are surrendered unreservedly into the hands of men who, it is provided by the Constitution itself, shall never be "questioned" as to any disposal they make of them.

Thus the Constitution (Art. I, Sec. 6) provides that, "for any speech or debate (or vote), in either house, they (the senators and representatives) shall not be questioned in any other place."

The whole law-making power is given to these senators and representatives (when acting by a two-thirds vote)[v]; and this provision protects them from all responsibility for the laws they make.

The Constitution also enables them to secure the execution of all their laws, by giving them power to withhold the salaries of, and to impeach and remove, all judicial and executive officers, who refuse to execute them.

Thus the whole power of the government is in their hands, and they are made utterly irresponsible for the use they make of it. What is this but absolute, irresponsible power?

It is no answer to this view of the case to say that these men are under oath to use their power only within certain limits; for what care they, or what should they care, for oaths or limits, when it is expressly provided, by the Constitution itself, that they shall never be "questioned," or held to any responsibility whatever, for violating their oaths, or transgressing those limits?

Neither is it any answer to this view of the case to say that the particular individuals holding this power can be changed once in two or six years; for the power of each set of men is absolute during the term for which they hold it; and when they can hold it no longer, they are succeeded only by men whose power will be equally absolute and irresponsible.

Neither is it any answer to this view of the case to say that the men holding this absolute, irresponsible power, must be men chosen by the people (or portions of them) to hold it. A man is none the less a slave because he is allowed to choose a new master once in a term of years. Neither are a people any the less slaves because permitted periodically to choose new masters. What makes them slaves is the fact that they now are, and are always hereafter to be, in the hands of men whose power over them is, and always is to be, absolute and irresponsible.[vi]

The right of absolute and irresponsible dominion is the right of property, and the right of property is the right of absolute, irresponsible dominion. The two are identical; the one necessarily implying the other. Neither can exist without the other. If, therefore, Congress have that absolute and irresponsible law-making power, which the Constitution—according to their interpretation of it— gives them, it can only be because they own us as property. If they own us as property, they are our masters, and their will is our law. If they do not own us as property, they are not our masters, and their will, as such, is of no authority over us.

But these men who claim and exercise this absolute and irresponsible dominion over us, dare not be consistent, and claim either to be our masters, or to own us as property. They say they are only our servants, agents, attorneys, and representatives. But this declaration involves an absurdity, a contradiction. No man can be my servant, agent, attorney, or representative, and be, at the same time, uncontrollable by me, and irresponsible to me for his acts. It is of no importance that I appointed him, and put all power in his hands. If I made him uncontrollable by me, and irresponsible to me, he is no longer my servant, agent, attorney, or representative. If I gave him absolute, irresponsible power over my property, I gave him the property. If I gave him absolute, irresponsible power over myself, I made him my master, and gave myself to him as a slave. And it is of no importance whether I called him master or servant, agent or owner. The only question is, what power did I put into his hands? Was it an absolute and irresponsible one? or a limited and responsible one?

For still another reason they are neither our servants, agents, attorneys, nor representatives. And that reason is, that we do not make ourselves responsible for their acts. If a man is my servant, agent, or attorney, I necessarily make myself responsible for all his acts done within the limits of the power I have intrusted to him. If I have intrusted him, as my agent, with either absolute power, or any power at all, over the persons or properties of other men than myself, I thereby necessarily make myself responsible to those other persons for any injuries he may do them, so long as he acts within the limits of the power I have granted him. But no individual who may be injured in his person or property, by acts of Congress, can come to the individual electors, and hold them responsible for these acts of their so-called agents or representatives. This fact proves that these pretended agents of the people, of everybody, are really the agents of nobody.

If, then, nobody is individually responsible for the acts of Congress, the members of Congress are nobody's agents. And if they are nobody's agents, they are themselves individually responsible for their own acts, and for the acts of all whom they employ. And the authority they are exercising is simply their own individual authority; and, by the law of nature—the highest of all laws—anybody injured by their acts, anybody who is deprived by them of his property or his liberty, has the same right to hold them individually responsible, that he has to hold any other trespasser individually responsible. He has the same right to resist them, and their agents, that he has to resist any other trespassers.

VII

It is plain, then, that on general principles of law and reason—such principles as we all act upon in courts of justice and in common life—the Constitution is no contract; that it binds nobody, and never did bind anybody; and that all those who pretend to act by its authority, are really acting without any legitimate authority at all; that, on general principles of law and reason, they are mere usurpers, and that everybody not only has the right, but is morally bound, to treat them as such.

If the people of this country wish to maintain such a government as the Constitution describes, there is no reason in the world why they should not sign the instrument itself, and thus make known their wishes in an open, authentic manner; in such manner as the common sense and experience of mankind have shown to be reasonable and necessary in such cases; *and in such manner as to make themselves (as they ought to do) individually responsible for the acts of the government.* But the people have never been asked to sign it. And the only reason why they have never been asked to sign it, has been that it has been known that they never would sign it; that they were neither such fools nor knaves as they must needs have been to be willing to sign it; that (at least as it has been practically interpreted) it is not what any sensible and honest man wants for himself; nor such as he has any right to impose upon others. It is, to all moral intents and purposes, as destitute of obligation as the compacts which robbers and thieves and pirates enter into with each other, but never sign.

If any considerable number of the people believe the Constitution to be good, why do they not sign it themselves, and make laws for, and administer them upon, each other; leaving all other persons (who do not interfere with them) in peace? Until they have tried the experiment for themselves, how can they have the face to impose the Constitution upon, or even to recommend it to, others? Plainly the reason for such absurd and inconsistent conduct is that they want the Constitution, not solely for any honest or legitimate use it can be of to themselves or others, but for the dishonest and illegitimate power it gives them over the persons and properties of others. But for this latter reason, all their eulogiums on the Constitution, all their exhortations, and all their expenditures of money and blood to sustain it, would be wanting.

VIII

The Constitution itself, then, being of no authority, on what authority does our government practically rest? On what ground can those who pretend to administer it, claim the right to seize men's property, to restrain them of their natural liberty of action, industry, and trade, and to kill all who deny their authority to dispose of men's properties, liberties, and lives at their pleasure or discretion?

The most they can say, in answer to this question, is, that some half, two-thirds, or three-fourths, of the male adults of the country have a *tacit understanding* that they will maintain a government under the Constitution; that they will select, by ballot, the persons to administer it; and that those persons who may receive a majority, or a plurality, of their ballots, shall act as their representatives, and administer the Constitution in their name, and by their authority.

But this tacit understanding (admitting it to exist) cannot at all justify the conclusion drawn from it. A tacit understanding between A, B, and C, that they will, by ballot, depute D as their agent, to deprive me of my property, liberty, or life, cannot at all authorize D to do so. He is none the less a robber, tyrant, and murderer, because he claims to act as their agent, than he would be if he avowedly acted on his own responsibility alone.

Neither am I bound to recognize him as their agent, nor can he legitimately claim to be their agent, when he brings no *written* authority from them accrediting him as such. I am under no obligation to take his word as to who his principals may be, or whether he has any. Bringing no credentials, I have a right to say he has no such authority even as he claims to have: and that he is therefore intending to rob, enslave, or murder me on his own account.

This tacit understanding, therefore, among the voters of the country, amounts to nothing as an authority to their agents. Neither do the ballots by which they select their agents, avail any more than does their tacit understanding; for their ballots are given in secret, and therefore in a way to avoid any personal responsibility for the acts of their agents.

No body of men can be said to authorize a man to act as their agent, to the injury of a third person, unless they do it in so open and authentic a manner as to make themselves personally responsible for his acts. None of the voters in this country appoint their political agents in any open, authentic manner, or in any manner to make themselves responsible for their acts. Therefore these pretended agents cannot legitimately claim to be really agents. Somebody must be responsible for the acts of these pretended agents; and if they cannot show any open and authentic credentials from their principals, they cannot, in law or reason, be said to have any principals. The maxim applies here, that what does not appear, does not exist. If they can show no principals, they have none.

But even these pretended agents do not themselves know who their pretended principals are. These latter act in secret; for acting by secret ballot is acting in secret as much as if they were to meet in secret conclave in the darkness of the night. And they are personally as much unknown to the agents they select, as they are to others. No pretended agent therefore can ever know by whose ballots he is selected, or consequently who his real principals are. Not knowing who his principals are, he has no right to say that he has any. He can, at most, say only that he is the agent of a secret band of robbers and murderers, who are bound by that faith which prevails among confederates in crime, to stand by him, if his acts, done in their name, shall be resisted.

Men honestly engaged in attempting to establish justice in the world, have no occasion thus to act in secret; or to appoint agents to do acts for which they (the principals) are not willing to be responsible.

The secret ballot makes a secret government; and a secret government is a secret band of robbers and murderers. Open despotism is better than this. The single despot stands out in the face of all men, and says: I am the State: My will is law: I am your master: I take the responsibility of my acts: The only arbiter I acknowledge is the sword: If any one denies my right, let him try conclusions with me.

But a secret government is little less than a government of assassins. Under it, a man knows not who his tyrants are, until they have struck, and perhaps not then. He may *guess*, beforehand, as to some of his immediate neighbors. But he really knows nothing. The man to whom he would most naturally fly for protection, may prove an enemy, when the time of trial comes.

This is the kind of government we have; and it is the only one we are likely to have, until men are ready to say: We will consent to no Constitution, except such an one as we are neither ashamed nor afraid to sign; and we will authorize no government to do anything in our name which we are not willing to be personally responsible for.

IX

What is the motive to the secret ballot? This, and only this: Like other confederates in crime, those who use it are not friends, but enemies; and they are afraid to be known, and to have their individual doings known, even to each other. They can contrive to bring about a sufficient understanding to enable them to act in concert against other persons; but beyond this they have no confidence, and no friendship, among themselves. In fact, they are engaged quite as much in schemes for plundering each other, as in plundering those who are not of them. And it is perfectly well understood among them that the strongest party among them will, in certain contingencies, murder each other by the hundreds of thousands (as they lately did do) to accomplish their purposes against each other. Hence they dare not be known, and have their individual doings known, even to each other. And this is avowedly the only reason for the ballot: for a secret government; a government by secret bands of robbers and murderers. And we are insane enough to call this liberty! To be a member of this secret band of robbers and murderers is esteemed a privilege and an honor! Without this privilege, a man is considered a slave; but with it a free man! With it he is considered a free man, because he has the same power to secretly (by secret ballot) procure the robbery, enslavement, and murder of another man, and that other man has to procure his robbery, enslavement, and murder. And this they call equal rights!

If any number of men, many or few, claim the right to govern the people of this country, let them make and sign an open compact with each other to do so. Let them thus make themselves individually known to those whom they propose to govern. And let them thus openly take the legitimate responsibility of their acts. How many of those who now support the Constitution, will ever do this? How many will ever dare openly proclaim their right to govern? or take the legitimate responsibility of their acts? Not one!

<h1 style="text-align:center">X</h1>

It is obvious that, on general principles of law and reason, there exists no such thing as a government created by, or resting upon, any consent, compact, or agreement of "the people of the United States" with each other; that the only visible, tangible, responsible government that exists, is that of a few individuals only, who act in concert, and call themselves by the several names of senators, representatives, presidents, judges, marshals, treasurers, collectors, generals, colonels, captains, etc., etc.

On general principles of law and reason, it is of no importance whatever that those few individuals profess to be the agents and representatives of "the people of the United States"; since they can show no credentials from the people themselves; they were never appointed as agents or representatives in any open, authentic manner; they do not themselves know, and have no means of knowing, and cannot prove, who their principals (as they call them) are individually; and consequently cannot, in law or reason, be said to have any principals at all.

It is obvious, too, that if these alleged principals ever did appoint these pretended agents, or representatives, they appointed them secretly (by secret ballot), and in a way to avoid all personal responsibility for their acts; that, at most, these alleged principals put these pretended agents forward for the most criminal purposes, viz: to plunder the people of their property, and restrain them of their liberty; and that the only authority that these alleged principals have for so doing, is simply a *tacit understanding* among themselves that they will imprison, shoot, or hang every man who resists the exactions and restraints which their agents or representatives may impose upon them.

Thus it is obvious that the only visible, tangible government we have is made up of these professed agents or representatives of a secret band of robbers and murderers, who, to cover up, or gloss over, their robberies and murders, have taken to themselves the title of "the people of the United States"; and who, on the pretense of being "the people of the United States," assert their right to subject to their dominion, and to control and dispose of at their pleasure, all property and persons found in the United States.

XI

On general principles of law and reason, the oaths which these pretended agents of the people take "to support the Constitution," are of no validity or obligation. And why? For this, if for no other reason, viz., *that they are given to nobody.* There is no privity (as the lawyers say)—that is, no mutual recognition, consent, and agreement—between those who take these oaths, and any other persons.

If I go upon Boston Common, and in the presence of a hundred thousand people, men, women and children, with whom I have no contract on the subject, take an oath that I will enforce upon them the laws of Moses, of Lycurgus, of Solon, of Justinian, or of Alfred, that oath is, on general principles of law and reason, of no obligation. It is of no obligation, not merely because it is intrinsically a criminal one, *but also because it is given to nobody*, and consequently pledges my faith to nobody. It is merely given to the winds.

It would not alter the case at all to say that, among these hundred thousand persons, in whose presence the oath was taken, there were two, three, or five thousand male adults, who had *secretly*—by secret ballot, and in a way to avoid making themselves *individually* known to me, or to the remainder of the hundred thousand—designated me as their agent to rule, control, plunder, and, if need be, murder, these hundred thousand people. The fact that they had designated me

106

secretly, and in a manner to prevent my knowing them individually, prevents all privity between them and me; and consequently makes it impossible that there can be any contract, or pledge of faith, on my part towards them; for it is impossible that I can pledge my faith, in any legal sense, to a man whom I neither know, nor have any means of knowing, individually.

So far as I am concerned, then, these two, three, or five thousand persons are a secret band of robbers and murderers, who have secretly, and in a way to save themselves from all responsibility for my acts, designated me as their agent; and have, through some other agent, or pretended agent, made their wishes known to me. But being, nevertheless, individually unknown to me, and having no open, authentic contract with me, my oath is, on general principles of law and reason, of no validity as a pledge of faith to them. And being no pledge of faith to them, it is no pledge of faith to anybody. It is mere idle wind. At most, it is only a pledge of faith to an unknown band of robbers and murderers, whose instrument for plundering and murdering other people, I thus publicly confess myself to be. And it has no other obligation than a similar oath given to any other unknown body of pirates, robbers, and murderers.

For these reasons the oaths taken by members of Congress, "to support the Constitution," are, on general principles of law and reason, of no validity. They are not only criminal in themselves, and therefore void; but they are also void for the further reason *that they are given to nobody.*

It cannot be said that, in any legitimate or legal sense, they are given to "the people of the United States"; because neither the whole, nor any large proportion of the whole, people of the United States ever, either openly or secretly, appointed or designated these men as their agents to carry the Constitution into effect. The great body of the people—that is, men, women and children—were never asked, or even permitted, to signify, in any *formal* manner, either openly or secretly, their choice or wish on the subject. The most that these members of Congress can say, in favor of their appointment, is simply this: Each one can say for himself:

I have evidence satisfactory to myself, that there exists, scattered throughout the country, a band of men, having a tacit understanding with each other, and calling themselves "the people of the United States," whose general purposes are to control and plunder each other, and all other persons in the country, and, so far as they can, even in neighboring countries; and to kill every man who shall attempt to defend his person and property against their schemes of plunder and dominion. Who these men are, *individually*, I have no certain means of knowing, for they sign no papers, and give no open, authentic evidence of their individual membership. They are not known individually even to each other. They are apparently as much afraid of being individually known to each other, as of being known to other persons. Hence they ordinarily have no mode either of exercising, or of making known, their individual membership, otherwise than by giving their votes secretly for certain agents to do their will. But although these men are individually unknown, both to each other and to other persons, it is generally understood in the country that none but male persons, of the age of twenty-one years and upwards, can be members. It is also generally understood that *all* male persons, born in the country, having certain complexions, and (in some localities) certain amounts of property, and (in certain cases) even persons of foreign birth, are *permitted* to be members. But it appears that usually not more than one half, two-thirds, or, in some cases, three-fourths, of all who are thus permitted to become members of the band, ever exercise, or consequently prove, their actual membership, in the only mode in which they ordinarily can exercise or prove it, viz., by giving their votes secretly for the officers or agents of the band. The number of these secret votes, so far as we have any account of them, varies greatly from year to year, thus tending to prove that the band, instead of being a permanent organization, is a merely *pro tempore* affair with those who choose to act with it for the time being. The gross number of these secret votes, or what purports to be their gross number, in different localities, is occasionally published. Whether these reports are accurate or not, we have no means of knowing. It is generally supposed that great frauds are often committed in depositing them. They are understood to be received and counted by certain men, who are themselves appointed for that purpose by the same secret process by which all other officers and agents of the band are selected. According to the reports of these receivers of votes (for whose accuracy or honesty, however, I cannot vouch), and according to my best knowledge of the whole number of male persons "in my district," who (it is supposed) were permitted to vote, it would appear that one-half, two-thirds or three-fourths actually did vote. Who the men were, individually, who cast these votes, I have no knowledge, for the whole thing was done secretly. But of the secret votes thus given for what they call a "member of Congress," the receivers reported that I had a majority, or at least a larger number than any other one person. And it is only by virtue of such a designation that I am now here to act in concert with other persons similarly selected in other parts of the country. It is understood among those who sent me here, that all the persons so selected, will, on coming together at the City of Washington, take an oath in each other's presence "to support the Constitution of the United States." By this is meant a certain paper that was drawn up eighty years ago. It was never signed by anybody, and apparently has no obligation, and never had any obligation, as a contract. In fact, few persons ever read it, and doubtless much the largest number of those who voted for me and the others, never even saw it, or now pretend to know what it means. Nevertheless, it is often spoken of in the country as "the Constitution of the United States"; and for some reason or another, the men who sent me here, seem to expect that I, and all with whom I act, will swear to carry this Constitution into effect. I am therefore ready to take this oath, and to co-operate with all others, similarly selected, who are ready to take the same oath.

This is the most that any member of Congress can say in proof that he has any constituency; that he represents anybody; that his oath "to support the Constitution," *is given to anybody*, or pledges his faith to *anybody*. He has no open, written, or other authentic evidence, such as is required in all other cases, that he was ever appointed the agent or representative of anybody. He has no written power of attorney from any single individual. He has no such legal knowledge as is required in all other cases, by which he can identify a single one of those who pretend to have appointed him to represent them.

Of course his oath, professedly given to them, "to support the Constitution," is, on general principles of law and reason, an oath given to nobody. It pledges his faith to nobody. If he fails to fulfil his oath, not a single person can come forward, and say to him, you have betrayed me, or broken faith with me.

No one can come forward and say to him: I appointed you my attorney to act for me. I required you to swear that, as my attorney, you would support the Constitution. You promised me that you would do so; and now you have forfeited the oath you gave to me. No single individual can say this.

No open, avowed, or responsible association, or body of men, can come forward and say to him: We appointed you our attorney, to act for us. We required you to swear that, as our attorney, you would support the Constitution. You promised us that you would do so; and now you have forfeited the oath you gave to us.

No open, avowed, or responsible association, or body of men, can say this to him; because there is no such association or body of men in existence. If any one should assert that there is such an association, let him prove, if he can, who compose it. Let him produce, if he can, any open, written, or other authentic contract, signed or agreed to by these men; forming themselves into an association; making themselves known as such to the world; appointing him as their agent; and making themselves individually, or as an association, responsible for his acts, done by their authority. Until all this can be shown, no one can say that, in any legitimate sense, there is any such association; or that he is their agent; or that he ever gave his oath to them; or ever pledged his faith to them.

On general principles of law and reason, it would be a sufficient answer for him to say, to all individuals, and all pretended associations of individuals, who should accuse him of a breach of faith to them:

I never knew you. Where is your evidence that you, either individually or collectively, ever appointed me your attorney? that you ever required me to swear to you, that, as your attorney, I would support the Constitution? or that I have now broken any faith I ever pledged to you? You may, or you may not, be members of that secret band of robbers and murderers, who act in secret; appoint their agents by a secret ballot; who keep themselves individually unknown even to the agents they thus appoint; and who, therefore, cannot claim that they have any agents; or that any of their pretended agents ever gave his oath, or pledged his faith, to them. I repudiate you altogether. My oath was given to others, with whom you have nothing to do; or it was idle wind, given only to the idle winds. Begone!

XII

For the same reasons, the oaths of all the other pretended agents of this secret band of robbers and murderers are, on general principles of law and reason, equally destitute of obligation. They are given to nobody; but only to the winds.

The oaths of the tax-gatherers and treasurers of the band, are, on general principles of law and reason, of no validity. If any tax gatherer, for example, should put the money he receives into his own pocket, and refuse to part with it, the members of this band could not say to him: You collected that money as our agent, and for our uses; and you swore to pay it over to us, or to those we should appoint to receive it. You have betrayed us, and broken faith with us.

It would be a sufficient answer for him to say to them:

I never knew you. You never made yourselves individually known to me. I never gave my oath to you, as individuals. You may, or you may not, be members of that secret band, who appoint agents to rob and murder other people; but who are cautious not to make themselves individually known, either to such agents, or to those whom their agents are commissioned to rob. If you are members of that band, you have given me no proof that you ever commissioned me to rob others for your benefit. I never knew you, as individuals, and of course never promised you that I would pay over to you the proceeds of my robberies. I committed my robberies on my own account, and for my own profit. If you thought I was fool enough to allow you to keep yourselves concealed, and use me as your tool for robbing other persons; or that I would take all the personal risk of the robberies, and pay over the proceeds to you, you were particularly simple. As I took all the risk of my robberies, I propose to take all the profits. Begone! You are fools, as well as villains. If I gave my oath to anybody, I gave it to other persons than you. But I really gave it to nobody. I only gave it to the winds. It answered my purposes at the time. It enabled me to get the money I was after, and now I propose to keep it. If you expected me to pay it over to you, you relied only upon that honor that is said to prevail among thieves. You now understand that that is a very poor reliance. I trust you may become wise enough to never rely upon it again. If I have any duty in the matter, it is to give back the money to those from whom I took it; not to pay it over to such villains as you.

XIII

On general principles of law and reason, the oaths which foreigners take, on coming here, and being "naturalized" (as it is called), are of no validity. They are necessarily given to nobody; because there is no open, authentic association, to which they can join themselves; or to whom, as individuals, they can pledge their faith. No such association, or organization, as "the people of the United States," having ever been formed by any open, written, authentic, or voluntary contract, there is, on general principles of law and reason, no such association, or organization, in existence. And all oaths that purport to be given to such an association are necessarily given only to the winds. They cannot be said to be given to any man, or body of men, as individuals, because no man, or body of men, can come forward *with any proof* that the oaths were given to them, as individuals, or to any association of which they are members. To say that there is a tacit understanding among a portion of the male adults of the country, that they will call themselves "the people of the United States," and that they will act in concert in subjecting the remainder of the people of the United States to their dominion; but that they will keep themselves personally concealed by doing all their acts secretly, is wholly insufficient, on general principles of law and reason, to prove the existence of any such association, or organization, as "the people of the United States"; or consequently to prove that the oaths of foreigners were given to any such association.

XIV

On general principles of law and reason, all the oaths which, since the war, have been given by Southern men, that they will obey the laws of Congress, support the Union, and the like, are of no validity. Such oaths are invalid, not only because they were extorted by military power, and threats of confiscation, and because they are in contravention of men's natural right to do as they please about supporting the government, *but also because they were given to nobody.* They were nominally given to "the United States." But being nominally given to "the United States," they were necessarily given to nobody, because, on general principles of law and reason, there were no "United States," to whom the oaths could be given. That is to say, there was no open, authentic, avowed, legitimate association, corporation, or body of men, known as "the United States," or as "the people of the United States," to whom the oaths could have been given. If anybody says there was such a corporation, let him state who were the individuals that composed it, and how and when they became a corporation. Were Mr. A, Mr. B, and Mr. C members of it? If so, where are their signatures? Where the evidence of their membership? Where the record? Where the open, authentic proof? There is none. Therefore, in law and reason, there was no such corporation.

On general principles of law and reason, every corporation, association, or organized body of men, having a legitimate corporate existence, and legitimate corporate rights, must consist of certain known individuals, who can prove, by legitimate and reasonable evidence, their membership. But nothing of this kind can be proved in regard to the corporation, or body of men, who call themselves "the United States." Not a man of them, in all the Northern States, can prove by any legitimate evidence, such as is required to prove membership in other legal corporations, that he himself, or any other man whom he can name, is a member of any corporation or association called "the United States," or "the people of the United States," or, consequently, that there is any such corporation. And since no such corporation can be proved to exist, it cannot of course be proved that the oaths of Southern men were given to any such corporation. The most that can be claimed is that the oaths were given to a secret band of robbers and murderers, who called themselves "the United States," and extorted those oaths. But that certainly is not enough to prove that the oaths are of any obligation.

XV

On general principles of law and reason, the oaths of soldiers, that they will serve a given number of years, that they will obey the orders of their superior officers, that they will bear true allegiance to the government, and so forth, are of no obligation. Independently of the criminality of an oath, that, for a given number of years, he will kill all whom he may be commanded to kill, without exercising his own judgment or conscience as to the justice or necessity of such killing, there is this further reason why a soldier's oath is of no obligation, viz., that, like all the other oaths that have now been mentioned, it is given to nobody. There being, in no legitimate sense, any such corporation, or nation, as "the United States," nor, consequently, in any legitimate sense, any such government as "the government of the United States," a soldier's oath given to, or contract made with, such nation or government, is necessarily an oath given to, or a contract made with, nobody. Consequently such oath or contract can be of no obligation.

XVI

On general principles of law and reason, the treaties, so called, which purport to be entered into with other nations, by persons calling themselves ambassadors, secretaries, presidents, and senators of the United States, in the name, and in behalf, of "the people of the United States," are of no validity. These so-called ambassadors, secretaries, presidents, and senators, who claim to be the agents of "the people of the United States," for making these treaties, can show no open, written, or other authentic evidence that either the whole "people of the United States," or any other open, avowed, responsible body of men, calling themselves by that name, ever authorized these pretended ambassadors and others to make treaties in the name of, or binding upon any one of, "the people of the United States," or any other open, avowed, responsible body of men, calling themselves by that name, ever authorized these pretended ambassadors, secretaries, and others, in their name and behalf, to recognize certain other persons, calling themselves emperors, kings, queens, and the like, as the rightful rulers, sovereigns, masters, or representatives of the different peoples whom they assume to govern, to represent, and to bind.

The "nations," as they are called, with whom our pretended ambassadors, secretaries, presidents, and senators profess to make treaties, are as much myths as our own. On general principles of law and reason, there are no such "nations." That is to say, neither the whole people of England, for example, nor any open, avowed, responsible body of men, calling themselves by that name, ever, by any open, written, or other authentic contract with each other, formed themselves into any bona fide, legitimate association or organization, or authorized any king, queen, or other representative to make treaties in their name, or to bind them, either individually, or as an association, by such treaties.

Our pretended treaties, then, being made with no legitimate or bona fide nations, or representatives of nations, and being made, on our part, by persons who have no legitimate authority to act for us, have intrinsically no more validity than a pretended treaty made by the Man in the Moon with the king of the Pleiades.

<h1 style="text-align:center">XVII</h1>

On general principles of law and reason, debts contracted in the name of "the United States," or of "the people of the United States," are of no validity. It is utterly absurd to pretend that debts to the amount of twenty-five hundred millions of dollars are binding upon thirty-five or forty millions of people, when there is not a particle of legitimate evidence—such as would be required to prove a private debt—that can be produced against any one of them, that either he, or his properly authorized attorney, ever contracted to pay one cent.

Certainly, neither the whole people of the United States, nor any number of them, ever separately or individually contracted to pay a cent of these debts.

Certainly, also, neither the whole people of the United States, nor any number of them, ever, by any open, written, or other authentic and voluntary contract, united themselves as a firm, corporation, or association, by the name of "the United States," or "the people of the United States," and authorized their agents to contract debts in their name.

Certainly, too, there is in existence no such firm, corporation, or association as "the United States," or "the people of the United States," formed by any open, written, or other authentic and voluntary contract, and having corporate property with which to pay these debts.

How, then, is it possible, on any general principle of law or reason, that debts that are binding upon nobody individually, can be binding upon forty millions of people collectively, when, on general and legitimate principles of law and reason, these forty millions of people neither have, nor ever had, any corporate property? never made any corporate or individual contract? and neither have, nor ever had, any corporate existence?

Who, then, created these debts, in the name of "the United States"? Why, at most, only a few persons, calling themselves "members of Congress," etc., who pretended to represent "the people of the United States," but who really represented only a secret band of robbers and murderers, who wanted money to carry on the robberies and murders in which they were then engaged; and who intended to extort from the future people of the United States, by robbery and threats of murder (and real murder, if that should prove necessary), the means to pay these debts.

This band of robbers and murderers, who were the real principals in contracting these debts, is a secret one, because its members have never entered into any open, written, avowed, or authentic contract, by which they may be individually known to the world, or even to each other. Their real or pretended representatives, who contracted these debts in their name, were selected (if selected at all) for that purpose secretly (by secret ballot), and in a way to furnish evidence against none of the principals *individually*; and these principals were really known *individually* neither to their pretended representatives who contracted these debts in their behalf, nor to those who lent the money. The money, therefore, was all borrowed and lent in the dark; that is, by men who did not see each other's faces, or know each other's names; who could not then, and cannot now, identify each other as principals in the transactions; and who consequently can prove no contract with each other.

Furthermore, the money was all lent and borrowed for criminal purposes; that is, for purposes of robbery and murder; and for this reason the contracts were all intrinsically void; and would have been so, even though the real parties, borrowers and lenders, had come face to face, and made their contracts openly, in their own proper names.

Furthermore, this secret band of robbers and murderers, who were the real borrowers of this money, having no legitimate corporate existence, have no corporate property with which to pay these debts. They do indeed pretend to own large tracts of wild lands, lying between the Atlantic and Pacific Oceans, and between the Gulf of Mexico and the North Pole. But, on general principles of law and reason, they might as well pretend to own the Atlantic and Pacific Oceans themselves; or the atmosphere and the sunlight; and to hold them, and dispose of them, for the payment of these debts.

Having no corporate property with which to pay what purports to be their corporate debts, this secret band of robbers and murderers are really bankrupt. They have nothing to pay with. In fact, they do not propose to pay their debts otherwise than from the proceeds of their future robberies and murders. These are confessedly their sole reliance; and were known to be such by the lenders of the money, at the time the money was lent. And it was, therefore, virtually a part of the contract, that the money should be repaid only from the proceeds of these future robberies and murders. For this reason, if for no other, the contracts were void from the beginning.

In fact, these apparently two classes, borrowers and lenders, were really one and the same class. They borrowed and lent money from and to themselves. They themselves were not only part and parcel, but the very life and soul, of this secret band of robbers and murderers, who borrowed and spent the money. Individually they furnished money for a common enterprise; taking, in return, what purported to be corporate promises for individual loans. The only excuse they had for taking these so-called corporate promises of, for individual loans by, the same parties, was that they might have some apparent excuse for the future robberies of the band (that is, to pay the debts of the corporation), and that they might also know what shares they were to be respectively entitled to out of the proceeds of their future robberies.

Finally, if these debts had been created for the most innocent and honest purposes, and in the most open and honest manner, by the real parties to the contracts, these parties could thereby have bound nobody but themselves, and no property but their own. They could have bound nobody that should have come after them, and no property subsequently created by, or belonging to, other persons.

XVIII

The Constitution having never been signed by anybody; and there being no other open, written, or authentic contract between any parties whatever, by virtue of which the United States government, so called, is maintained; and it being well known that none but male persons, of twenty-one years of age and upwards, are allowed any voice in the government; and it being also well known that a large number of these adult persons seldom or never vote at all; and that all those who do vote, do so secretly (by secret ballot), and in a way to prevent their individual votes being known, either to the world, or even to each other; and consequently in a way to make no one openly responsible for the acts of their agents, or representatives,—all these things being known, the questions arise: *Who* compose the real governing power in the country? Who are the men, *the responsible men*, who rob us of our property? Restrain us of our liberty? Subject us to their arbitrary dominion? And devastate our homes, and shoot us down by the hundreds of thousands, if we resist? How shall we find these men? How shall we know them from others? How shall we defend ourselves and our property against them? Who, of our neighbors, are members of this secret band of robbers and murderers? How can we know which are *their* houses, that we may burn or demolish them? Which *their* property, that we may destroy it? Which their persons, that we may kill them, and rid the world and ourselves of such tyrants and monsters?

These are questions that must be answered, before men can be free; before they can protect themselves against this secret band of robbers and murderers, who now plunder, enslave, and destroy them.

The answer to these questions is, that only those who have the will and the power to shoot down their fellow men, are the real rulers in this, as in all other (so-called) civilized countries; for by no others will civilized men be robbed, or enslaved.

Among savages, mere physical strength, on the part of one man, may enable him to rob, enslave, or kill another man. Among barbarians, mere physical strength, on the part of a body of men, disciplined, and acting in concert, though with very little money or other wealth, may, under some circumstances, enable them to rob, enslave, or kill another body of men, as numerous, or perhaps even more numerous, than themselves. And among both savages and barbarians, mere want may sometimes compel one man to sell himself as a slave to another. But with (so-called) civilized peoples, among whom knowledge, wealth, and the means of acting in concert, have become diffused; and who have invented such weapons and other means of defense as to render mere physical strength of less importance; and by whom soldiers in any requisite number, and other instrumentalities of war in any requisite amount, can always be had for money, the question of war, and consequently the question of power, is little else than a mere question of money. As a necessary consequence, those who stand ready to furnish this money, are the real rulers. It is so in Europe, and it is so in this country.

In Europe, the nominal rulers, the emperors and kings and parliaments, are anything but the real rulers of their respective countries. They are little or nothing else than mere tools, employed by the wealthy to rob, enslave, and (if need be) murder those who have less wealth, or none at all.

The Rothschilds, and that class of money-lenders of whom they are the representatives and agents—men who never think of lending a shilling to their next-door neighbors, for purposes of honest industry, unless upon the most ample security, and at the highest rate of interest—stand ready, at all times, to lend money in unlimited amounts to those robbers and murderers, who call themselves governments, to be expended in shooting down those who do not submit quietly to being robbed and enslaved.

They lend their money in this manner, knowing that it is to be expended in murdering their fellow men, for simply seeking their liberty and their rights; knowing also that neither the interest nor the principal will ever be paid, except as it will be extorted under terror of the repetition of such murders as those for which the money lent is to be expended.

These money-lenders, the Rothschilds, for example, say to themselves: If we lend a hundred millions sterling to the queen and parliament of England, it will enable them to murder twenty, fifty, or a hundred thousand people in England, Ireland, or India; and the terror inspired by such wholesale murder, will enable them to keep the whole people of those countries in subjection for twenty, or perhaps fifty, years to come; to control all their trade and industry; and to extort from them large amounts of money, under the name of taxes; and from the wealth thus extorted from them, they (the queen and parliament) can afford to pay us a higher rate of interest for our money than we can get in any other way. Or, if we lend this sum to the emperor of Austria, it will enable him to murder so many of his people as to strike terror into the rest, and thus enable him to keep them in subjection, and extort money from them, for twenty or fifty years to come. And they say the same in regard to the emperor of Russia, the king of Prussia, the emperor of France, or any other ruler, so called, who, in their judgment, will be able, by murdering a reasonable portion of his people, to keep the rest in subjection, and extort money from them, for a long time to come, to pay the interest and principal of the money lent him.

And why are these men so ready to lend money for murdering their fellow men? Solely for this reason, viz., that such loans are considered better investments than loans for purposes of honest industry. They pay higher rates of interest; and it is less trouble to look after them. This is the whole matter.

The question of making these loans is, with these lenders, a mere question of pecuniary profit. They lend money to be expended in robbing, enslaving, and murdering their fellow men, solely because, on the whole, such loans pay better than any others. They are no respecters of persons, no superstitious fools, that reverence monarchs. They care no more for a king, or an emperor, than they do for a beggar, except as he is a better customer, and can pay them better interest for their money. If they doubt his ability to make his murders successful for maintaining his power, and thus extorting money from his people in future, they dismiss him as unceremoniously as they would dismiss any other hopeless bankrupt, who should want to borrow money to save himself from open insolvency.

When these great lenders of blood-money, like the Rothschilds, have loaned vast sums in this way, for purposes of murder, to an emperor or a king, they sell out the bonds taken by them, in small amounts, to anybody, and everybody, who are disposed to buy them at satisfactory prices, to hold as investments. They (the Rothschilds) thus soon get back their money, with great profits; and are now ready to lend money in the same way again to any other robber and murderer, called an emperor or a king, who, they think, is likely to be successful in his robberies and murders, and able to pay a good price for the money necessary to carry them on.

This business of lending blood-money is one of the most thoroughly sordid, cold-blooded, and criminal that was ever carried on, to any considerable extent, amongst human beings. It is like lending money to slave traders, or to common robbers and pirates, to be repaid out of their plunder. And the men who loan money to governments, so called, for the purpose of enabling the latter to rob, enslave, and murder their people, are among the greatest villains that the world has ever seen. And they as much deserve to be hunted and killed (if they cannot otherwise be got rid of) as any slave traders, robbers, or pirates that ever lived.

When these emperors and kings, so-called, have obtained their loans, they proceed to hire and train immense numbers of professional murderers, called soldiers, and employ them in shooting down all who resist their demands for money. In fact, most of them keep large bodies of these murderers constantly in their service, as their only means of enforcing their extortions. There are now, I think, four or five millions of these professional murderers constantly employed by the so-called sovereigns of Europe. The enslaved people are, of course, forced to support and pay all these murderers, as well as to submit to all the other extortions which these murderers are employed to enforce.

It is only in this way that most of the so-called governments of Europe are maintained. These so-called governments are in reality only great bands of robbers and murderers, organized, disciplined, and constantly on the alert. And the so-called sovereigns, in these different governments, are simply the heads, or chiefs, of different bands of robbers and murderers. And these heads or chiefs are dependent upon the lenders of blood-money for the means to carry on their robberies and murders. They could not sustain themselves a moment but for the loans made to them by these blood-money loan-mongers. And their first care is to maintain their credit with them; for they know their end is come, the instant their credit with them fails. Consequently the first proceeds of their extortions are scrupulously applied to the payment of the interest on their loans.

In addition to paying the interest on their bonds, they perhaps grant to the holders of them great monopolies in banking, like the Banks of England, of France, and of Vienna; with the agreement that these banks shall furnish money whenever, in sudden emergencies, it may be necessary to shoot down more of their people. Perhaps also, by means of tariffs on competing imports, they give great monopolies to certain branches of industry, in which these lenders of blood-money are engaged. They also, by unequal taxation, exempt wholly or partially the property of these loan-mongers, and throw corresponding burdens upon those who are too poor and weak to resist.

Thus it is evident that all these men, who call themselves by the high-sounding names of Emperors, Kings, Sovereigns, Monarchs, Most Christian Majesties, Most Catholic Majesties, High Mightinesses, Most Serene and Potent Princes, and the like, and who claim to rule "by the grace of God," by "Divine Right"—that is, by special authority from Heaven—are intrinsically not only the merest miscreants and wretches, engaged solely in plundering, enslaving, and murdering their fellow men, but that they are also the merest hangers on, the servile, obsequious, fawning dependents and tools of these blood-money loan-mongers, on whom they rely for the means to carry on their crimes. These loan-mongers, like the Rothschilds, laugh in their sleeves, and say to themselves: These despicable creatures, who call themselves emperors, and kings, and majesties, and most serene and potent princes; who profess to wear crowns, and sit on thrones; who deck themselves with ribbons, and feathers, and jewels; and surround themselves with hired flatterers and lickspittles; and whom we suffer to strut around, and palm themselves off, upon fools and slaves, as sovereigns and lawgivers specially appointed by Almighty God; and to hold themselves out as the sole fountains of honors, and dignities, and wealth, and power—all these miscreants and imposters know that we make them, and use them; that in us they live, move, and have their being; that we require them (as the price of their positions) to take upon themselves all the labor, all the danger, and all the odium of all the crimes they commit for our profit; and that we will unmake them, strip them of their gewgaws, and send them out into the world as beggars, or give them over to the vengeance of the people they have enslaved, the moment they refuse to commit any crime we require of them, or to pay over to us such share of the proceeds of their robberies as we see fit to demand.

XIX

Now, what is true in Europe, is substantially true in this country. The difference is the immaterial one, that, in this country, there is no visible, permanent head, or chief, of these robbers and murderers, who call themselves "the government." That is to say, there is no one man, who calls himself the state, or even emperor, king, or sovereign; no one who claims that he and his children rule "by the Grace of God," by "Divine Right," or by special appointment from Heaven. There are only certain men, who call themselves presidents, senators, and representatives, and claim to be the authorized agents, for the time being, or for certain short periods, of all "the people of the United States"; but who can show no credentials, or powers of attorney, or any other open, authentic evidence that they are so; and who notoriously are not so; but are really only the agents of a secret band of robbers and murderers, whom they themselves do not know, and have no means of knowing, individually; but who, they trust, will openly or secretly, when the crisis comes, sustain them in all their usurpations and crimes.

What is important to be noticed is, that these so-called presidents, senators, and representatives, these pretended agents of all "the people of the United States," the moment their exactions meet with any formidable resistance from any portion of "the people" themselves, are obliged, like their co-robbers and murderers in Europe, to fly at once to the lenders of blood money, for the means to sustain their power. And they borrow their money on the same principle, and for the same purpose, viz., to be expended in shooting down all those "people of the United States"—their own constituents and principals, as they profess to call them—who resist the robberies and enslavement which these borrowers of the money are practising upon them. And they expect to repay the loans, if at all, only from the proceeds of the future robberies, which they anticipate it will be easy for them and their successors to perpetrate through a long series of years, upon their pretended principals, if they can but shoot down now some hundreds of thousands of them, and thus strike terror into the rest.

Perhaps the facts were never made more evident, in any country on the globe, than in our own, that these soulless blood-money loan-mongers are the real rulers; that they rule from the most sordid and mercenary motives; that the ostensible government, the presidents, senators, and representatives, so called, are merely their tools; and that no ideas of, or regard for, justice or liberty had anything to do in inducing them to lend their money for the war. In proof of all this, look at the following facts.

Nearly a hundred years ago we professed to have got rid of all that religious superstition, inculcated by a servile and corrupt priesthood in Europe, that rulers, so called, derived their authority directly from Heaven; and that it was consequently a religious duty on the part of the people to obey them. We professed long ago to have learned that governments could rightfully exist only by the free will, and on the voluntary support, of those who might choose to sustain them. We all professed to have known long ago, that the only legitimate objects of government were the maintenance of liberty and justice equally for all. All this we had professed for nearly a hundred years. And we professed to look with pity and contempt upon those ignorant, superstitious, and enslaved peoples of Europe, who were so easily kept in subjection by the frauds and force of priests and kings.

Notwithstanding all this, that we had learned, and known, and professed, for nearly a century, these lenders of blood money had, for a long series of years previous to the war, been the willing accomplices of the slave-holders in perverting the government from the purposes of liberty and justice, to the greatest of crimes. They had been such accomplices *for a purely pecuniary consideration*, to wit, a control of the markets in the South; in other words, the privilege of holding the slave-holders themselves in industrial and commercial subjection to the manufacturers and merchants of the North (who afterwards furnished the money for the war). And these Northern merchants and manufacturers, these lenders of blood-money, were willing to continue to be the accomplices of the slave-holders in the future, for the same pecuniary consideration. But the slave-holders, either doubting the fidelity of their Northern allies, or feeling themselves strong enough to keep their slaves in subjection without Northern assistance, would no longer pay the price which these Northern men demanded. And it was to enforce this price in the future—that is, to monopolize the Southern markets, to maintain their industrial and commercial control over the South—that these Northern manufacturers and merchants lent some of the profits of their former monopolies for the war, in order to secure to themselves the same, or greater, monopolies in the future. These—and not any love of liberty or justice—were the motives on which the money for the war was lent by the North. In short, the North said to the slave-holders: If you will not pay us our price (give us control of your markets) for our assistance against your slaves, we will secure the same price (keep control of your markets) by helping your slaves against you, and using them as our tools for maintaining dominion over you; for the control of your markets we will have, whether the tools we use for that purpose be black or white, and be the cost, in blood and money, what it may.

On this principle, and from this motive, and not from any love of liberty, or justice, the money was lent in enormous amounts, and at enormous rates of interest. And it was only by means of these loans that the objects of the war were accomplished.

And now these lenders of blood-money demand their pay; and the government, so called, becomes their tool, their servile, slavish, villainous tool, to extort it from the labor of the enslaved people both of the North and the South. It is to be extorted by every form of direct, and indirect, and unequal taxation. Not only the nominal debt and interest—enormous as the latter was—are to be paid in full; but these holders of the debt are to be paid still further—and perhaps doubly, triply, or quadruply paid—by such tariffs on imports as will enable our home manufacturers to realize enormous prices for their commodities; also by such monopolies in banking as will enable them to keep control of, and thus enslave and plunder, the industry and trade of the great body of the Northern people themselves. In short, the industrial and commercial slavery of the great body of the people, North and South, black and white, is the price which these lenders of blood money demand, and insist upon, and are determined to secure, in return for the money lent for the war.

This programme having been fully arranged and systematized, they put their sword into the hands of the chief murderer of the war, and charge him to carry their scheme into effect. And now he, speaking as their organ, says: "*Let us have peace.*"

The meaning of this is: Submit quietly to all the robbery and slavery we have arranged for you, and you can have "peace." But in case you resist, the same lenders of blood-money, who furnished the means to subdue the South, will furnish the means again to subdue you.

These are the terms on which alone this government, or, with few exceptions, any other, ever gives "peace" to its people.

The whole affair, on the part of those who furnished the money, has been, and now is, a deliberate scheme of robbery and murder; not merely to monopolize the markets of the South, but also to monopolize the currency, and thus control the industry and trade, and thus plunder and enslave the laborers, of both North and South. And Congress and the president are today the merest tools for these purposes. They are obliged to be, for they know that their own power, as rulers, so-called, is at an end, the moment their credit with the blood-money loan-mongers fails. They are like a bankrupt in the hands of an extortioner. They dare not say nay to any demand made upon them. And to hide at once, if possible, both their servility and their crimes, they attempt to divert public attention, by crying out that they have "Abolished Slavery!" That they have "Saved the Country!" That they have "Preserved our Glorious Union!" and that, in now paying the "National Debt," as they call it (as if the people themselves, *all of them who are to be taxed for its payment*, had really and voluntarily joined in contracting it), they are simply "Maintaining the National Honor!"

By "maintaining the national honor," they mean simply that they themselves, open robbers and murderers, assume to be the nation, and will keep faith with those who lend them the money necessary to enable them to crush the great body of the people under their feet; and will faithfully appropriate, from the proceeds of their future robberies and murders, enough to pay all their loans, principal and interest.

The pretense that the "abolition of slavery" was either a motive or justification for the war, is a fraud of the same character with that of "maintaining the national honor." Who, but such usurpers, robbers, and murderers as they, ever established slavery? Or what government, except one resting upon the sword, like the one we now have, was ever capable of maintaining slavery? And why did these men abolish slavery? Not from any love of liberty in general—not as an act of justice to the black man himself, but only "as a war measure," and because they wanted his assistance, and that of his friends, in carrying on the war they had undertaken for maintaining and intensifying that political, commercial, and industrial slavery, to which they have subjected the great body of the people, both white and black. And yet these imposters now cry out that they have abolished the chattel slavery of the black man—although that was not the motive of the war—as if they thought they could thereby conceal, atone for, or justify that other slavery which they were fighting to perpetuate, and to render more rigorous and inexorable than it ever was before. There was no difference of principle—but only of degree—between the slavery they boast they have abolished, and the slavery they were fighting to preserve; for all restraints upon men's natural liberty, not necessary for the simple maintenance of justice, are of the nature of slavery, and differ from each other only in degree.

If their object had really been to abolish slavery, or maintain liberty or justice generally, they had only to say: All, whether white or black, who want the protection of this government, shall have it; and all who do not want it, will be left in peace, so long as they leave us in peace. Had they said this, slavery would necessarily have been abolished at once; the war would have been saved; and a thousand times nobler union than we have ever had would have been the result. It would have been a voluntary union of free men; such a union as will one day exist among all men, the world over, if the several nations, so called, shall ever get rid of the usurpers, robbers, and murderers, called governments, that now plunder, enslave, and destroy them.

Still another of the frauds of these men is, that they are now establishing, and that the war was designed to establish, "a government of consent." The only idea they have ever manifested as to what is a government of consent, is this—that it is one to which everybody must consent, or be shot. This idea was the dominant one on which the war was carried on; and it is the dominant one, now that we have got what is called "peace."

Their pretenses that they have "Saved the Country," and "Preserved our Glorious Union," are frauds like all the rest of their pretenses. By them they mean simply that they have subjugated, and maintained their power over, an unwilling people. This they call "Saving the Country"; as if an enslaved and subjugated people—or as if any people kept in subjection by the sword (as it is intended that all of us shall be hereafter)—could be said to have any country. This, too, they call "Preserving our Glorious Union"; as if there could be said to be any Union, glorious or inglorious, that was not voluntary. Or as if there could be said to be any union between masters and slaves; between those who conquer, and those who are subjugated.

All these cries of having "abolished slavery," of having "saved the country," of having "preserved the union," of establishing "a government of consent," and of "maintaining the national honor," are all gross, shameless, transparent cheats—so transparent that they ought to deceive no one—when uttered as justifications for the war, or for the government that has succeeded the war, or for now compelling the people to pay the cost of the war, or for compelling anybody to support a government that he does not want.

The lesson taught by all these facts is this: As long as mankind continue to pay "national debts," so-called—that is, so long as they are such dupes and cowards as to pay for being cheated, plundered, enslaved, and murdered—so long there will be enough to lend the money for those purposes; and with that money a plenty of tools, called soldiers, can be hired to keep them in subjection. But when they refuse any longer to pay for being thus cheated, plundered, enslaved, and murdered, they will cease to have cheats, and usurpers, and robbers, and murderers and blood-money loan-mongers for masters.

APPENDIX

Inasmuch as the Constitution was never signed, nor agreed to, by anybody, as a contract, and therefore never bound anybody, and is now binding upon nobody; and is, moreover, such an one as no people can ever hereafter be expected to consent to, except as they may be forced to do so at the point of the bayonet, it is perhaps of no importance what its true legal meaning, as a contract, is. Nevertheless, the writer thinks it proper to say that, in his opinion, the Constitution is no such instrument as it has generally been assumed to be; but that by false interpretations, and naked usurpations, the government has been made in practice a very widely, and almost wholly, different thing from what the Constitution itself purports to authorize. He has heretofore written much, and could write much more, to prove that such is the truth. But whether the Constitution really be one thing, or another, this much is certain—that it has either authorized such a government as we have had, or has been powerless to prevent it. In either case, it is unfit to exist.

---

[i] *See "No Treason, No. 2"*

[ii] *Suppose it be "the best government on earth," does that prove its own goodness, or only the badness of all other governments?*

[iii] *The very men who drafted it, never signed it in any way to bind themselves by it, as a contract. And not one of them probably ever would have signed it in any way to bind himself by it, as a contract.*

[iv] *I have personally examined the statute books of the following States, viz.: Maine, New Hampshire, Vermont, Massachusetts, Rhode Island, Connecticut, New York, New Jersey, Pennsylvania, Delaware, Virginia, North Carolina, South Carolina, Georgia, Florida, Alabama, Mississippi, Tennessee, Kentucky, Ohio, Michigan, Indians, Illinois, Wisconsin, Texas, Arkansas, Missouri, Iowa, Minnesota, Nebraska, Kansas, Nevada, California, and Oregon, and find that in all these States the English statute has been re-enacted, sometimes with modifications, but generally enlarging its operations, and is now in force.*

The following are some of the provisions of the Massachusetts statute:

"No action shall be brought in any of the following cases, that is to say: . . . .

"To charge a person upon a special promise to answer for the debt, default, or misdoings of another: . . . .

"Upon a contract for the sale of lands, tenements, hereditaments, or of any interest in, or concerning them; or

"*Upon an agreement that is not to be performed within one year from the writing thereof:*
"*Unless the promise, contract, or agreement, upon which such action is brought, or some memorandum or note thereof, is in writing, and signed by the party to be charged therewith, or by some person thereunto by him awfully authorized:* . . . .
"*No contract for the sale of goods, wares, or merchandise, for the price of fifty dollars or more, shall be good or valid, unless the purchaser accepts and receives part of the goods so sold, or gives something in earnest to bind the bargain, or in part payment; or unless some note or memorandum in writing of the bargain is made and signed by the party to be charged thereby, or by some person thereunto by him lawfully authorized.*"
v And this two-thirds vote may be but two-thirds of a quorum—that is two-thirds of a majority—instead of two-thirds of the whole.
vi Of what appreciable value is it to any man, as an individual, that he is allowed a voice in choosing these public masters? His voice is only one of several millions.

Chapter 9

JOHANN MOST
from
*The Science of Revolutionary Warfare: A Little Handbook of Instruction in the
Use and Preparation of Nitroglycerine, Dynamite, Gun-Cotton, Fulminating
Mercury, Bombs, Fuses, Poisons, Etc., Etc.* (1883)

*German-born anarchist Johann Most was the primary proponent of
achieving a free, anarchist society through violent revolution. The term
"anarchist" is largely synonymous with "terrorist" in the United
Kingdom, and it is due to Most that this came to be. He popularized the
concept and term of "the propaganda of the deed," meaning using
assassination or bombs as a means of advancing one's political position.
Almost a century before the publication of explosives manual* The
Anarchist Cookbook, *the translation of Most's* The Science of
Revolutionary Warfare *became an enormous free-speech concern. His
work was nothing less than a clear manual for the everyday
revolutionary on how to build dynamite and other explosives. Here is the
introduction to Most's provocative work.*

Today, the importance of explosives as an instrument for carrying
out revolutions oriented to social justice is obvious. Anyone can see
that these materials will be the decisive factor in the next period of
world history. It therefore makes sense for revolutionaries in all
countries to acquire explosives and to learn the skills needed to use
them in real situations.

It seems to us that far too much time and money has been wasted on false approaches to this objective. Many people obtained expensive text-books meant for professional chemists and not for the layman, and were unable to understand them. Some individuals may have learned a little in this way, especially in cases where they were able to consult an expert. Everything learned is worth something, so their time was not entirely wasted.

We, along with some other people, went a step further, and arranged for popularized versions of technical papers on the production of explosives to be published. However, we found that these also were not well understood. Here and there, people started experimenting on the basis of this material, but the results were usually not very encouraging.

The equipment they worked with was expensive and fragile, and easily damaged beyond repair when used by unskilled people. The necessary raw materials, when bought from ordinary retailers, usually turned out to be of inferior quality. Upgrading or purifying these raw materials would once again have called for expensive equipment and economic demands beyond the means of the man in the street. It would have been still more difficult to make the materials, both for financial reasons and due to the lack of expertise.

We do know some people who have made something resembling gun cotton. Some have even succeeded—after their fifth or sixth mixing rig blew up—in making small quantities of nitroglycerine, and converting it into dynamite. These fortunate ones were then faced with the fact that all their efforts and sacrifices had resulted in something of theoretical value only, since one cannot accomplish much with small quantities, and the method was too expensive anyway.

To manufacture large quantities of dynamite, one must have a rather expensive setup. Several rooms are needed, so it cannot be done in a private apartment. In fact, it is necessary to locate the workshop away from any neighbors, because dynamite manufacture produces a strong smell that would soon betray the operation. Although people have not given up experimenting, we conclude that the demand for dynamite and other explosives required for revolutionary purposes cannot be met on a do-it-yourself basis, and that it is a much better idea to obtain it ready-made, from regular industrial sources.

Not an ounce of the dynamite that has actually been used by revolutionaries anywhere in the world was home-made. Imperial, royal and republican (government) arsenals have had to do the providing. No matter how well-guarded they are, the authorities can never completely prevent the disappearance of some of their stores, generally before the material is actually delivered and locked up in the arsenal. On the other hand, dynamite is used for many purposes, so that it is nonsense to believe that it cannot be obtained from conventional suppliers.

Everything can be had for money, and that includes dynamite. Revolutionaries with money will be able to get it, and without money they can neither buy it nor make it. So the slogan is, "Save your pennies!!" You may object that nothing can be made out of nothing, and that resources are in the hands of others. This becomes a question of appropriating them...

Once we are in an era when things are really happening, it would be stupid to consider amateur dynamite production. Dynamite factories and explosives warehouses can be seized just like anything else. The skilled workers there would work just as well for us as for anyone else, if we pay them properly. Summing up, we shall from now on not focus our attention on making dynamite, about which there has been so much talk and so little to be seen, and occupy ourselves with how to obtain large quantities of ready-made dynamite.

Chapter 10

LOUIS LINGG
from
Famous Speeches of Our Martyrs, Delivered in Court: When asked if they had anything to say why sentence of death should not be passed upon them, October 7, 8 and 9, 1886 (1886)

On May 4, 1886, a still-unknown person threw a bomb at a labor demonstration in Chicago's Haymarket Square. In the ensuing chaos dozens were injured and several killed, including seven police officers. As a result of this, eight anarchists were arrested in connection as part of a conspiracy, even though most of them hadn't actually been there at the time. Four of the men would later be hanged for the events; two sentenced to life; and one to fifteen years. Bombs were found in the eighth man's, Louis Lingg's, home, for which his attorney's weak excuse was that Lingg had the right to have bombs in his house. Through the ages this has become popularized as Lingg supposedly proclaiming, "I couldn't have thrown that bomb. I was at home making bombs." Lingg could be regarded as the mythical Che Guevara figure of his day, with his outraged defiance at the court inspiring an entire generation of young revolutionaries. Rather than hanging, Lingg smuggled a blasting cap into his prison cell and blew off his jaw, writing "Hurray for anarchy!" on the wall in German with his own blood before dying. All the Haymarket martyrs were posthumously pardoned, and a monument later raised in their honor.

Court of Justice! With the same irony with which you have regarded my efforts to win in this "free land of America," a livelihood such as humankind is worthy to enjoy, do you now, after condemning me to death, concede me the liberty of making a final speech.

I accept your concession; but it is only for the purpose of exposing the injustice, the calumnies and the outrages which have been heaped upon me.

You have accused me of murder, and convicted me: What proof have you brought that I am guilty?

In the first place, you have brought this fellow Seliger to testify against me. Him I have helped to make bombs, and you have further proven that with the assistance of another, I took those bombs to No. 58 Clybourn Avenue, but what you have not proven—even with the assistance of your bought "squealer," Seliger, who would appear to have acted such a prominent part in the affair—is that any of those bombs were taken to the Haymarket.

A couple of chemists also, have been brought here as specialists, yet they could only state that the metal of which the Haymarket bomb was made bore a certain resemblance to those bombs of mine, and your Mr. Ingham has vainly endeavored to deny that the bombs were quite different. He had to admit that there was a difference of a full half-inch in their diameters, although he suppressed the fact that there was also a difference of a quarter of an inch in the thickness of the shell. This is the kind of evidence upon which you have convicted me.

It is not murder, however, of which you have convicted me. The judge has stated that much only this morning in his resume of the case, and Grinnell has repeatedly asserted that we were being tried not for murder, but for anarchy, so the condemnation is—that I am an Anarchist!

What is Anarchy?

This is a subject which my comrades have explained with sufficient clearness, and it is unnecessary for me to go over it again. They have told you plainly enough what our aims are. The State's attorney, however, has not given you that information. He has merely criticized and condemned, not the doctrines of Anarchy, but our methods of giving them practical effect, and even here he has maintained a discreet silence as to the fact that those methods were forced upon us by the brutality of the police. Grinnell's own proffered remedy for our grievances is the ballot and combination of trades unions, and Ingham has even avowed the desirability of a six-hour movement! But the fact is, that at every attempt to wield the ballot, at every endeavor to combine the efforts of workingmen, you have displayed the brutal violence of the police club, and this is why I have recommended rude force, to combat the ruder force of the police.

You have charged me with despising "law and order." What does your "law and order" amount to? Its representatives are the police, and they have thieves in their ranks. Here sits Captain Schaack. He has himself admitted to me that my hat and books have been stolen from him in his office—stolen by policemen. These are your defenders of property rights!

The detectives again, who arrested me, forced their way into my room like housebreakers, under false pretenses, giving the name of a carpenter, Lorenz, of Burlington Street. They have sworn that I was alone in my room, therein perjuring themselves. You have not subpoenaed this lady, Mrs. Klein, who was present, and could have sworn that the aforesaid detectives broke into my room under false pretenses, and that their testimonies are perjured.

But let us go further. In Schaack we have a captain of the police, and he also has perjured himself. He has sworn that I admitted to him being present at the Monday night meeting, whereas I distinctly informed him that I was at a carpenters' meeting at Zepf's Hall. He has sworn again that I told him that I also learned to make bombs from Herr Most's book. That, also, is a perjury.

Let us go still a step higher among these representatives of law and order. Grinnell and his associates have permitted perjury, and I say that they have done it knowingly. The proof has been adduced by my counsel, and with my own eyes I have seen Grinnell point out to Gilmer, eight days before he came upon the stand, the persons of the men whom he was to swear against.

While I, as I have stated above, believe in force for the sake of winning for myself and fellow-workmen a livelihood such as men ought to have, Grinnell, on the other hand, through his police and other rogues, has suborned perjury in order to murder seven men, of whom I am one.

Grinnell had the pitiful courage here in the courtroom, where I could not defend myself, to call me a coward! The scoundrel! A fellow who has leagued himself with a parcel of base, hireling knaves, to bring me to the gallows. Why? For no earthly reason save a contemptible selfishness—a desire to "rise in the world"—to "make money," forsooth.

This wretch—who, by means of the perjuries of other wretches is going to murder seven men—is the fellow who calls me "coward"! And yet you blame me for despising such "defenders of the law"— such unspeakable hypocrites!

Anarchy means no domination or authority of one man over another, yet you call that "disorder." A system which advocates no such "order" as shall require the services of rogues and thieves to defend it you call "disorder."

The Judge himself was forced to admit that the State's attorney had not been able to connect me with the bombthrowing. The latter knows how to get around it, however. He charges me with being a "conspirator." How does he prove it? Simply by declaring the International Working People's Association to be a "conspiracy." I was a member of that body, so he has the charge securely fastened on me. Excellent! Nothing is too difficult for the genius of a State's attorney!

It is hardly incumbent upon me to review the relations which I occupy to my companions in misfortune. I can say truly and openly that I am not as intimate with my fellow prisoners as I am with Captain Schaack.

The universal misery, the ravages of the capitalistic hyena have brought us together in our agitation, not as persons, but as workers in the same cause. Such is the "conspiracy" of which you have convicted me.

I protest against the conviction, against the decision of the court. I do not recognize your law, jumbled together as it is by the nobodies of bygone centuries, and I do not recognize the decision of the court. My own counsel have conclusively proven from the decisions of equally high courts that a new trial must be granted us. The State's attorney quotes three times as many decisions from perhaps still higher courts to prove the opposite, and I am convinced that if, in another trial, these decisions should be supported by twenty-one volumes, they will adduce one hundred in support of the contrary, if it is Anarchists who are to be tried. And not even under such a law— a law that a schoolboy must despise—not even by such methods have they been able to "legally" convict us. They have suborned perjury to boot.

I tell you frankly and openly, I am for force. I have already told Captain Schaack, "if they use cannons against us, we shall use dynamite against them."

I repeat that I am the enemy of the "order" of today, and I repeat that, with all my powers, so long as breath remains in me, I shall combat it. I declare again, frankly and openly, that I am in favor of using force. I have told Captain Schaack, and I stand by it, "if you cannonade us, we shall dynamite you." You laugh! Perhaps you think, "you'll throw no more bombs"; but let me assure you that I die happy on the gallows, so confident am I that the hundreds and thousands to whom I have spoken will remember my words; and when you shall have hanged us, then—mark my words—they will do the bomb throwing! In this hope do I say to you: I despise you. I despise your order, your laws, your force-propped authority. Hang me for it!

Chapter 11

BENJAMIN R. TUCKER
State Socialism and Anarchism: How Far They Agree, And Wherein They Differ (1888)

Individualist anarchist and publisher Benjamin R. Tucker was one of the most important radicals in American history. His long-running periodical Liberty *was home to essays from anarchists and socialists of all stripes, at a time where socialism did not necessarily have the contemporary meaning of government control. In the same way that there are many answers as to what anarchism would look like in practice, socialism too had numerous variants. Here Tucker tries to define and contrast the two concepts.*

In the summer of 1886, shortly after the bomb-throwing at Chicago, the author of this volume received an invitation from the editor of the *North American Review* to furnish him a paper on Anarchism. In response the above article was sent him. A few days later the author received a letter announcing the acceptance of his paper, the editor volunteering the declaration that it was the ablest article he had received during his editorship of the *Review*. The next number of the *Review* bore the announcement, on the second page of its cover, that the article (giving its title and the name of the author) would appear at an early date. Month after month went by, and the article did not appear. Repeated letters of inquiry failed to bring any explanation.

Finally, after nearly a year had elapsed, the author wrote to the editor that he had prepared the article, not to be pigeon-holed, but to be printed, and that he wished the matter to be acted on immediately. In reply he received his manuscript and a check for seventy-five dollars. Thereupon he made a few slight changes in the article and delivered it on several occasions as a lecture, after which it was printed in *Liberty* of March 10, 1888.

Probably no agitation has ever attained the magnitude, either in the number of its recruits or the area of its influence, which has been attained by Modern Socialism, and at the same time been so little understood and so misunderstood, not only by the hostile and the indifferent, but by the friendly, and even by the great mass of its adherents themselves. This unfortunate and highly dangerous state of things is due partly to the fact that the human relationships which this movement—if anything so chaotic can be called a movement— aims to transform, involve no special class or classes, but literally all mankind; partly to the fact that these relationships are infinitely more varied and complex in their nature than those with which any special reform has ever been called upon to deal; and partly to the fact that the great moulding forces of society, the channels of information and enlightenment, are well-nigh exclusively under the control of those whose immediate pecuniary interests are antagonistic to the bottom claim of Socialism that labor should be put in possession of its own.

Almost the only persons who may be said to comprehend even approximately the significance, principles, and purposes of Socialism are the chief leaders of the extreme wings of the Socialistic forces, and perhaps a few of the money kings themselves. It is a subject of which it has lately become quite the fashion for preacher, professor, and penny-a-liner to treat, and, for the most part, woeful work they have made with it, exciting the derision and pity of those competent to judge. That those prominent in the intermediate Socialistic divisions do not fully understand what they are about is evident from the positions they occupy. If they did; if they were consistent, logical thinkers; if they were what the French call consequent men,—their reasoning faculties would long since have driven them to one extreme or the other.

For it is a curious fact that the two extremes of the vast army now under consideration, though united, as has been hinted above, by the common claim that labor shall be put in possession of its own, are more diametrically opposed to each other in their fundamental principles of social action and their methods of reaching the ends aimed at than either is to their common enemy, the existing society. They are based on two principles the history of whose conflict is almost equivalent to the history of the world since man came into it; and all intermediate parties, including that of the upholders of the existing society, are based upon a compromise between them. It is clear, then, that any intelligent, deep-rooted opposition to the prevailing order of things must come from one or the other of these extremes, for anything from any other source, far from being revolutionary in character, could be only in the nature of such superficial modification as would be utterly unable to concentrate upon itself the degree of attention and interest now bestowed upon Modern Socialism.

The two principles referred to are **Authority** and **Liberty**, and the names of the two schools of Socialistic thought which fully and unreservedly represent one or the other of them are, respectively, State Socialism and Anarchism. Whoso knows what these two schools want and how they propose to get it understands the Socialistic movement. For, just as it has been said that there is no half-way house between Rome and Reason, so it may be said that there is no half-way house between State Socialism and Anarchism. There are, in fact, two currents steadily flowing from the center of the Socialistic forces which are concentrating them on the left and on the right; and, if Socialism is to prevail, it is among the possibilities that, after this movement of separation has been completed and the existing order have been crushed out between the two camps, the ultimate and bitterer conflict will be still to come. In that case all the eight-hour men, all the trades-unionists, all the Knights of Labor, all the land nationalizationists, all the greenbackers, and, in short, all the members of the thousand and one different battalions belonging to the great army of Labor, will have deserted their old posts, and, these being arrayed on the one side and the other, the great battle will begin. What a final victory for the State Socialists will mean, and what a final victory for the Anarchists will mean, it is the purpose of this paper to briefly state.

To do this intelligently, however, I must first describe the ground common to both, the features that make Socialists of each of them.

The economic principles of Modern Socialism are a logical deduction from the principle laid down by Adam Smith in the early chapters of his *Wealth of Nations,*—namely, that labor is the true measure of price. But Adam Smith, after stating this principle most clearly and concisely, immediately abandoned all further consideration of it to devote himself to showing what actually does measure price, and how, therefore, wealth is at present distributed. Since his day nearly all the political economists have followed his example by confining their function to the description of society as it is, in its industrial and commercial phases. Socialism, on the contrary, extends its function to the description of society as it should be, and the discovery of the means of making it what it should be. Half a century or more after Smith enunciated the principle above stated, Socialism picked it up where he had dropped it, and in following it to its logical conclusions, made it the basis of a new economic philosophy.

This seems to have been done independently by three different men, of three different nationalities, in three different languages: Josiah Warren, an American; Pierre J. Proudhon, a Frenchman; Karl Marx, a German Jew. That Warren and Proudhon arrived at their conclusions singly and unaided is certain; but whether Marx was not largely indebted to Proudhon for his economic ideas is questionable. However this may be, Marx's presentation of the ideas was in so many respects peculiarly his own that he is fairly entitled to the credit of originality. That the work of this interesting trio should have been done so nearly simultaneously would seem to indicate that Socialism was in the air, and that the time was ripe and the conditions favorable for the appearance of this new school of thought. So far as priority of time is concerned, the credit seems to belong to Warren, the American,—a fact which should be noted by the stump orators who are so fond of declaiming against Socialism as an imported article. Of the purest revolutionary blood, too, this Warren, for he descended from the Warren who fell at Bunker Hill.

From Smith's principle that labor is the true measure of price— or, as Warren phrased it, that cost is the proper limit of price—these three men made the following deductions: that the natural wage of labor is its product; that this wage, or product, is the only just source of income (leaving out, of course, gift, inheritance, etc.); that all who derive income from any other source abstract it directly or indirectly from the natural and just wage of labor; that this abstracting process generally takes one of three forms,—interest, rent, and profit; that these three constitute the trinity of usury, and are simply different methods of levying tribute for the use of capital; that, capital being simply stored-up labor which has already received its pay in full, its use ought to be gratuitous, on the principle that labor is the only basis of price; that the lender of capital is entitled to its return intact, and nothing more; that the only reason why the banker, the stockholder, the landlord, the manufacturer, and the merchant are able to exact usury from labor lies in the fact that they are backed by legal privilege, or monopoly; and that the only way to secure labor the enjoyment of its entire product, or natural wage, is to strike down monopoly.

It must not be inferred that either Warren, Proudhon, or Marx used exactly this phraseology, or followed exactly this line of thought, but it indicates definitely enough the fundamental ground taken by all three, and their substantial thought up to the limit to which they went in common. And, lest I may be accused of stating the positions and arguments of these men incorrectly, it may be well to say in advance that I have viewed them broadly, and that, for the purpose of sharp, vivid, and emphatic comparison and contrast, I have taken considerable liberty with their thought by rearranging it in an order, and often in a phraseology, of my own, but, I am satisfied, without, in so doing, misrepresenting them in any essential particular.

It was at this point—the necessity of striking down monopoly—that came the parting of their ways. Here the road forked. They found that they must turn either to the right or to the left,—follow either the path of Authority or the path of Liberty. Marx went one way; Warren and Proudhon the other. Thus were born State Socialism and Anarchism.

First, then, State Socialism, which may be described as *the doctrine that all the affairs of men should be managed by the government, regardless of individual choice.*

Marx, its founder, concluded that the only way to abolish the class monopolies was to centralize and consolidate all industrial and commercial interests, all productive and distributive agencies, in one vast monopoly in the hands of the State. The government must become banker, manufacturer, farmer, carrier, and merchant, and in these capacities must suffer no competition. Land, tools, and all instruments of production must be wrested from individual hands, and made the property of the collectivity. To the individual can belong only the products to be consumed, not the means of producing them. A man may own his clothes and his food, but not the sewing-machine which makes his shirts or the spade which digs his potatoes. Product and capital are essentially different things; the former belongs to individuals, the latter to society. Society must seize the capital which belongs to it, by the ballot if it can, by revolution if it must. Once in possession of it, it must administer it on the majority principle, though its organ, the State, utilize it in production and distribution, fix all prices by the amount of labor involved, and employ the whole people in its workshops, farms, stores, etc. The nation must be transformed into a vast bureaucracy, and every individual into a State official. Everything must be done on the cost principle, the people having no motive to make a profit out of themselves. Individuals not being allowed to own capital, no one can employ another, or even himself. Every man will be a wage-receiver, and the State the only wage-payer. He who will not work for the State must starve, or, more likely, go to prison. All freedom of trade must disappear. Competition must be utterly wiped out. All industrial and commercial activity must be centered in one vast, enormous, all-inclusive monopoly. The remedy for *monopolies* is **monopoly**.

Such is the economic programme of State Socialism as adopted from Karl Marx. The history of its growth and progress cannot be told here. In this country the parties that uphold it are known as the Socialistic Labor Party, which pretends to follow Karl Marx; the Nationalists, who follow Karl Marx filtered through Edward Bellamy; and the Christian Socialists, who follow Karl Marx filtered through Jesus Christ.

What other applications this principle of Authority, once adopted in the economic sphere, will develop is very evident. It means the absolute control by the majority of all individual conduct. The right of such control is already admitted by the State Socialists, though they maintain that, as a matter of fact, the individual would be allowed a much larger liberty than he now enjoys. But he would only be allowed it; he could not claim it as his own. There would be no foundation of society upon a guaranteed equality of the largest possible liberty. Such liberty as might exist would exist by sufferance and could be taken away at any moment. Constitutional guarantees would be of no avail. There would be but one article in the constitution of a State Socialistic country: The right of the majority is absolute.

The claim of the State Socialists, however, that this right would not be exercised in matters pertaining to the individual in the more intimate and private relations of his life is not borne out by the history of governments. It has ever been the tendency of power to add to itself, to enlarge its sphere, to encroach beyond the limits set for it; and where the habit of resisting such encroachment is not fostered, and the individual is not taught to be jealous of his rights, individuality gradually disappears and the government or State becomes the all-in-all. Control naturally accompanies responsibility. Under the system of State Socialism, therefore, which holds the community responsible for the health, wealth, and wisdom of the individual, it is evident that the community, through its majority expression, will insist more and more in prescribing the conditions of health, wealth, and wisdom, thus impairing and finally destroying individual independence and with it all sense of individual responsibility.

Whatever, then, the State Socialists may claim or disclaim, their system, if adopted, is doomed to end in a State religion, to the expense of which all must contribute and at the altar of which all must kneel; a State school of medicine, by whose practitioners the sick must invariably be treated; a State system of hygiene, prescribing what all must and must not eat, drink, wear, and do; a State code of morals, which will not content itself with punishing crime, but will prohibit what the majority decide to be vice; a State system of instruction, which will do away with all private schools, academies, and colleges; a State nursery, in which all children must be brought up in common at the public expense; and, finally, a State family, with an attempt at stirpiculture, or scientific breeding, in which no man and woman will be allowed to have children if the State prohibits them and no man and woman can refuse to have children if the State orders them. Thus will Authority achieve its acme and Monopoly be carried to its highest power.

Such is the ideal of the logical State Socialist, such the goal which lies at the end of the road that Karl Marx took. Let us now follow

the fortunes of Warren and Proudhon, who took the other road,—
the road of Liberty.

This brings us to Anarchism, which may be described as *the doctrine that all the affairs of men should be managed by individuals or voluntary associations, and that the State should be abolished.*

When Warren and Proudhon, in prosecuting their search for justice to labor, came face to face with the obstacle of class monopolies, they saw that these monopolies rested upon Authority, and concluded that the thing to be done was, not to strengthen this Authority and thus make monopoly universal, but to utterly uproot Authority and give full sway to the opposite principle, Liberty, by making competition, the antithesis of monopoly, universal. They saw in competition the great leveler of prices to the labor cost of production. In this they agreed with the political economists. The query then naturally presented itself why all prices do not fall to labor cost; where there is any room for incomes acquired otherwise than by labor; in a word, why the usurer, the receiver of interest, rent, and profit, exists. The answer was found in the present one-sidedness of competition. It was discovered that capital had so manipulated legislation that unlimited competition is allowed in supplying productive labor, thus keeping wages down to the starvation point, or as near it as practicable; that a great deal of competition is allowed in supplying distributive labor, or the labor of the mercantile classes, thus keeping, not the prices of goods, but the merchants' actual profits on them down to a point somewhat approximating equitable wages for the merchants' work; but that almost no competition at all is allowed in supplying capital, upon the aid of which both productive and distributive labor are dependent for their power of achievement, thus keeping the rate of interest on money and of house-rent and ground-rent at as high a point as the necessities of the people will bear.

On discovering this, Warren and Proudhon charged the political economists with being afraid of their own doctrine. The Manchester men were accused of being inconsistent. The believed in liberty to compete with the laborer in order to reduce his wages, but not in liberty to compete with the capitalist in order to reduce his usury. Laissez faire was very good sauce for the goose, labor, but was very poor sauce for the gander, capital. But how to correct this inconsistency, how to serve this gander with this sauce, how to put capital at the service of business men and laborers at cost, or free of usury,—that was the problem.

Marx, as we have seen, solved it by declaring capital to be a different thing from product, and maintaining that it belonged to society and should be seized by society and employed for the benefit of all alike. Proudhon scoffed at this distinction between capital and product. He maintained that capital and product are not different kinds of wealth, but simply alternate conditions or functions of the same wealth; that all wealth undergoes an incessant transformation from capital into product and from product back into capital, the process repeating itself interminably; that capital and product are purely social terms; that what is product to one man immediately becomes capital to another, and vice versa; that if there were but one person in the world, all wealth would be to him at once capital and product; that the fruit of A's toil is his product, which, when sold to B, becomes B's capital (unless B is an unproductive consumer, in which case it is merely wasted wealth, outside the view of social economy); that a steam-engine is just as much product as a coat, and that a coat is just as much capital as a steam-engine; and that the same laws of equity govern the possession of the one that govern the possession of the other.

For these and other reasons Proudhon and Warren found themselves unable to sanction any such plan as the seizure of capital by society. But, though opposed to socializing the ownership of capital, they aimed nevertheless to socialize its effects by making its use beneficial to all instead of a means of impoverishing the many to enrich the few. And when the light burst in upon them, they saw that this could be done by subjecting capital to the natural law of competition, thus bringing the price of its own use down to cost,— that is, to nothing beyond the expenses incidental to handling and transferring it. So they raised the banner of Absolute Free Trade; free trade at home, as well as with foreign countries; the logical carrying out of the Manchester doctrine; laissez faire the universal rule. Under this banner they began their fight upon monopolies, whether the all-inclusive monopoly of the State Socialists, or the various class monopolies that now prevail.

Of the latter they distinguished four of principal importance: the money monopoly, the land monopoly, the tariff monopoly, and the patent monopoly.

First in the importance of its evil influence they considered the money monopoly, which consists of the privilege given by the government to certain individuals, or to individuals holding certain kinds of property, of issuing the circulating medium, a privilege which is now enforced in this country by a national tax of ten per cent., upon all other persons who attempt to furnish a circulating medium, and by State laws making it a criminal offense to issue notes as currency. It is claimed that the holders of this privilege control the rate of interest, the rate of rent of houses and buildings, and the prices of goods,—the first directly, and the second and third indirectly. For, say Proudhon and Warren, if the business of banking were made free to all, more and more persons would enter into it until the competition should become sharp enough to reduce the price of lending money to the labor cost, which statistics show to be less than three-fourths of one per cent. In that case the thousands of people who are now deterred from going into business by the ruinously high rates which they must pay for capital with which to start and carry on business will find their difficulties removed. If they have property which they do not desire to convert into money by sale, a bank will take it as collateral for a loan of a certain proportion of its market value at less than one per cent. discount. If they have no property, but are industrious, honest, and capable, they will generally be able to get their individual notes endorsed by a sufficient number of known and solvent parties; and on such business paper they will be able to get a loan at a bank on similarly favorable terms. Thus interest will fall at a blow. The banks will really not be lending capital at all, but will be doing business on the capital of their customers, the business consisting in an exchange of the known and widely available credits of the banks for the unknown and unavailable, but equality good, credits of the customers and a charge therefor of less than one per cent., not as interest for the use of capital, but as pay for the labor of running the banks. This facility of acquiring capital will give an unheard of impetus to business, and consequently create an unprecedented demand for labor,—a demand which will always be in excess of the supply, directly to the contrary of the present condition of the labor market. Then will be seen an exemplification of the words of Richard Cobden that, when two laborers are after one employer, wages fall, but when two employers are after one laborer, wages rise. Labor will then be in a position to dictate its wages, and will thus secure its natural wage, its entire product. Thus the same blow that strikes interest down will send wages up. But this is not all. Down will go profits also. For merchants, instead of buying at high prices on credit, will borrow money of the banks at less than one per cent., buy at low prices for cash, and correspondingly reduce the prices of their goods to their customers. And with the rest will go house-rent. For no one who can borrow capital at one per cent. with which to build a house of his own will consent to pay rent to a landlord at a higher rate than that. Such is the vast claim made by Proudhon and Warren as to the results of the simple abolition of the money monopoly.

Second in importance comes the land monopoly, the evil effects of which are seen principally in exclusively agricultural countries, like Ireland. This monopoly consists in the enforcement by government of land titles which do not rest upon personal occupancy and cultivation. It was obvious to Warren and Proudhon that, as soon as individualists should no longer be protected by their fellows in anything but personal occupancy and cultivation of land, ground-rent would disappear, and so usury have one less leg to stand on. Their followers of to-day are disposed to modify this claim to the extent of admitting that the very small fraction of ground-rent which rests, not on monopoly, but on superiority of soil or site, will continue to exist for a time and perhaps forever, though tending constantly to a minimum under conditions of freedom. But the inequality of soils which gives rise to the economic rent of land, like the inequality of human skill which gives rise to the economic rent of ability, is not a cause for serious alarm even to the most thorough opponent of usury, as its nature is not that of a germ from which other and graver inequalities may spring, but rather that of a decaying branch which may finally wither and fall.

Third, the tariff monopoly, which consists in fostering production at high prices and under unfavorable conditions by visiting with the penalty of taxation those who patronize production at low prices and under favorable conditions. The evil to which this monopoly gives rise might more properly be called *mis*usury than usury, because it compels labor to pay, not exactly for the use of capital, but rather for the misuse of capital. The abolition of this monopoly would result in a great reduction in the prices of all articles taxed, and this saving to the laborers who consume these articles would be another step toward securing to the laborer his natural wage, his entire product. Proudhon admitted, however, that to abolish this monopoly before abolishing the money monopoly would be a cruel and disastrous policy, first, because the evil of scarcity of money, created by the money monopoly, would be intensified by the flow of money out of the country which would be involved in an excess of imports over exports, and, second, because that fraction of the laborers of the country which is now employed in the protected industries would be turned adrift to face starvation without the benefit of the insatiable demand for labor which a competitive money system would create. Free trade in money at home, making money and work abundant, was insisted upon by Proudhon as a prior condition of free trade in goods with foreign countries.

Fourth, the patent monopoly, which consists in protecting inventors and authors against competition for a period long enough to enable them to extort from the people a reward enormously in excess of the labor measure of their services,—in other words, in giving certain people a right of property for a term of years in laws and facts of Nature, and the power to exact tribute from others for the use of this natural wealth, which should be open to all. The abolition of this monopoly would fill its beneficiaries with a wholesome fear of competition which would cause them to be satisfied with pay for their services equal to that which other laborers get for theirs, and to secure it by placing their products and works on the market at the outset at prices so low that their lines of business would be no more tempting to competitors than any other lines.

The development of the economic programme which consists in the destruction of these monopolies and the substitution for them of the freest competition led its authors to a perception of the fact that all their thought rested upon a very fundamental principle, the freedom of the individual, his right of sovereignty over himself, his products, and his affairs, and of rebellion against the dictation of external authority. Just as the idea of taking capital away from individuals and giving it to the government started Marx in a path which ends in making the government everything and the individual nothing, so the idea of taking capital away from government-protected monopolies and putting it within easy reach of all individuals started Warren and Proudhon in a path which ends in making the individual everything and the government nothing. If the individual has a right to govern himself, all external government is tyranny. Hence the necessity of abolishing the State. This was the logical conclusion to which Warren and Proudhon were forced, and it became the fundamental article of their political philosophy. It is the doctrine which Proudhon named An-archism, a word derived from the Greek, and meaning, not necessarily absence of order, as is generally supposed, but an absence of rule. The Anarchists are simply unterrified Jeffersonian Democrats. They believe that the best government is that which governs least, and that that which governs least is no government at all. Even the simple police function of protecting person and property they deny to governments supported by compulsory taxation. Protection they look upon as a thing to be secured, as long as it is necessary, by voluntary association and cooperation for self-defence, or as a commodity to be purchased, like any other commodity, of those who offer the best article at the lowest price. In their view it is in itself an invasion of the individual to compel him to pay for or suffer a protection against invasion that he has not asked for and does not desire. And they further claim that protection will become a drug in the market, after poverty and consequently crime have disappeared through the realization of their economic programme. Compulsory taxation is to them the life-principle of all the monopolies, and passive, but organized, resistance to the tax-collector they contemplate, when the proper time comes, as one of the most effective methods of accomplishing their purposes.

Their attitude on this is a key to their attitude on all other questions of a political or social nature. In religion they are atheistic as far as their own opinions are concerned, for they look upon divine authority and the religious sanction of morality as the chief pretexts put forward by the privileged classes for the exercise of human authority. If God exists, said Proudhon, he is man's enemy. And in contrast to Voltaire's famous epigram, If God did not exist, it would be necessary to invent him, the great Russian Nihilist, Mikhail Bakunin, placed this antithetical proposition: If God existed, it would be necessary to abolish him. But although, viewing the divine hierarchy as a contradiction of Anarchy, they do not believe in it, the Anarchists none the less firmly believe in the liberty to believe in it. Any denial of religious freedom they squarely oppose.

Upholding thus the right of every individual to be or select his own priest, they likewise uphold his right to be or select his own doctor. No monopoly in theology, no monopoly in medicine. Competition everywhere and always; spiritual advice and medical advice alike to stand or fall on their own merits. And not only in medicine, but in hygiene, must this principle of liberty be followed. The individual may decide for himself not only what to do to get well, but what to do to keep well. No external power must dictate to him what he must and must not eat, drink, wear, or do.

Nor does the Anarchistic scheme furnish any code of morals to be imposed upon the individual. Mind your own business is its only moral law. Interference with another's business is a crime and the only crime, and as such may properly be resisted. In accordance with this view the Anarchists look upon attempts to arbitrarily suppress vice as in themselves crimes. They believe liberty and the resultant social well-being to be a sure cure for all the vices. But they recognize the right of the drunkard, the gambler, the rake, and the harlot to live their lives until they shall freely choose to abandon them.

In the matter of the maintenance and rearing of children the Anarchists would neither institute the communistic nursery which the State Socialists favor nor keep the communistic school system which now prevails. The nurse and the teacher, like the doctor and the preacher, must be selected voluntarily, and their services must be paid for by those who patronize them. Parental rights must not be taken away, and parental responsibilities must not be foisted upon others.

Even in so delicate a matter as that of the relations of the sexes the Anarchists do not shrink from the application of their principle. They acknowledge and defend the right of any man and woman, or any men and women, to love each other for as long or as short a time as they can, will, or may. To them legal marriage and legal divorce are equal absurdities. They look forward to a time when every individual, whether man or woman, shall be self-supporting, and when each shall have an independent home of his or her own, whether it be a separate house or rooms in a house with others; when the love relations between these independent individuals shall be as varied as are individual inclinations and attractions; and when the children born of these relations shall belong exclusively to the mothers until old enough to belong to themselves.

Such are the main features of the Anarchistic social ideal. There is wide difference of opinion among those who hold it as to the best method of obtaining it. Time forbids the treatment of that phase of the subject here. I will simply call attention to the fact that it is an ideal utterly inconsistent with that of those Communists who falsely call themselves Anarchists while at the same time advocating a regime of Archism fully as despotic as that of the State Socialists themselves. And it is an ideal that can be as little advanced by Prince Kropotkine as retarded by the brooms of those Mrs. Partingtons of the bench who sentence them to prison; an ideal which the martyrs of Chicago did far more to help by their glorious death upon the gallows for the common cause of Socialism than by their unfortunate advocacy during their lives, in the name of Anarchism, of force as a revolutionary agent and authority as a safeguard of the new social order. The Anarchists believe in liberty both as an end and means, and are hostile to anything that antagonizes it.

I should not undertake to summarize this altogether too summary exposition of Socialism from the standpoint of Anarchism, did I not find the task already accomplished for me by a brilliant French journalist and historian, Ernest Lesigne, in the form of a series of crisp antithesis; by reading which to you as a conclusion of this lecture I hope to deepen the impression which it has been my endeavor to make.

"There are two Socialisms.

"One is communistic, the other solidaritarian.

"One is dictatorial, the other libertarian.

"One is metaphysical, the other positive.

"One is dogmatic, the other scientific.

"One is emotional, the other reflective.

"One is destructive, the other constructive.

"Both are in pursuit of the greatest possible welfare for all.

"One aims to establish happiness for all, the other to enable each to be happy in his own way.

"The first regards the State as a society sui generis, of an especial essence, the product of a sort of divine right outside of and above all society, with special rights and able to exact special obediences; the second considers the State as an association like any other, generally managed worse than others.

"The first proclaims the sovereignty of the State, the second

155

recognizes no sort of sovereign.

"One wishes all monopolies to be held by the State; the other wishes the abolition of all monopolies.

"One wishes the governed class to become the governing class; the other wishes the disappearance of classes.

"Both declare that the existing state of things cannot last.

"The first considers revolutions as the indispensable agent of evolutions; the second teaches that repression alone turns evolutions into revolution.

"The first has faith in a cataclysm.

"The second knows that social progress will result from the free play of individual efforts.

"Both understand that we are entering upon a new historic phase.

"One wishes that there should be none but proletaires.

"The other wishes that there should be no more proletaires.

"The first wishes to take everything away from everybody.

"The second wishes to leave each in possession of its own.

"The one wishes to expropriate everybody.

"The other wishes everybody to be a proprietor.

"The first says: 'Do as the government wishes.'

"The second says: 'Do as you wish yourself.'

"The former threatens with despotism.

"The latter promises liberty.

"The former makes the citizen the subject of the State.

"The latter makes the State the employee of the citizen.

"One proclaims that labor pains will be necessary to the birth of a new world.

"The other declares that real progress will not cause suffering to any one.

"The first has confidence in social war.

"The other believes only in the works of peace.

"One aspires to command, to regulate, to legislate.

"The other wishes to attain the minimum of command, of regulation, of legislation.

"One would be followed by the most atrocious of reactions.

"The other opens unlimited horizons to progress.

"The first will fail; the other will succeed.

"Both desire equality.

"One by lowering heads that are too high.

"The other by raising heads that are too low.

"One sees equality under a common yoke.

"The other will secure equality in complete liberty.

"One is intolerant, the other tolerant.

"One frightens, the other reassures.

"The first wishes to instruct everybody.

"The second wishes to enable everybody to instruct himself.

"The first wishes to support everybody.

"The second wishes to enable everybody to support himself.

"One says:

"The land to the State.

"The mine to the State.

"The tool to the State.

"The product to the State.

"The other says:

"The land to the cultivator.

"The mine to the miner.

"The tool to the laborer.

"The product to the producer.

"There are only these two Socialisms.

"One is the infancy of Socialism; the other is its manhood.

"One is already the past; the other is the future.

"One will give place to the other.

"To-day each of us must choose for the one or the other of these two Socialisms, or else confess that he is not a Socialist."

Chapter 12

PETER KROPOTKIN
from
The Conquest of Bread (1892)

No one has done as much to flesh out what anarcho-communism would look like in practice as Peter Kropotkin. Kropotkin regarded anarchism as the evolved alternative to the might-makes-right, social-Darwinist worldview, and is quoted as saying "Competition is the law of the jungle, but cooperation is the law of civilization." He envisioned a peaceful society where everyone would work to the benefit of all, where kindness and compassion motivated humanity. Despite claims that he was utterly naive, it is violence that is by far the exception in interpersonal human interaction. Kropotkin's The Conquest of Bread *remains the classic text elucidating the ancom perspective.*

ANARCHIST COMMUNISM

I

Every society which has abolished private property will be forced, we maintain, to organize itself on the lines of Communistic Anarchy. Anarchy leads to Communism, and Communism to Anarchy, both alike being expressions of the predominant tendency in modern societies, the pursuit of equality.

Time was when a peasant family could consider the corn which it grew, or the woollen garments woven in the cottage, as the products of its own toil. But even then this way of looking at things was not quite correct. There were the roads and the bridges made in common, the swamps drained by common toil, and the communal pastures enclosed by hedges which were kept in repair by each and all. If the looms for weaving or the dyes for colouring fabrics were improved, all profited; so even in those days a peasant family could not live alone, but was dependent in a thousand ways on the village or the commune.

But nowadays, in the present state of industry, when everything is interdependent, when each branch of production is knit up with all the rest, the attempt to claim an Individualist origin for the products of industry is absolutely untenable. The astonishing perfection attained by the textile or mining industries in civilized countries is due to the simultaneous development of a thousand other industries, great and small, to the extension of the railroad system, to inter-oceanic navigation, to the manual skill of thousands of workers, to a certain standard of culture reached by the working classes as a whole, to the labours, in short, of men in every corner of the globe.

The Italians who died of cholera while making the Suez Canal, or of anchylosis in the St. Gothard Tunnel, and the Americans mowed down by shot and shell while fighting for the abolition of slavery have helped to develop the cotton industry in France and England, as well as the work-girls who languish in the factories of Manchester and Rouen, and the inventor who (following the suggestion of some worker) succeeds in improving the looms.

How, then, shall we estimate the share of each in the riches which ALL contribute to amass?

Looking at production from this general, synthetic point of view, we cannot hold with the Collectivists that payment proportionate to the hours of labour rendered by each would be an ideal arrangement, or even a step in the right direction.

Without discussing whether exchange value of goods is really measured in existing societies by the amount of work necessary to produce it—according to the doctrine of Smith and Ricardo, in whose footsteps Marx has followed—suffice it to say here, leaving ourselves free to return to the subject later, that the Collectivist ideal appears to us untenable in a society which considers the instruments of labour as a common inheritance. Starting from this principle, such a society would find itself forced from the very outset to abandon all forms of wages.

The mitigated individualism of the collectivist system certainly could not maintain itself alongside a partial communism—the socialization of land and the instruments of production. A new form of property requires a new form of remuneration. A new method of production cannot exist side by side with the old forms of consumption, any more than it can adapt itself to the old forms of political organization.

The wage system arises out of the individual ownership of the land and the instruments of labour. It was the necessary condition for the development of capitalist production, and will perish with it, in spite of the attempt to disguise it as "profit-sharing." The common possession of the instruments of labour must necessarily bring with it the enjoyment in common of the fruits of common labour.

We hold further that Communism is not only desirable, but that existing societies, founded on Individualism, *are inevitably impelled in the direction of Communism*. The development of Individualism during the last three centuries is explained by the efforts of the individual to protect himself from the tyranny of Capital and of the State. For a time he imagined, and those who expressed his thought for him declared, that he could free himself entirely from the State and from society. "By means of money," he said, "I can buy all that I need." But the individual was on a wrong tack, and modern history has taught him to recognize that, without the help of all, he can do nothing, although his strong-boxes are full of gold.

In fact, alongside this current of Individualism, we find in all modern history a tendency, on the one hand, to retain all that remains of the partial Communism of antiquity, and, on the other, to establish the Communist principle in the thousand developments of modern life.

As soon as the communes of the tenth, eleventh, and twelfth centuries had succeeded in emancipating themselves from their lords, ecclesiastical or lay, their communal labour and communal consumption began to extend and develop rapidly. The township—and not private persons—freighted ships and equipped expeditions, and the benefit arising from the foreign trade did not accrue to individuals, but was shared by all. The townships also bought provisions for their citizens. Traces of these institutions have lingered on into the nineteenth century, and the folk piously cherish the memory of them in their legends.

All that has disappeared. But the rural township still struggles to preserve the last traces of this Communism, and it succeeds—except when the State throws its heavy sword into the balance.

Meanwhile new organizations, based on the same principle—*to every man according to his needs*—spring up under a thousand different forms; for without a certain leaven of Communism the present societies could not exist. In spite of the narrowly egoistic turn given to men's minds by the commercial system, the tendency towards Communism is constantly appearing, and influences our activities in a variety of ways.

The bridges, for the use of which a toll was levied in the old days, are now become public property and free to all; so are the high roads, except in the East, where a toll is still exacted from the traveller for every mile of his journey. Museums, free libraries, free schools, free meals for children; parks and gardens open to all; streets paved and lighted, free to all; water supplied to every house without measure or stint—all such arrangements are founded on the principle: "Take what you need."

The tramways and railways have already introduced monthly and annual season tickets, without limiting the number of journeys taken; and two nations, Hungary and Russia, have introduced on their railways the zone system, which permits the holder to travel five hundred or a thousand miles for the same price. It is but a short step from that to a uniform charge, such as already prevails in the postal service. In all these innovations, and a thousand others, the tendency is not to measure the individual consumption. One man wants to travel a thousand miles, another five hundred. These are personal requirements. There is no sufficient reason why one should pay twice as much as the other because his need is twice as great. Such are the signs which appear even now in our individualist societies.

Moreover, there is a tendency, though still a feeble one, to consider the needs of the individual, irrespective of his past or possible services to the community. We are beginning to think of society as a whole, each part of which is so intimately bound up with the others that a service rendered to one is a service rendered to all.

When you go into a public library—not indeed the National Library of Paris, but, say, into the British Museum or the Berlin

Library—the librarian does not ask what services you have rendered to society before giving you the book, or the fifty books which you require, and he comes to your assistance if you do not know how to manage the catalogue. By means of uniform credentials—and very often a contribution of work is preferred—the scientific society opens its museums, its gardens, its library, its laboratories, and its annual conversaziones to each of its members, whether he be a Darwin, or a simple amateur.

At St. Petersburg, if you are pursuing an invention, you go into a special laboratory or a workshop, where you are given a place, a carpenter's bench, a turning lathe, all the necessary tools and scientific instruments, provided only you know how to use them; and you are allowed to work there as long as you please. There are the tools; interest others in your idea, join with fellow workers skilled in various crafts, or work alone if you prefer it. Invent a flying machine, or invent nothing—that is your own affair. You are pursuing an idea—that is enough.

In the same way, those who man the lifeboat do not ask credentials from the crew of a sinking ship; they launch their boat, risk their lives in the raging waves, and sometimes perish, all to save men whom they do not even know. And what need to know them? "They are human beings, and they need our aid—that is enough, that establishes their right—To the rescue!"

Thus we find a tendency, eminently communistic, springing up on all sides, and in various guises, in the very heart of theoretically individualist societies.

Suppose that one of our great cities, so egotistic in ordinary times, were visited to-morrow by some calamity—a siege, for instance—that same selfish city would decide that the first needs to satisfy were those of the children and the aged. Without asking what services they had rendered, or were likely to render to society, it would first of all feed them. Then the combatants would be cared for, irrespective of the courage or the intelligence which each has displayed, and thousands of men and women would outvie each other in unselfish devotion to the wounded.

This tendency exists and is felt as soon as the most pressing needs of each are satisfied, and in proportion as the productive power of the race increases. It becomes an active force every time a great idea comes to oust the mean preoccupations of everyday life.

How can we doubt, then, that when the instruments of production are placed at the service of all, when business is conducted on Communist principles, when labour, having recovered its place of honour in society, produces much more than is necessary to all—how can we doubt but that this force (already so powerful) will enlarge its sphere of action till it becomes the ruling principle of social life?

Following these indications, and considering further the practical side of expropriation, of which we shall speak in the following chapters, we are convinced that our first obligation, when the revolution shall have broken the power upholding the present system, will be to realize Communism without delay.

But ours is neither the Communism of Fourier and the Phalansteriens, nor of the German State-Socialists. It is Anarchist Communism,—Communism without government—the Communism of the Free. It is the synthesis of the two ideals pursued by humanity throughout the ages—Economic and Political Liberty.

II

In taking "Anarchy" for our ideal of political organization we are only giving expression to another marked tendency of human progress. Whenever European societies have developed up to a certain point they have shaken off the yoke of authority and substituted a system founded roughly more or less on the principles of individual liberty. And history shows us that these periods of partial or general revolution, when the governments were overthrown, were also periods of sudden progress both in the economic and the intellectual field. Now it is the enfranchisement of the communes, whose monuments, produced by the free labour of the guilds, have never been surpassed; now it is the peasant rising which brought about the Reformation and imperilled the papacy; and then again it is the society, free for a brief space, which was created at the other side of the Atlantic by the malcontents from the Old World.

Further, if we observe the present development of civilized peoples we see, most unmistakably, a movement ever more and more marked to limit the sphere of action of the Government, and to allow more and more liberty to the individual. This evolution is going on before our eyes, though cumbered by the ruins and rubbish of old institutions and old superstitions. Like all evolutions, it only waits a revolution to overthrow the old obstacles which block the way, that it may find free scope in a regenerated society.

After having striven long in vain to solve the insoluble problem—the problem of constructing a government "which will constrain the individual to obedience without itself ceasing to be the servant of society," men at last attempt to free themselves from every form of government and to satisfy their need for organization by a free contract between individuals and groups pursuing the same aim. The independence of each small territorial unit becomes a pressing need; mutual agreement replaces law, and everywhere regulates individual interests in view of a common object.

All that was once looked on as a function of the Government is to-day called in question. Things are arranged more easily and more satisfactorily without the intervention of the State. And in studying the progress made in this direction, we are led to conclude that the tendency of the human race is to reduce Government interference to zero; in fact, to abolish the State, the personification of injustice, oppression, and monopoly.

We can already catch glimpses of a world in which the bonds which bind the individual are no longer laws, but social habits—the result of the need felt by each one of us to seek the support, the co-operation, the sympathy of his neighbours.

Assuredly the idea of a society without a State will give rise to at least as many objections as the political economy of a society without private capital. We have all been brought up from our childhood to regard the State as a sort of Providence; all our education, the Roman history we learned at school, the Byzantine code which we studied later under the name of Roman law, and the various sciences taught at the universities, accustom us to believe in Government and in the virtues of the State providential.

To maintain this superstition whole systems of philosophy have been elaborated and taught; all politics are based on this principle; and each politician, whatever his colours, comes forward and says to the people, "Give me the power, and I both can and will free you from the miseries which press so heavily upon you."

From the cradle to the grave all our actions are guided by this principle. Open any book on sociology or jurisprudence, and you will find there the Government, its organization, its acts, filling so large a place that we come to believe that there is nothing outside the Government and the world of statesmen.

The press teaches us the same in every conceivable way. Whole columns are devoted to parliamentary debates and to political intrigues. The vast every day life of a nation is barely mentioned in a few lines when dealing with economic subjects, law, or in "divers facts" relating to police cases. And when you read these newspapers, you hardly think of the incalculable number of beings—all humanity, so to say—who grow up and die, who know sorrow, who work and consume, think and create outside the few encumbering personages who have been so magnified that humanity is hidden by their shadows enlarged by our ignorance.

And yet as soon as we pass from printed matter; to life itself, as soon as we throw a glance at society, we are struck by the infinitesimal part played by the Government. Balzac already remarked how millions of peasants spend the whole of their lives without knowing anything about the State, save the heavy taxes they are compelled to pay. Every day millions of transactions are made without Government intervention, and the greatest of them—those of commerce and of the Exchange—are carried on in such a way that the Government could not be appealed to if one of the contracting parties had the intention of not fulfilling his agreement. Should you speak to a man who understands commerce he will tell you that the everyday business transacted by merchants would be absolutely impossible were it not based on mutual confidence. The habit of keeping his word, the desire not to lose his credit, amply suffice to maintain this relative honesty. The man who does not feel the slightest remorse when poisoning his customers with noxious drugs covered with pompous labels thinks he is in honour bound to keep his engagements. Now, if this relative morality has developed under present conditions, when enrichment is the only incentive and the only aim, can we doubt its rapid progress when appropriation of the fruits of others' labour will no longer be the basis of society?

Another striking fact, which especially characterizes our generation, speaks still more in favour of our ideas. It is the continual extension of the field of enterprise due to private initiative, and the prodigious development of free groups of all kinds. We shall discuss this more at length in the chapter devoted to *Free Agreement*. Suffice it to mention that the facts are so numerous and so customary that they are the essence of the second half of the nineteenth century, even though political and socialist writers ignore them, always preferring to talk to us about the functions of Government.

These organizations, free and infinitely varied, are so natural an outcome of our civilization; they expand so rapidly and group themselves with so much ease; they are so necessary a result of the continual growth of the needs of civilized man; and lastly, they so advantageously replace governmental interference that we must recognize in them a factor of growing importance in the life of societies. If they do not yet spread over the whole of the manifestations of life, it is that they find an insurmountable obstacle in the poverty of the worker, in the casts of present society, in the private appropriation of capital, and in the State. Abolish these obstacles and you will see them covering the immense field of civilized man's activity.

The history of the last fifty years furnishes a living proof that Representative Government is impotent to discharge the functions we have sought to assign to it. In days to come the nineteenth century will be quoted as having witnessed the failure of parliamentarianism.

But this impotence is becoming evident to all; the faults of parliamentarianism, and the inherent vices of the representative principle, are self-evident, and the few thinkers who have made a critical study of them (J. S. Mill and Leverdays) did but give literary form to the popular dissatisfaction. It is not difficult, indeed, to see the absurdity of naming a few men and saying to them, "Make laws regulating all our spheres of activity, although not one of you knows anything about them!"

We are beginning to see that government by majorities means abandoning all the affairs of the country to the tide-waiters who make up the majorities in the House and in election committees; to those, in a word, who have no opinion of their own. But mankind is seeking and already finding new issues.

The International Postal Union, the railway unions, and the learned societies give us examples of solutions based on free agreement in place and stead of law.

To-day, when groups scattered far and wide wish to organize themselves for some object or other, they no longer elect an international parliament of Jacks-of-all-trades. No, where it is not possible to meet directly or come to an agreement by correspondence, delegates versed in the question at issue are sent to treat, with the instructions: "Endeavour to come to an agreement on such or such a question and then return not with a law in your pocket, but with a proposition of agreement which we may or may not accept."

Such is the method of the great industrial companies, the learned societies, and the associations of every description, which already cover Europe and the United States. And such should be the method of an emancipated society. While bringing about expropriation, society cannot continue to organize itself on the principle of parliamentary representation. A society founded on serfdom is in keeping with absolute monarchy; a society based on the wage system and the exploitation of the masses by the capitalists finds its political expression in parliamentarianism. But a free society, regaining possession of the common inheritance, must seek, in free groups and free federations of groups, a new organization, in harmony with the new economic phase of history.

Every economic phase has a political phase corresponding to it, and it would be impossible to touch property without finding at the same time a new mode of political life.

EXPROPRIATION

I

It is told of Rothschild that, seeing his fortune threatened by the Revolution of 1848, he hit upon the following stratagem: "I am quite willing to admit," said he, "that my fortune has been accumulated at the expense of others, but if it were divided to-morrow among the millions of Europe, the share of each would only amount to five shillings. Very well, then, I undertake to render to each his five shillings if he asks me for it."

Having given due publicity to his promise, our millionaire proceeded as usual to stroll quietly through the streets of Frankfort. Three or four passers-by asked for their five shillings, which he disbursed with a sardonic smile. His stratagem succeeded, and the family of the millionaire is still in possession of its wealth.

It is in much the same fashion that the shrewd heads among the middle classes reason when they say, "Ah, Expropriation! I know what that means. You take all the overcoats and lay them in a heap, and every one is free to help himself and fight for the best."

But such jests are irrelevant as well as flippant. What we want is not a redistribution of overcoats, although it must be said that even in such a case, the shivering folk would see advantage in it. Nor do we want to divide up the wealth of the Rothschilds. What we do want is so to arrange things that every human being born into the world shall be ensured the opportunity in the first instance of learning some useful occupation, and of becoming skilled in it; next, that he shall be free to work at his trade without asking leave of master or owner, and without handing over to landlord or capitalist the lion's share of what he produces. As to the wealth held by the Rothschilds or the Vanderbilts, it will serve us to organize our system of communal production.

The day when the labourer may till the ground without paying away half of what he produces, the day when the machines necessary to prepare the soil for rich harvests are at the free disposal of the cultivators, the day when the worker in the factory produces for the community and not the monopolist—that day will see the workers clothed and fed, and there will be no more Rothschilds or other exploiters.

No one will then have to sell his working power for a wage that only represents a fraction of what he produces.

"So far so good," say our critics, "but you will have Rothschilds coming in from outside. How are you to prevent a person from amassing millions in China and then settling amongst you? How are you going to prevent such a one from surrounding himself with lackeys and wage-slaves—from exploiting them and enriching himself at their expense?"

"You cannot bring about a revolution all over the world at the same time. Well, then, are you going to establish custom-houses on your frontiers to search all who enter your country and confiscate the money they bring with them?—Anarchist policemen firing on travellers would be a fine spectacle!"

But at the root of this argument there is a great error. Those who propound it have never paused to inquire whence come the fortunes of the rich. A little thought would, however, suffice to show them that these fortunes have their beginnings in the poverty of the poor. When there are no longer any destitute there will no longer be any rich to exploit them.

Let us glance for a moment at the Middle Ages, when great fortunes began to spring up.

A feudal baron seizes on a fertile valley. But as long as the fertile valley is empty of folk our baron is not rich. His land brings him in nothing; he might as well possess a property in the moon.

What does our baron do to enrich himself? He looks out for peasants—for poor peasants!

If every peasant-farmer had a piece of land, free from rent and taxes, if he had in addition the tools and the stock necessary for farm labour, who would plough the lands of the baron? Everyone would look after his own. But there are thousands of destitute persons ruined by wars, or drought, or pestilence. They have neither horse nor plough. (Iron was costly in the Middle Ages, and a draughthorse still more so.)

All these destitute creatures are trying to better their condition. One day they see on the road at the confines of our baron's estate a notice-board indicating by certain signs adapted to their comprehension that the labourer who is willing to settle on this estate will receive the tools and materials to build his cottage and sow his fields, and a portion of land rent free for a certain number of years. The number of years is represented by so many crosses on the sign-board, and the peasant understands the meaning of these crosses.

So the poor wretches swarm over the baron's lands, making roads, draining marshes, building villages. In nine years he begins to tax them. Five years later he increases the rent. Then he doubles it. The peasant accepts these new conditions because he cannot find better ones elsewhere; and little by little, with the aid of laws made by the barons, the poverty of the peasant becomes the source of the landlord's wealth. And it is not only the lord of the manor who preys upon him. A whole host of usurers swoop down upon the villages, multiplying as the wretchedness of the peasants increases. That is how things went in the Middle Ages. And to-day is it not still the same thing? If there were free lands which the peasant could cultivate if he pleased, would he pay £50 to some "shabble of a duke" for condescending to sell him a scrap? Would he burden himself with a lease which absorbed a third of the produce? Would he—on the *métayer* system—consent to give the half of his harvest to the landowner?

But he has nothing. So he will accept any conditions, if only he can keep body and soul together, while he tills the soil and enriches the landlord.

So in the nineteenth century, just as in the Middle Ages, the poverty of the peasant is a source of wealth to the landed proprietor.

II

The landlord owes his riches to the poverty of the peasants, and the wealth of the capitalist comes from the same source.

Take the case of a citizen of the middle class, who somehow or other finds himself in possession of £20,000. He could, of course, spend his money at the rate of £2,000 a year, a mere bagatelle in these days of fantastic, senseless luxury. But then he would have nothing left at the end of ten years. So, being a "practical person," he prefers to keep his fortune intact, and win for himself a snug little annual income as well.

This is very easy in our society, for the good reason that the towns and villages swarm with workers who have not the wherewithal to live for a month, or even a fortnight. So our worthy citizen starts a factory. The banks hasten to lend him another £20,000, especially if he has a reputation for "business ability"; and with this round sum he can command the labour of five hundred hands.

If all the men and women in the country-side had their daily bread sure and their daily needs already satisfied, who would work for our capitalist at a wage of half a crown a day, while the commodities one produces in a day sell in the market for a crown or more?

Unhappily—we know it all too well—the poor quarters of our towns and the neighbouring villages are full of needy wretches, whose children clamour for bread. So, before the factory is well finished, the workers hasten to offer themselves. Where a hundred are required three hundred besiege the doors, and from the time his mill is started the owner, if he only has average business capacities, will clear £40 a year out of each mill-hand he employs.

He is thus able to lay by a snug little fortune; and if he chooses a lucrative trade and has "business talents" he will soon increase his income by doubling the number of the men he exploits.

So he becomes a personage of importance. He can afford to give dinners to other personages—to the local magnates, the civic, legal, and political dignitaries. With his money he can "marry money"; by and by he may pick and choose places for his children, and later on perhaps get something good from the Government—a contract for the army or for the police. His gold breeds gold; till at last a war, or even a rumour of war, or a speculation on the Stock Exchange, gives him his great opportunity.

Nine-tenths of the great fortunes made in the United States are (as Henry George has shown in his "Social Problems") the result of knavery on a large scale, assisted by the State. In Europe, nine-tenths of the fortunes made in our monarchies and republics have the same origin. There are not two ways of becoming a millionaire.

This is the secret of wealth; find the starving and destitute, pay them half a crown, and make them produce five shillings worth in the day, amass a fortune by these means, and then increase it by some lucky hit, made with the help of the State.

Need we go on to speak of small fortunes attributed by the economists to forethought and frugality, when we know that mere saving in itself brings in nothing, so long as the pence saved are not used to exploit the famishing?

Take a shoemaker, for instance. Grant that his work is well paid, that he has plenty of custom, and that by dint of strict frugality he contrives to lay by from eighteen pence to two shillings a day, perhaps two pounds a month.

Grant that our shoemaker is never ill, that he does not half starve himself, in spite of his passion for economy; that he does not marry or that he has no children; that he does not die of consumption; suppose anything and everything you please!

Well, at the age of fifty he will not have scraped together £800; and he will not have enough to live on during his old age, when he is past work. Assuredly this is not how great fortunes are made. But suppose our shoemaker, as soon as he has laid by a few pence, thriftily conveys them to the savings bank, and that the savings bank lends them to the capitalist who is just about to "employ labour," i.e. to exploit the poor. Then our shoemaker takes an apprentice, the child of some poor wretch, who will think himself lucky if in five years time his son has learned the trade and is able to earn his living.

Meanwhile our shoemaker does not lose by him, and if trade is brisk he soon takes a second, and then a third apprentice. By and by he will take two or three working men—poor wretches, thankful to receive half a crown a day for work that is worth five shillings, and if

172

our shoemaker is "in luck," that is to say, if he is keen enough and mean enough, his working men and apprentices will bring him in nearly one pound a day, over and above the product of his own toil. He can then enlarge his business. He will gradually become rich, and no longer have any need to stint himself in the necessaries of life. He will leave a snug little fortune to his son.

That is what people call "being economical and having frugal, temperate habits." At bottom it is nothing more nor less than grinding the face of the poor.

Commerce seems an exception to this rule. "Such a man," we are told, "buys tea in China, brings it to France, and realizes a profit of thirty per cent on his original outlay. He has exploited nobody."

Nevertheless the case is analogous. If our merchant had carried his bales on his back, well and good! In early medieval times that was exactly how foreign trade was conducted, and so no one reached such giddy heights of fortune as in our days. Very few and very hardly earned were the gold coins which the medieval merchant gained from a long and dangerous voyage. It was less the love of money than the thirst of travel and adventure that inspired his undertakings.

Nowadays the method is simpler. A merchant who has some capital need not stir from his desk to become wealthy. He telegraphs to an agent telling him to buy a hundred tons of tea; he freights a ship, and in a few weeks, in three months if it is a sailing ship, the vessel brings him his cargo. He does not even take the risks of the voyage, for his tea and his vessel are insured, and if he has expended four thousand pounds he will receive more than five thousand; that is to say, if he has not attempted to speculate in some novel commodities, in which case he runs a chance of either doubling his fortune or losing it altogether.

Now, how could he find men willing to cross the sea, to travel to China and back, to endure hardship and slavish toil and to risk their lives for a miserable pittance? How could he find dock labourers willing to load and unload his ships for "starvation wages"? How? Because they are needy and starving. Go to the seaports, visit the cook-shops and taverns on the quays, and look at these men who have come to hire themselves, crowding round the dock-gates, which they besiege from early dawn, hoping to be allowed to work on the vessels. Look at these sailors, happy to be hired for a long voyage, after weeks and months of waiting. All their lives long they have gone to the sea in ships, and they will sail in others still, until they have perished in the waves.

Enter their homes, look at their wives and children in rags, living one knows not how till the father's return, and you will have the answer to the question. Multiply examples, choose them where you will, consider the origin of all fortunes, large or small, whether arising out of commerce, finance, manufactures, or the land. Everywhere you will find that the wealth of the wealthy springs from the poverty of the poor. This is why an anarchist society need not fear the advent of a Rothschild who would settle in its midst. If every member of the community knows that after a few hours of productive toil he will have a right to all the pleasures that civilization procures, and to those deeper sources of enjoyment which art and science offer to all who seek them, he will not sell his strength for a starvation wage. No one will volunteer to work for the enrichment of your Rothschild. His golden guineas will be only so many pieces of metal—useful for various purposes, but incapable of breeding more.

In answering the above objection we have at the same time indicated the scope of Expropriation. It must apply to everything that enables any man—be he financier, mill-owner, or landlord—to appropriate the product of others' toil. Our formula is simple and comprehensive.

We do not want to rob any one of his coat, but we wish to give to the workers all those things the lack of which makes them fall an easy prey to the exploiter, and we will do our utmost that none shall lack aught, that not a single man shall be forced to sell the strength of his right arm to obtain a bare subsistence for himself and his babes. This is what we mean when we talk of Expropriation; this will be our duty during the Revolution, for whose coming we look, not two hundred years hence, but soon, very soon.

III

The ideas of Anarchism in general and of Expropriation in particular find much more sympathy than we are apt to imagine among men of independent character, and those for whom idleness is not the supreme ideal. "Still," our friends often warn us, "take care you do not go too far! Humanity cannot be changed in a day, so do not be in too great a hurry with your schemes of Expropriation and Anarchy, or you will be in danger of achieving no permanent result."

Now, what we fear with regard to Expropriation is exactly the contrary. We are afraid of not going far enough, of carrying out Expropriation on too small a scale to be lasting. We would not have the revolutionary impulse arrested in mid-career, to exhaust itself in half measures, which would content no one, and while producing a tremendous confusion in society, and stopping its customary activities, would have no vital power—would merely spread general discontent and inevitably prepare the way for the triumph of reaction.

There are, in fact, in a modern State established relations which it is practically impossible to modify if one attacks them only in detail. There are wheels within wheels in our economic organization—the machinery is so complex and interdependent that no one part can be modified without disturbing the whole. This becomes clear as soon as an attempt is made to expropriate anything.

Let us suppose that in a certain country a limited form of expropriation is effected. For example, that, as it has been suggested more than once, only the property of the great landlords is socialized, whilst the factories are left untouched; or that, in a certain city, house property is taken over by the Commune, but everything else is left in private ownership; or that, in some manufacturing centre, the factories are communalized, but the land is not interfered with.

The same result would follow in each case—a terrible shattering of the industrial system, without the means of reorganizing it on new lines. Industry and finance would be at a deadlock, yet a return to the first principles of justice would not have been achieved, and society would find itself powerless to construct a harmonious whole.

If agriculture could free itself from great landowners, while industry still remained the bondslave of the capitalist, the merchant, and the banker, nothing would be accomplished. The peasant suffers to-day not only in having to pay rent to the landlord; he is oppressed on all hands by existing conditions. He is exploited by the tradesman, who makes him pay half a crown for a spade which, measured by the labour spent on it, is not worth more than sixpence. He is taxed by the State, which cannot do without its formidable hierarchy of officials, and finds it necessary to maintain an expensive army, because the traders of all nations are perpetually fighting for the markets, and any day a little quarrel arising from the exploitation of some part of Asia or Africa may result in war.

Then again the peasant suffers from the depopulation of country places: the young people are attracted to the large manufacturing towns by the bait of high wages paid temporarily by the producers of articles of luxury, or by the attractions of a more stirring life. The artificial protection of industry, the industrial exploitation of foreign countries, the prevalence of stock-jobbing, the difficulty of improving the soil and the machinery of production—all these agencies combine nowadays to work against agriculture, which is burdened not only by rent, but by the whole complex of conditions in a society based on exploitation. Thus, even if the expropriation of land were accomplished, and every one were free to till the soil and cultivate it to the best advantage, without paying rent, agriculture, even though it should enjoy—which can by no means be taken for granted—a momentary prosperity, would soon fall back into the slough in which it finds itself to-day. The whole thing would have to be begun over again, with increased difficulties.

The same holds true of industry. Take the converse case: instead of turning the agricultural labourers into peasant-proprietors, make over the factories to those who work in them. Abolish the master-manufacturers, but leave the landlord his land, the banker his money, the merchant his Exchange, maintain the swarm of idlers who live on the toil of the workmen, the thousand and one middlemen, the State with its numberless officials, and industry would come to a standstill. Finding no purchasers in the mass of peasants who would remain poor; not possessing the raw material, and unable to export their produce, partly on account of the stoppage of trade, and still more so because industries spread all over the world, the manufacturers would feel unable to struggle, and thousands of workers would be thrown upon the streets. These starving crowds would be ready and willing to submit to the first schemer who came to exploit them; they would even consent to return to the old slavery, if only under promise of work.

Or, finally, suppose you oust the landowners, and hand over the mills and factories to the worker, without interfering with the swarm of middlemen who drain the product of our manufacturers, and speculate in corn and flour, meat and groceries, in our great centres of commerce. Then, as soon as exchange is arrested, the great cities are left without bread, and others find no buyers for their articles of luxury, a terrible counter-revolution will take place—a counter-revolution treading upon the slain, sweeping the towns and villages with shot and shell; there would be proscriptions, panic, flight, tend all the terrors of the guillotine, as it was in France in 1815, 1848, and 1871.

All is interdependent in a civilized society; it is impossible to reform any one thing without altering the whole. Therefore, on the day we strike at private property, under any one of its forms, territorial or industrial, we shall be obliged to attack them all. The very success of the Revolution will demand it.

Besides, we could not, if we would, confine ourselves to a partial expropriation. Once the principle of the "Divine Right of Property" is shaken, no amount of theorizing will prevent its overthrow, here by the slaves of the toil, there by the slaves of the machine.

If a great town, Paris for example, were to confine itself to taking possession of the dwelling houses or the factories, it would be forced also to deny the right of the bankers to levy upon the Commune a tax amounting to £2,000,000 in the form of interest for former loans. The great city would be obliged to put itself in touch with the rural districts, and its influence would inevitably urge the peasants to free themselves from the landowner. It would be necessary to communalize the railways, that the citizens might get food and work, and lastly, to prevent the waste of supplies, and to guard against the trust of corn-speculators, like those to whom the Commune of 1793 fell a prey, it would have to place in the hands of the City the work of stocking its warehouses with commodities, and apportioning the produce.

Nevertheless, some Socialists still seek to establish a distinction. "Of course," they say, "the soil, the mines, the mills, and manufactures must be expropriated, these are the instruments of production, and it is right we should consider them public property. But articles of consumption—food, clothes, and dwellings—should remain private property."

Popular common sense has got the better of this subtle distinction. We are not savages who can live in the woods, without other shelter than the branches. The civilized man needs a roof, a room, a hearth, and a bed. It is true that the bed, the room, and the house is a home of idleness for the non-producer. But for the worker, a room, properly heated and lighted, is as much an instrument of production as the tool or the machine. It is the place where the nerves and sinews gather strength for the work of the morrow. The rest of the workman is the daily repairing of the machine.

The same argument applies even more obviously to food. The so-called economists of whom we speak would hardly deny that the coal burnt in a machine is as necessary to production as the raw material itself. How then can food, without which the human machine could do no work, be excluded from the list of things indispensable to the producer? Can this be a relic of religious metaphysics? The rich man's feast is indeed a matter of luxury, but the food of the worker is just as much a part of production as the fuel burnt by the steam-engine.

The same with clothing. If the economists who draw this distinction between articles of production and of consumption dressed themselves in the fashion of New Guinea, we could understand their objection. But men who could not write a word without a shirt on their back are not in a position to draw such a hard and fast line between their shirt and their pen. And though the dainty gowns of their dames must certainly rank as objects of luxury, there is nevertheless a certain quantity of linen, cotton, and woollen stuff which is a necessity of life to the producer. The shirt and shoes in which he goes to his work, his cap and the jacket he slips on after the day's toil is over, these are as necessary to him as the hammer to the anvil.

Whether we like it or not, this is what the people mean by a revolution. As soon as they have made a clean sweep of the Government, they will seek first of all to ensure to themselves decent dwellings and sufficient food and clothes—free of capitalist rent.

And the people will be right. The methods of the people will be much more in accordance with science than those of the economists who draw so many distinctions between instruments of production and articles of consumption. The people understand that this is just the point where the Revolution ought to begin; and they will lay the foundations of the only economic science worthy the name—a science which might be called *"The Study of the Needs of Humanity, and of the Economic Means to satisfy them."*

Chapter 13

LEO TOLSTOY
from
The Slavery of Our Times (1900)

Tolstoy is universally regarded as one of the great novelists of all time, with both War and Peace *and* Anna Karenina *still held up as masterpieces of fiction. Few are aware that he was also an explicit committed anarchist. In his non-fiction Tolstoy set out to explain how a stateless society is superior, as well as possible mechanisms to transition to such a preferable form of human organization.*

WHAT ARE GOVERNMENTS?

IS IT POSSIBLE TO EXIST WITHOUT GOVERNMENTS?

The cause of the miserable condition of the workers is slavery. The cause of slavery is legislation. Legislation rests on organized violence.

It follows that an improvement in the condition of the people is possible only through the abolition of organized violence.

"But organized violence is government, and how can we live without governments? Without governments there will be chaos, anarchy; all the achievements of civilization will perish, and people will revert to their primitive barbarism."

It is usual,—not only for those to whom the existing order is profitable, but even for those to whom it is evidently unprofitable, but who are so accustomed to it they cannot imagine life without governmental violence,—to say we must not dare to touch the existing order of things. The destruction of government will, say they, produce the greatest misfortunes—riot, theft, and murder—till finally the worst men will again seize power and enslave all the good people. But not to mention the fact that all this—i.e. riots, thefts and murders, followed by the rule of the wicked and the enslavement of the good—all this is what has happened and is happening, the anticipation that the disturbance of the existing order will produce riots and disorder does not prove the present order to be good.

"Only touch the present order and the greatest evils will follow."

Only touch one brick of the thousand bricks piled into a narrow column several yards high and all the bricks will tumble down and smash! But the fact that any brick extracted or any push administered will destroy such a column and smash the bricks certainly does not prove it to be wise to keep the bricks in such an unnatural and inconvenient position. On the contrary, it shows that bricks should not be piled in such a column, but that they should be rearranged so that they may lie firmly, and so that they can be made use of without destroying the whole erection. It is the same with the present state organizations. The state organization is extremely artificial and unstable, and the fact that the least push may destroy it not only does not prove that it is necessary, but, on the contrary, shows that, if once upon a time it was necessary it is now absolutely unnecessary, and is, therefore, harmful and dangerous.

It is harmful and dangerous because the effect of this organization on all the evil that exists in society is not to lessen and correct, but rather to strengthen and confirm that evil. It is strengthened and confirmed by being either justified and put in attractive forms or secreted.

All that well being of the people which we see in so-called well-governed states, ruled by violence, is but an appearance—a fiction. Everything that would disturb the external appearance of well-being—all the hungry people, the sick, the revoltingly vicious—are all hidden away where they cannot be seen. But the fact that we do not see them does not show that they do not exist; on the contrary, the more they are hidden the more there will be of them, and the more cruel towards them will those be who are the cause of their condition. It is true that every interruption, and yet more, every stoppage of governmental action, i.e. of organized violence, disturb this external appearance of well-being in our life, but such disturbance does not produce disorder, but merely displays what was hidden, and makes possible its amendment.

Until now, say till almost the end of the nineteenth century, people thought and believed that they could not live without Governments. But life flows onward, and the conditions of life and people's views change. And notwithstanding the efforts of Governments to keep people in that childish condition in which an injured man feels as if it were better for him to have some one to complain to, people— especially the labouring people, both in Europe and in Russia—are more and more emerging from childhood and beginning to understand the true conditions of their life.

"You tell us but that for you we shall be conquered by neighboring nations: by the Chinese or the Japanese," men of the people now say, "but we read the papers, and know that no one is threatening to attack us, and that it is only you who govern us who, for some aims, unintelligible to us, exasperate each other, and then, under pretence of defending your own people, ruin us with taxes for the maintenance of the fleet, for armaments, or for strategical railways, which are only required to gratify your ambition and vanity; and then you arrange wars with one another, as you have now done against the peaceful Chinese. You say that you defend landed property for our advantage; but your defense has this effect: that all the land either has passed or is passing into the control of rich banking companies, which do not work, while we, the immense majority of the people, are being deprived of land and left in the power of those who do not labour. You with your laws of landed property do not defend landed property, but take it from those who work it. You say you secure to each man the produce of his labour, but you do just the reverse; all those who produce articles of value are, thanks to your pseudo-protection, placed in such a position that they not only never receive the value of their labour, but are all their lives long in complete subjection to and in the power of non-workers."

Thus do people, at the end of the century, begin to understand and to speak. And this awakening from the lethargy in which governments have kept them is going on in some rapidly increasing ratio. Within the last five or six years the public opinion of the common folk, not only in the towns, but in the villages, and not only in Europe, but also among us in Russia, has altered amazingly.

It is said that without governments we should not have those institutions, enlightening, educational and public, that are needful for all.

But why should we suppose this? Why think that non-official people could not arrange their life themselves as well as government people arrange it, not for themselves, but for others?

We see, on the contrary, that in the most diverse matters people in our times arrange their own lives incomparably better than those who govern them arrange for them. Without the least help from government, and often in spite of the interference of government, people organize all sorts of social undertakings—workmen's unions, co-operative societies, railway companies, *artels*, and syndicates. If collections for public works are needed, why should we suppose that free people could not without violence voluntarily collect the necessary means, and carry out all that is carried out by means of taxes, if only the undertakings in question are really useful for everybody? Why suppose that there cannot be tribunals without violence? Trial by people trusted by the disputants has always existed and will exist, and needs no violence. We are so depraved by long-continued slavery that we can hardly imagine administration without violence. And yet, again, that is not true: Russian communes migrating to distant regions, where our government leaves them alone, arrange their own taxation, administration, tribunals, and police, and always prosper until government violence interferes with their administration. And in the same way, there is no reason to suppose that people could not, by common consent, decide how the land is to be apportioned for use.

I have known people—Cossacks of the Oural—who have lived without acknowledging private property in land. And there was such well-being and order in their commune as does not exist in society, where landed property is defended by violence. And I now know communes that live without acknowledging the right of individuals to private property. Within my recollection the whole Russian peasantry did not accept the idea of landed property. The defense of landed property by governmental violence not merely does not abolish the struggle for landed property, but, on the contrary, strengthens that struggle, and in many cases causes it.

Were it not for the defense of landed property, and its consequent rise in price, people would not be crowded into such narrow spaces, but would scatter over the free land, of which there is still so much in the world. But as it is, a continual struggle goes on for landed property; a struggle with the weapons government furnishes by means of its laws of landed property. And in this struggle it is not those who work on the land, but always those who take part in governmental violence, that have the advantage.

It is the same with reference to things produced by labour. Things really produced by a man's own labour, and that he needs, are always defended by custom, by public opinion, by feelings of justice and reciprocity, and they do not need to be protected by violence.

Tens of thousands of acres of forest lands belonging to one proprietor—while thousands of people close by have no fuel—need protection by violence. So, too, do factories and works where several generations of workmen have been defrauded, are still being defrauded. Yet more do hundreds of thousands of bushels of grain, belonging to one owner, who has held them back till a famine has come, to sell them at triple price. But no man, however depraved— except a rich man or a Government official—would take from a countryman living by his own labour the harvest he has raised or the cow he has bred, and from which he gets milk for his children, or the *sokhas*, the scythes, and the spades he has made and uses. If even a man were found who did take from another articles the latter had made and required, such a man would rouse against himself such indignation from every one living in similar circumstances that he would hardly find his action profitable for himself. A man so immoral as to do it under such circumstances would be sure to do it under the strictest system of property defense by violence. It is generally said, "Only attempt to abolish the rights of property in land and in the produce of labour, and no one will take the trouble to work, lacking the assurance that he will not be deprived of what he has produced." We should say just the opposite: the defense by violence of the rights of property immorally obtained, which is now customary, if it has not quite destroyed, has considerably weakened people's natural consciousness of justice in the matter of using articles, i.e. the natural and innate right of property, without which humanity could not exist, and which has always existed and still exists among all men.

And, therefore, there is no reason to anticipate that people will not be able to arrange their lives without organized violence.

Of course, it may be said that horses and bulls must be guided by the violence of rational beings—men; but why must men be guided, not by some higher beings, but by people such as themselves? Why ought people to be subject to the violence of just those people who are in power at a given time? What proves that these people are wiser than those on whom they inflict violence?

The fact that they allow themselves to use violence toward human beings indicates that they are not only not more wise, but are less wise than those who submit to them. The examinations in China for the office of Mandarin do not, we know, ensure that the wisest and best people should be placed in power. And just as little is this ensured by inheritance, or the whole machinery of promotions in rank, or the elections in constitutional countries. On the contrary, power is always seized by those who are less conscientious and less moral.

It is said, "How can people live without governments, i.e. without violence?" But it should, on the contrary, be asked, "How can people who are rational live, acknowledging that the vital bond of their social life is violence, and not reasonable agreement?"

One of two things: either people are rational beings or they are irrational beings. If they are irrational beings, then they are all irrational, and then everything among them is decided by violence; and there is no reason why certain people should and others should not have a right to use violence. And in that case governmental violence has no justification. But if men are rational beings, then their relations should be based on reason, and not on the violence of those who happen to have seized power. And in that case, again, governmental violence has no justification.

HOW CAN GOVERNMENTS BE ABOLISHED?

Slavery results from laws, laws are made by governments, and, therefore, people can only be freed from slavery by the abolition of Governments.

But how can Governments be abolished?

All attempts to get rid of Governments by violence have hitherto, always and everywhere, resulted only in this: that in place of the deposed Governments new ones established themselves, often more cruel than those they replaced.

Not to mention past attempts to abolish Governments by violence, according to the Socialist theory, the coming abolition of the rule of the capitalists, i.e. the communalisation of the means of production and the new economic order of society, is also to be carried out by a fresh organization of violence, and will have to be maintained by the same means. So that attempts to abolish violence by violence neither have in the past nor, evidently, can in the future emancipate people from violence nor, consequently, from slavery.

It cannot be otherwise.

Apart from outbursts of revenge or anger, violence is used only in order to compel some people, against their own will, to do the will of others. But the necessity to do what other people wish against your own will is slavery. And, therefore, as long as any violence, designed to compel some people to do the will of others, exists there will be slavery.

All the attempts to abolish slavery by violence are like extinguishing fire with fire, stopping water with water, or filling up one hole by digging another.

Therefore, the means of escape from slavery, if such means exist, must be found, not in setting up fresh violence, but in abolishing whatever renders governmental violence possible. And the possibility of governmental violence, like every other violence perpetrated by a small number of people upon a larger number, has always depended, and still depends, simply on the fact that the small number are armed while the large number are unarmed, or that the small number are better armed than the large number.

That has been the case in all the conquests: it was thus the Greeks, the Romans, the Knights, and Pizarros conquered nations, and it is thus that people are now conquered in Africa and Asia. And in this same way in times of peace all governments hold their subjects in subjection.

As of old, so now, people rule over other people only because some are armed and others are not.

In olden times the warriors, with their chiefs, fell upon the defenseless inhabitants, subdued them and robbed them, and all divided the spoils in proportion to their participation, courage and cruelty; and each warrior saw clearly that the violence he perpetrated was profitable to him. Now, armed men (taken chiefly from the working classes) attack defenseless people: men on strikes, rioters, or the inhabitants of other countries, and subdue them and rob them (i.e. make them yield the fruits of their labour), not for themselves, but for people who do not even take a share in the subjugation.

The difference between the conquerors and the governments is only that the conquerors have themselves, with their soldiers, attacked the unarmed inhabitants and have, in cases of insubordination, carried their threats to torture and to kill into execution; while the governments, in cases of insubordination, do not themselves torture or execute the unarmed inhabitants, but oblige others to do it who have been deceived and specially brutalized for the purpose, and who are chosen from among the very people on whom the Government inflicts violence. Thus, violence was formerly inflicted by personal effort, by the courage, cruelty and agility of the conquerors themselves; but now violence is inflicted by means of fraud.

So that if formerly, in order to get rid of armed violence, it was necessary to arm oneself and to oppose armed violence by armed violence, now when people are subdued, not by direct violence, but by fraud, in order to abolish violence it is only necessary to expose the deception which enables a small number of people to exercise violence upon a larger number.

The deception by means of which this is done consists in the fact that the small number who rule, on obtaining power from their predecessors, who were installed by conquest, say to the majority: "There are a lot of you, but you are stupid and uneducated, and cannot either govern yourselves or organize your public affairs, and, therefore, we will take those cares on ourselves; we will protect you from foreign foes, and arrange and maintain internal peace among you; we will set up courts of justice, arrange for you and take care of public institutions: schools, roads, and the postal service and in general we will take care of your well-being; and in return for all this you only have to fulfil those slight demands which we make, and, among other things, you must give into our complete control a small part of your incomes, and you must yourselves enter the armies which are needed for your own safety and government."

And most people agree to this, not because they have weighed the advantages and disadvantages of these conditions (they never have a chance to do that), but because from their very birth they have found themselves in conditions such as these.

If doubts suggest themselves to some people as to whether all this is necessary, each one thinks only about himself, and fears to suffer if he refuses to accept these conditions; each one hopes to take advantage of them for his own profit, and every one agrees, thinking that by paying a small part of his means to the Government, and by consenting to military service, he cannot do himself very much harm.

But as soon as the Governments have the money and the soldiers, instead of fulfilling their promises to defend their subjects from foreign enemies, and to arrange things for their benefit, they do all they can to provoke the neighbouring nations and to produce war; and they not only do not promote the internal well-being of their people, but they ruin and corrupt them.

In the Arabian nights there is a story of a traveller who, being cast upon an uninhabited island, found a little old man with withered legs sitting on the ground by the side of a stream. The old man asked the traveller to take him on his shoulders and to carry him over the stream. The traveler consented; but no sooner was the old man settled on the traveler's shoulders than the former twined his legs round the latter's neck and would not get off again. Having control of the traveler, the old man drove him about as he liked, plucked fruit from the trees and ate it himself, not giving any to his bearer, and abused him in every way.

This is just what happens with the people who give soldiers and money to the Governments. With the money the Governments buy guns, and hire, or train by education, subservient, brutalized military commanders. And these commanders, by means of an artful system of stupefaction, perfected in the course of ages and called discipline, make those who have been taken as soldiers into a disciplined army. Discipline consists in this, that people who are subjected to this training, and remain under it for some time, are completely deprived of all that is valuable in human life, and of man's chief attribute— rational freedom—and become submissive machine-like instruments of murder in the hands of their organised, hierarchical stratocracy. And it is in this disciplined army that the essence of the fraud dwells, which gives to modern Governments dominion over the peoples. When the governments have in their power this instrument of violence and murder, that possesses no will of its own, the whole people are in their hands, and they do not let them go again, and not only prey upon them, but also abuse them, instilling into the people, by means of a pseudo-religious and patriotic education, loyalty to and even adoration of, themselves, i.e. of the very men who torment the whole people by keeping them in slavery.

It is not for nothing that all the kings, emperors, and presidents esteem discipline so highly, are so afraid of any breach of discipline, and attach the highest importance to reviews, maneuvers, parades, ceremonial marches and other such nonsense. They know that it all maintains discipline, and that not only their power, but their very existence depends on discipline.

Discipline armies are the means by which they, without using their own hands, accomplish the greatest atrocities, the possibility of perpetrating which give them power over the people.

And, therefore, the only means to destroy Governments is not force, but it is the exposure of this fraud. It is necessary people should understand: First, that in Christendom there is no need to protect the peoples one from another; that all the enmity of the peoples, one to another, are produced by the Governments themselves, and that armies are only needed by the small number of those who rule for the people it is not only unnecessary, but it is in the highest degree harmful, serving as the instrument to enslave them. Secondly, it is necessary that people should understand that the discipline which is so highly esteemed by all the governments is the greatest of crimes that man can commit, and is a clear indication of the criminality of the aims of governments. Discipline is the suppression of reason and of freedom in man, and can have no other aim than preparation for the performance of crimes such as no man can commit while in a normal condition. It is not even needed for war, when the war is defensive and national, as the Boers have recently shown. It is wanted and wanted only for the purpose indicated by William II.: for the committal of the greatest crimes, fratricide and parricide.

The terrible old man who sat on the traveler's shoulders behaved as the Governments do. He mocked him and insulted him, knowing that as long as he sat on the traveler's neck the latter was in his power.

And it is just this fraud, by means of which a small number of unworthy people, called the Government, have power over the people, and not only impoverish them, but do what is the most harmful of all actions—pervert whole generations from childhood upwards; just this terrible fraud which should be exposed, in order that the abolition of Government and of the slavery that results from it may become possible.

The German writer, Eugene Schmitt, in the newspaper *Ohne Staat*, that he published in Budapest, wrote an article that was profoundly true and bold, not only in expression, but in thought. In it he showed that Governments, justifying their existence on the ground that they ensure a certain kind of safety to their subjects, are like the Calabrian robber-chief who collected a regular tax from all who wished to travel in safety along the highways. Schmitt was committed for trial for that article, but was acquitted by the jury.

We are so hypnotized by the governments that such a comparison seems to us an exaggeration, a paradox, or a joke; but in reality it is not a paradox or a joke; the only inaccuracy in the comparison is that the activity of all the Governments is many times more inhuman and, above all, more harmful than the activity of the Calabrian robber. The robber generally plundered the rich; the Governments generally plunder the poor and protect those rich who assist in their crimes. The robber doing his work risked his life, while the Governments risk nothing, but base their whole activity on lies and deception. The robber did not compel any one to join his band, the Governments generally enroll their soldiers by force. All who paid the tax to the robber had equal security from danger. But in the state, the more any one takes part in the organized fraud the more he receives not merely of protection, but also of reward. Most of all, the emperors, kings and presidents are protected (with their perpetual body-guards), and they can spend the largest share of the money collected from the taxpaying subjects. Next in the scale of participation in the governmental crimes come the commanders-in-chief, the ministers, the heads of police, governors, and so on, down to the policemen, who are least protected, and who receive the smallest salaries of all. Those who do not take any part in the crimes of government, who refuse to serve, to pay taxes, or to go to law, are subjected to violence; as among the robbers. The robber does not intentionally vitiate people; but the governments, to accomplish their ends, vitiate whole generations from childhood to manhood with false religions and patriotic instruction. Above all, not even the most cruel robber, no Stenka Razin or Cartouche can be compared for cruelty, pitilessness and ingenuity in torturing, I will not say with the villain kings notorious for their cruelty,—John the Terrible, Louis XI., the Elizabeths, etc.,—but even with the present constitutional and Liberal Governments, with their solitary cells, disciplinary battalions, suppressions of revolts, and their massacres in war.

Towards Governments, as towards Churches, it is impossible to feel otherwise than with veneration or aversion.

Until a man has understood what a Government is and until he has understood what a Church is he cannot but feel veneration towards those institutions. As long as he is guided by them his vanity makes it necessary for him to think that what guides him is something primal, great and holy; but as soon as he understands that what guides him is not something primal and holy, but that it is a fraud carried out by unworthy people, who, under the pretence of guiding him, make use of him for their own personal ends, he cannot but at once feel aversion towards these people, and the more important the side of his life that has been guided the more aversion will he feel.

People cannot but feel this when they have understood what Governments are.

People must feel that their participation in the criminal activity of Governments, whether by giving part of their work in the form of money, or by direct participation in military service, is not, as is generally supposed, an indifferent action, but, besides being harmful to one's self and to one's brothers, is a participation in the crimes unceasingly committed by all Governments and a preparation for new crimes, which Governments are always preparing by maintaining disciplined armies.

The age of veneration for governments, notwithstanding all the hypnotic influence they employ to maintain their position, is more and more passing away. And it is time for people to understand that Governments not only are not necessary, but are harmful and most highly immoral institutions, in which a self-respecting, honest man cannot and must not take part, and the advantages of which he cannot and should not enjoy.

And as soon as people clearly understand that, they will naturally cease to take part in such deeds, i.e. cease to give the Governments soldiers and money. And as soon as a majority of people ceases to do this the fraud which enslaves people will be abolished.

Only in this way can people be freed from slavery.

WHAT SHOULD EACH MAN DO?

"But all these are general considerations, and whether they are correct or not, they are inapplicable to life," will be the remark made by people accustomed to their position, and who do not consider it possible, or who do not wish, to change it.

"Tell us what to do, and how to organize society," is what people of the well-to-do classes usually say.

People of the well-to-do classes are so accustomed to their role of slave owners that when there is talk of improving the workers' condition, they at once begin, like our serf owners before the emancipation, to devise all sorts of plans for their slaves; but it never occurs to them that they have no right to dispose of other people, and that if they really wish to do good to people, the one thing they can and should do is to cease to do the evil they are now doing. And the evil they do is very definite and clear. It is not merely that they employ compulsory slave labour, and do not wish to cease from employing it, but that they also take part in establishing and maintaining this compulsion of labour. That is what they should cease to do.

The working people are also so perverted by their compulsory slavery that it seems to most of them that if their position is a bad one, it is the fault of the masters, who pay them too little and who own the means of production. It does not enter their heads that their bad position depends entirely on themselves, and that if only they wish to improve their own and their brothers' positions, and not merely each to do the best he can for himself, the great thing for them to do is themselves to cease to do evil. And the evil that they do is that, desiring to improve their material position by the same means which have brought them into bondage,—the workers (for the sake of satisfying the habits they have adopted), sacrificing their human dignity and freedom, accept humiliating and immoral employment or produce unnecessary and harmful articles, and, above all, they maintain Governments,—taking part in them by paying taxes and by direct service—and thus they enslave themselves.

In order that the state of things may be improved, both the well-to-do classes and the workers must understand that improvement cannot be effected by safeguarding one's own interests. Service involves sacrifice, and, therefore, if people really wish to improve the position of their brother men, and not merely their own, they must be ready not only to alter the way of life to which they are accustomed, and to lose those advantages which they have held, but they must be ready for an intense struggle, not against governments, but against themselves and their families, and must be ready to suffer persecution for non-fulfillment of the demands of Government.

And, therefore, the reply to the question—What is it we must do?—is very simple, and not merely definite, but always in the highest degree applicable and practicable for each man, though it is not what is expected by those who, like people of the well-to-do classes, are fully convinced that they are appointed to correct not themselves (they are already good), but to teach and correct other people; and by those who, like the workmen, are sure that not they (but only the capitalists) are in fault for their present bad position, and think that things can only be put right by taking from the capitalists the things they use, and arranging so that all might make use of those conveniences of life which are now only used by the rich. The answer is very definite, applicable, and practicable, for it demands the activity of that one person over whom each of us has real, rightful, and unquestionable power, namely, oneself; and it consists in this, that if a man—whether slave or slave owner—really wishes to better not *his* position alone, but the position of people in general, he must not himself do those wrong things which enslave him and his brothers. And in order not to do the evil which produces misery for himself and for his brothers, *he should, first of all, neither willingly nor under compulsion take any part in Governmental activity, and should, therefore, be neither a soldier, nor a Field-Marshal, nor a Minister-of-State, nor a tax- collector, nor a witness, nor an alderman, nor a juryman, nor a governor, nor a Member of Parliament, nor, in fact, hold any office connected with violence.* That is one thing.

Secondly, *such a man should not voluntarily pay taxes to governments, either directly or indirectly; nor should he accept money collected by taxes, either as salary, or as pension, or as a reward; nor should he make use of governmental institutions, supported by taxes collected by violence from the people.* That is the second thing.

Thirdly, *a man who desires not to promote his own well-being alone, but to better the position of people in general, should not appeal to Governmental violence for the protection of his own possessions in land or in other things, nor to defend him and his near ones; but should only possess land and all products of his own or other people's toil, in so far as others do not claim them from him.*

"But such an activity is impossible; to refuse all participation in Governmental affairs means to refuse to live"—is what people will say. "A man who refuses military service will be imprisoned; a man who does not pay taxes will be punished and the tax will be collected from his property; a man who, having no other means of livelihood, refuses Government service, will perish of hunger with his family; the same will befall a man who rejects Governmental protection for his property and his person; not to make use of things that are taxed or of Government institutions, is quite impossible, as the most necessary articles are often taxed; and just in the same way it is impossible to do without Government institutions, such as the post, the roads, etc."

It is quite true that it is difficult for a man of our times to stand aside from all participation in Governmental violence. But the fact that not every one can so arrange his life as not to participate in some degree in Governmental violence does not at all show that it is not possible to free one's self from it more and more. Not every man will have the strength to refuse conscription (though there are and will be such men), but each man can abstain from voluntarily entering the army, the police force, and the judicial or revenue service; and can give the preference to a worse paid private service rather than to a better paid public service. Not every man will have the strength to renounce his landed estates (though there are people who do that), but every man can, understanding the wrongfulness of such property, diminish its extent. Not every man can renounce the possession of capital (there are some who do) or the use of articles defended by violence, but each man can, by diminishing his own requirements, be less and less in need of articles which provoke other people to envy. Not every official can renounce his Government salary (though there are men who prefer hunger to dishonest Governmental employment), but every one can prefer a smaller salary to a larger one for the sake of having duties less bound up with violence; not every one can refuse to make use of Government schools (though there are some who do), but every one can give the preference to private schools, and each can make less and less use of articles that are taxed, and of Government institutions.

Between the existing order, based on brute force, and the ideal of a society based on reasonable agreement confirmed by custom, there are an infinite number of steps, which mankind are ascending, and the approach to the ideal is only accomplished to the extent to which people free themselves from participation in violence, from taking advantage of it, and from being accustomed to it.

We do not know and cannot see, still less, like the pseudo-scientific men, foretell, in what way this gradual weakening of governments and emancipation of people will come about; nor do we know what new forms man's life will take as the gradual emancipation progresses, but we certainly do know that the life of people who, having understood the criminality and harmfulness of the activity of Governments, strive not to make use of them, or to take part in them, will be quite different and more in accord with the law of life and our own consciences than the present life, in which people themselves participating in Governmental violence and taking advantage of it, make a pretence of struggling against it, and try to destroy the old violence by new violence.

The chief thing is that the present arrangement of life is bad; about that all are agreed. The cause of the bad conditions and of the existing slavery lies in the violence used by Governments. There is only one way to abolish Governmental violence: that people should abstain from participating in violence. And, therefore, whether it be difficult or not, to abstain from participating in Governmental violence, and whether the good results of such abstinence will or will not be soon apparent,—are superfluous questions; because to liberate people from slavery there is only that one way,—and no other!

To what extent and when voluntary agreement, confirmed by custom, will replace violence in each society and in the whole world will depend on the strength and clearness of people's consciousness and on the number of individuals who make this consciousness their own. Each of us is a separate person, and each can be a participator in the general movement of humanity by his greater or lesser clearness of recognition of the aim before us, or he can be an opponent of progress. Each will have to make his choice: to oppose the will of God, building upon the sands the unstable house of his brief, illusive life,—or to join in the eternal, deathless movement of true life in accordance with God's will.

But perhaps I am mistaken, and the right conclusions to draw from human history are these, and the human race is not moving toward emancipation from slavery; perhaps it can be proved that violence is a needful factor of progress, and that the state, with its violence, is a necessary form of life, and that it will be worse for people if Governments are abolished and if the defense of our persons and property is abolished.

Let us grant it to be so, and say that all the foregoing reasoning is wrong; but besides the general considerations about the life of humanity, each man has also to face the question of his own life; and notwithstanding any considerations about the general laws of life, a man cannot do what he admits to be not merely harmful, but wrong.

"Very possibly the reasoning showing the state to be a necessary form of the development of the individual, and Governmental violence to be necessary for the good of Society, can all be deduced from history, and are all correct," each honest and sincere man of our times will reply; "but murder is an evil, that I know more certainly than any reasonings; by demanding that I should enter the army or pay for hiring and equipping soldiers, or for buying cannons and building ironclads, you wish to make me an accomplice in murder, and that I cannot and will not be. Neither do I wish, nor can I, make use of money you have collected from hungry people with threats of murder; nor do I wish to make use of land or capital defended by you, because I know that your defense rests on murder.

"I could do these things when I did not understand all their criminality, but when I have once seen it, I cannot avoid seeing it, and can no longer take part in these things.

"I know that we are all so bound up by violence that it is difficult to avoid it altogether, but I will, nevertheless, do all I can not to take part in it; I will not be an accomplice to it, and will try not to make use of what is obtained and defended by murder.

"I have but one life, and why should I, in this brief life of mine, act contrary to the voice of conscience and become a partner in your abominable deeds?—I cannot, and I will not.

"And what will come of this? I do not know. Only I think no harm can result from acting as my conscience demands."

So in our time should each honest and sincere man reply to all the arguments about the necessity of governments and of violence, and to every demand or invitation to take part in them.

The conclusion to which general reasoning should bring us, is thus confirmed to each individual, by that supreme and unimpeachable judge—the voice of conscience.

Chapter 14

ALEXANDER BERKMAN
Prisons and Crime (1906)

Inspired by his mentor Johann Most, Alexander Berkman decided to take matters into his own hands and engage in an attentat—*assassination—of Andrew Carnegie's lieutenant Henry Clay Frick in 1892. Frick was overseeing the Homestead strike in Pennsylvania, and matters had already turned deadly. Berkman failed to kill Frick, and his actions were disavowed by Most (and most). He ended up serving over a decade in prison, eventually penning* Prison Memoirs of an Anarchist. *How to deal with criminals is one of the biggest questions people have of the anarchist perspective. Here Berkman gives one possible anarchist framework with which to study the issue.*

Modern philanthropy has added a new role to the repertoire of penal institutions. While, formerly, the alleged necessity of prisons rested, solely, upon their penal and protective character, to-day a new function, claiming primary importance, has become embodied in these institutions—that of reformation.

Hence, three objects—reformative, penal, and protective—are now sought to be accomplished by means of enforced physical restraint, by incarceration of a more or less solitary character, for a specific, or more or less indefinite period.

Seeking to promote its own safety, society debars certain elements, called criminals, from participation in social life, by means of imprisonment. This temporary isolation of the offender exhausts the protective role of prisons. Entirely negative in character, does this protection benefit society? Does it protect?

Let us study some of its results.

First, let us investigate the penal and reformative phases of the prison question.

Punishment, as a social institution, has its origin in two sources; first, in the assumption that man is a free moral agent and, consequently, responsible for his demeanor, so far as he is supposed to be *compos mentis*; and, second, in the spirit of revenge, the retaliation of injury. Waiving, for the present, the debatable question as to man's free agency, let us analyze the second source.

The spirit of revenge is a purely animal proclivity, primarily manifesting itself where comparative physical development is combined with a certain degree of intelligence. Primitive man is compelled, by the conditions of his environment, to take the law into his own hands, so to speak, in furtherance of his instinctive desire of self-assertion, or protection, in coping with the animal or human aggressor, who is wont to injure or jeopardize his person or his interests. This proclivity, born of the instinct of self-preservation and developed in the battle for existence and supremacy, has become, with uncivilized man, a second instinct, almost as potent in its vitality as the source it primarily developed from, and occasionally even transcending the same in its ferocity and conquering, for the moment, the dictates of self-preservation.

Even animals possess the spirit of revenge. The ingenious methods frequently adopted by elephants in captivity, in avenging themselves upon some particularly hectoring spectator, are well known. Dogs and various other animals also often manifest the spirit of revenge. But it is with man, at certain stages of his intellectual development, that the spirit of revenge reaches its most pronounced character. Among barbaric and semi-civilized races the practice of personally avenging one's wrongs—actual or imaginary—plays an all-important role in the life of the individual. With them, revenge is a most vital matter, often attaining the character of religious fanaticism, the holy duty of avenging a particularly flagrant injury descending from father to son, from generation to generation, until the insult is extirpated with the blood of the offender or of his progeny. Whole tribes have often combined in assisting one of their members to avenge the death of a relative upon a hostile neighbor, and it is always the special privilege of the wronged to give the death-blow to the offender.

Even in certain European countries the old spirit of blood-revenge is still very strong. The semi-barbarians of the Caucasus, the ignorant peasants of Southern Italy, of Corsica and Sicily, still practice this form of personal vengeance; some of them, as the Tsherkessy, for instance, quite openly; others, as the Corsicans, seeking safety in secrecy. Even in our so-called enlightened countries the spirit of personal revenge, of sworn, eternal enmity, still exists. What are the secret organizations of the Mafia type, so common in all South European lands, but the manifestations of this spirit?! And what is the underlying principle of duelling in its various forms—from the armed combat to the fistic encounter—but this spirit of direct vengeance, the desire to personally avenge an insult or an injury, fancied or real; to wipe out the same, even with the blood of the antagonist. It is this spirit that actuates the enraged husband in attempting the life of the "robber of his honor and happiness." It is this spirit that is at the bottom of all lynch-law atrocities, the frenzied mob seeking to avenge the bereaved parent, the young widow or the outraged child.

Social progress, however, tends to check and eliminate the practice of direct, personal revenge. In so-called civilized communities the individual does not, as a rule, personally avenge his wrongs. He has delegated his "rights" in that direction to the State, the government; and it is one of the "duties" of the latter to avenge the wrongs of its citizens by punishing the guilty parties. Thus we see that punishment, as a social institution, is but another form of revenge, with the State in the role of the sole legal avenger of the collective citizen—the same well-defined spirit of barbarism in disguise. The penal powers of the State rest, theoretically, on the principle that, in organized society, "an injury to one is the concern of all"; in the wronged citizen society as a whole is attacked. The culprit must be punished in order to avenge outraged society, that "the majesty of the Law be vindicated." The principle that the punishment must be adequate to the crime still further proves the real character of the institution of punishment: it reveals the Old-Testamental spirit of "an eye for an eye, a tooth for a tooth,"—a spirit still alive in almost all so-called civilized countries, as witness capital punishment: a life for a life. The "criminal" is not punished for his offence, as such, but rather according to the nature, circumstances and character of the same, as viewed by society; in other words, the penalty is of a nature calculated to balance the intensity of the local spirit of revenge, aroused by the particular offence.

This, then, is the nature of punishment. Yet, strange to say—or naturally, perhaps—the results attained by penal institutions are the very opposite of the ends sought. The modern form of "civilized" revenge kills, figuratively speaking, the enemy of the individual citizen, but breeds in his place the enemy of society. The prisoner of the State no longer regards the person he injured as his particular enemy, as the barbarian does, fearing the wrath and revenge of the wronged one. Instead, he looks upon the State as his direct punisher; in the representatives of the law he sees his personal enemies. He nurtures his wrath, and wild thoughts of revenge fill his mind. His hate toward the persons, directly responsible, in his estimation, for his misfortune—the arresting officer, the jailer, the prosecuting attorney, judge and jury—gradually widens in scope, and the poor unfortunate becomes an enemy of society as a whole. Thus, while the penal institutions on the one hand protect society from the prisoner so long as he remains one, they cultivate, on the other hand, the germs of social hatred and enmity.

Deprived of his liberty, his rights, and the enjoyment of life; all his natural impulses, good and bad alike, suppressed; subjected to indignities and disciplined by harsh and often inhumanely severe methods, and generally maltreated and abused by official brutes whom he despises and hates, the young prisoner, utterly miserable, comes to curse the fact of his birth, the woman that bore him, and all those responsible, in his eyes, for his misery. He is brutalized by the treatment he receives and by the revolting sights he is forced to witness in prison. What manhood he may have possessed is soon eradicated by the "discipline." His impotent rage and bitterness are turned into hatred toward everything and everybody, growing in intensity as the years of misery come and go. He broods over his troubles and the desire to revenge himself grows in intensity, his until then perhaps undefined inclinations are turned into strong anti-social desires, which gradually become a fixed determination. Society had made him an outcast; it is his natural enemy. Nobody had shown him either kindness or mercy; he will be merciless to the world.

Then he is released. His former friends spurn him; he is no more recognized by his acquaintances; society points its finger at the ex-convict; he is looked upon with scorn, derision, and disgust; he is distrusted and abused. He has no money, and there is no charity for the "moral leper." He finds himself a social Ishmael, with everybody's hand turned against him—and he turns his hand against everybody else.

The penal and protective functions of prisons thus defeat their own ends. Their work is not merely unprofitable, it is worse than useless; it is positively and absolutely detrimental to the best interests of society.

It is no better with the reformative phase of penal institutions. The penal character of all prisons—workhouses, penitentiaries, state prisons—excludes all possibility of a reformative nature. The promiscuous mingling of prisoners in the same institution, without regard to the relative criminality of the inmates, converts prisons into veritable schools of crime and immorality.

The same is true of reformatories. These institutions, specifically designed to reform, do as a rule produce the vilest degeneration. The reason is obvious. Reformatories, the same as ordinary prisons, use physical restraint and are purely penal institutions—the very idea of punishment precludes true reformation. Reformation that does not emanate from the voluntary impulse of the inmate, one which is the result of fear—the fear of consequences and of probable punishment—is no real reformation; it lacks the very essentials of the latter, and so soon as the fear has been conquered, or temporarily emancipated from, the influence of the pseudo-reformation will vanish like smoke. Kindness alone is truly reformative, but this quality is an unknown quantity in the treatment of prisoners, both young and old.

Some time ago I read the account of a boy, thirteen years old, who had been confined in chains, night and day for three consecutive weeks, his particular offence being the terrible crime of an attempted escape from the Westchester, N. Y., Home for Indigent Children (Weeks case, Superintendent Pierce, Christmas, 1895). That was by no means an exceptional instance in that institution. Nor is the penal character of the latter exceptional. There is not a single prison or reformatory in the United States where either flogging and clubbing, or the straight-jacket, solitary confinement, and "reduced" diet (semi-starvation) are not practiced upon the unfortunate inmates. And though reformatories do not, as a rule, use the "means of persuasion" of the notorious Brockway, of Elmira, N. Y., yet flogging is practiced in some, and starvation and the dungeon are a permanent institution in all of them.

Aside from the penal character of reformatories and the derogatory influence the deprivation of liberty and enjoyment exercise on the youthful mind, the associations in those institutions preclude, in the majority of cases, all reformation. Even in the reformatories no attempt is made to classify the inmates according to the comparative gravity of their offenses, necessitating different modes of treatment and suitable companionship. In the so-called reform schools and reformatories children of all ages—from 5 to 25—are kept in the same institution, congregated for the several purposes of labor, learning and religious service, and allowed to mingle on the playing grounds and associate in the dormitories. The inmates are often classified according to age or stature, but no attention is paid to their relative depravity. The absurdity of such methods is simply astounding. Pause and consider. The youthful culprit who is such probably chiefly in consequence of bad associations, is put among the choicest assortment of viciousness and is expected to reform! And the fathers and mothers of the nation calmly look on, and either directly further this species of insanity or by their silence approve and encourage the State's work of breeding criminals. But such is human nature—we swear it is day-time, though it be pitch-dark; the old spirit of *credo quia absurdum est.*

It is unnecessary, however, to enlarge further upon the debasing influence those steeped in crime exert over their more innocent companions. Nor is it necessary to discuss further the reformative claims of reformatories. The fact that fully 60 per cent of the male prison population of the United States are graduates of "Reformatories" conclusively proves the reformative pretentions of the latter absolutely groundless. The rare cases of youthful prisoners having really reformed are in no sense due to the "beneficial" influence of imprisonment and of penal restraint, but rather to the innate powers of the individual himself.

Doubtless there exists no other institution among the diversified "achievements" of modern society, which, while assuming a most important role in the destinies of mankind, has proven a more reprehensible failure in point of attainment than the penal institutions. Millions of dollars are annually expended throughout the "civilized" world for the maintenance of these institutions, and notwithstanding each successive year witnesses additional appropriations for their improvement, yet the results tend to retrograde rather than advance the purports of their founding.

The money annually expended for the maintenance of prisons could be invested, with as much profit and less injury, in government bonds of the planet Mars, or sunk in the Atlantic. No amount of punishment can obviate crime, so long as prevailing conditions, in and out of prison, drive men to it.

Chapter 15

VOLTAIRINE DE CLEYRE
Anarchism & American Traditions (1909)

More popular with the unwashed masses than with true-blue Americans, in the 19th and early 20th century the anarchist idea was often caricatured as an invasive foreign ideology. Voltairine de Cleyre took pains to explain that anarchism and a hatred of the state is in fact far more American and had far more of a tradition on American soil than most ideas that were being bandied about in her time. In 1765—over a decade before the Declaration of Independence—Patrick Henry ("Give me liberty or give me death!") stood up in the Virginia House of Burgesses and basically said that King George was asking to be shot, and concluded with, "If this be treason, make the most of it!" Here de Cleyre makes the case that anarchism is more American than that foreign dessert, apple pie.

American traditions, begotten of religious rebellion, small self-sustaining communities, isolated conditions, and hard pioneer life, grew during the colonization period of one hundred and seventy years from the settling of Jamestown to the outburst of the Revolution. This was in fact the great constitution-making epoch, the period of charters guaranteeing more or less of liberty, the general tendency of which is well described by Wm. Penn in speaking of the charter for Pennsylvania: "I want to put it out of my power, or that of my successors, to do mischief."

The revolution is the sudden and unified consciousness of these traditions, their loud assertion, the blow dealt by their indomitable will against the counter force of tyranny, which has never entirely recovered from the blow, but which from then till now has gone on remolding and regrappling the instruments of governmental power, that the Revolution sought to shape and hold as defenses of liberty.

To the average American of today, the Revolution means the series of battles fought by the patriot army with the armies of England. The millions of school children who attend our public schools are taught to draw maps of the siege of Boston and the siege of Yorktown, to know the general plan of the several campaigns, to quote the number of prisoners of war surrendered with Burgoyne; they are required to remember the date when Washington crossed the Delaware on the ice; they are told to "Remember Paoli," to repeat "Molly Stark's a widow," to call General Wayne "Mad Anthony Wayne," and to execrate Benedict Arnold; they know that the Declaration of Independence was signed on the Fourth of July, 1776, and the Treaty of Paris in 1783; and then they think they have learned the Revolution—blessed be George Washington! They have no idea why it should have been called a "revolution" instead of the "English War," or any similar title: it's the name of it, that's all. And name-worship, both in child and man, has acquired such mastery of them, that the name "American Revolution" is held sacred, though it means to them nothing more than successful force, while the name "Revolution" applied to a further possibility, is a spectre detested and abhorred. In neither case have they any idea of the content of the word, save that of armed force. That has already happened, and long happened, which Jefferson foresaw when he wrote:

> "The spirit of the times may alter, will alter. Our rulers
> will become corrupt, our people careless. A single zealot
> may become persecutor, and better men be his victims. It
> can never be too often repeated that the time for fixing
> every essential right, on a legal basis, is while our rulers
> are honest, ourselves united. From the conclusion of this
> war we shall be going down hill. It will not then be
> necessary to resort every moment to the people for
> support. They will be forgotten, therefore, and their

206

rights disregarded. They will forget themselves in the sole faculty of making money, and will never think of uniting to effect a due respect for their rights. The shackles, therefore, which shall not be knocked off at the conclusion of this war, will be heavier and heavier, till our rights shall revive or expire in a convulsion."

To the men of that time, who voiced the spirit of that time, the battles that they fought were the least of the Revolution; they were the incidents of the hour, the things they met and faced as part of the game they were playing; but the stake they had in view, before, during, and after the war, the real Revolution, was a change in political institutions which should make of government not a thing apart, a superior power to stand over the people with a whip, but a serviceable agent, responsible, economical, and trustworthy (but never so much trusted as not to be continually watched), for the transaction of such business as was the common concern and to set the limits of the common concern at the line of where one man's liberty would encroach upon another's.

They thus took their starting point for deriving a minimum of government upon the same sociological ground that the modern Anarchist derives the no-government theory; viz., that equal liberty is the political ideal. The difference lies in the belief, on the one hand, that the closest approximation to equal liberty might be best secured by the rule of the majority in those matters involving united action of any kind (which rule of the majority they thought it possible to secure by a few simple arrangements for election), and, on the other hand, the belief that majority rule is both impossible and undesirable; that any government, no matter what its forms, will be manipulated by a very small minority, as the development of the States and United States governments has strikingly proved; that candidates will loudly profess allegiance to platforms before elections, which as officials in power they will openly disregard, to do as they please; and that even if the majority will could be imposed, it would also be subversive of equal liberty, which may be best secured by leaving to the voluntary association of those interested in the management of matters of common concern, without coercion of the uninterested or the opposed.

Among the fundamental likeness between the Revolutionary Republicans and the Anarchists is the recognition that the little must precede the great; that the local must be the basis of the general; that there can be a free federation only when there are free communities to federate; that the spirit of the latter is carried into the councils of the former, and a local tyranny may thus become an instrument for general enslavement. Convinced of the supreme importance of ridding the municipalities of the institutions of tyranny, the most strenuous advocates of independence, instead of spending their efforts mainly in the general Congress, devoted themselves to their home localities, endeavoring to work out of the minds of their neighbors and fellow-colonists the institutions of entailed property, of a State-Church, of a class-divided people, even the institution of African slavery itself. Though largely unsuccessful, it is to the measure of success they did achieve that we are indebted for such liberties as we do retain, and not to the general government. They tried to inculcate local initiative and independent action. The author of the Declaration of Independence, who in the fall of '76 declined a re-election to Congress in order to return to Virginia and do his work in his own local assembly, in arranging there for public education which he justly considered a matter of "common concern," said his advocacy of public schools was not with any "view to take its ordinary branches out of the hands of private enterprise, which manages so much better the concerns to which it is equal"; and in endeavoring to make clear the restrictions of the Constitution upon the functions of the general government, he likewise said:

> "Let the general government be reduced to foreign concerns only, and let our affairs be disentangled from those of all other nations, except as to commerce, which the merchants will manage for themselves, and the general government may be reduced to a very simple organization, and a very inexpensive one; a few plain duties to be performed by a few servants."

This then was the American tradition, that private enterprise manages better all that to which it IS equal. Anarchism declares that private enterprise, whether individual or cooperative, is equal to all the undertakings of society. And it quotes the particular two instances, Education and Commerce, which the governments of the States and of the United States have undertaken to manage and regulate, as the very two which in operation have done more to destroy American freedom and equality, to warp and distort American tradition, to make of government a mighty engine of tyranny, than any other cause, save the unforeseen developments of Manufacture.

It was the intention of the Revolutionists to establish a system of common education, which should make the teaching of history one of its principal branches; not with the intent of burdening the memories of our youth with the dates of battles or the speeches of generals, nor to make the Boston Tea Party Indians the one sacrosanct mob in all history, to be revered but never on any account to be imitated, but with the intent that every American should know to what conditions the masses of people had been brought by the operation of certain institutions, by what means they had wrung out their liberties, and how those liberties had again and again been filched from them by the use of governmental force, fraud, and privilege. Not to breed security, laudation, complacent indolence, passive acquiescence in the acts of a government protected by the label "home-made," but to beget a wakeful jealousy, a never-ending watchfulness of rulers, a determination to squelch every attempt of those entrusted with power to encroach upon the sphere of individual action—this was the prime motive of the revolutionists in endeavoring to provide for common education.

"Confidence," said the revolutionists who adopted the Kentucky Resolutions, "is everywhere the parent of despotism; free government is founded in jealousy, not in confidence; it is jealousy, not confidence, which prescribes limited constitutions to bind down those whom we are obliged to trust with power; our Constitution has accordingly fixed the limits to which, and no further, our confidence may go...In questions of power, let no more be heard of confidence in man, but bind him down from mischief by the chains of the Constitution."

These resolutions were especially applied to the passage of the Alien laws by the monarchist party during John Adams' administration, and were an indignant call from the State of Kentucky to repudiate the right of the general government to assume undelegated powers, for said they, to accept these laws would be "to be bound by laws made, not with our consent, but by others against our consent—that is, to surrender the form of government we have chosen, and to live under one deriving its powers from its own will, and not from our authority." Resolutions identical in spirit were also passed by Virginia, the following month; in those days the States still considered themselves supreme, the general government subordinate.

To inculcate this proud spirit of the supremacy of the people over their governors was to be the purpose of public education! Pick up today any common school history, and see how much of this spirit you will find therein. On the contrary, from cover to cover you will find nothing but the cheapest sort of patriotism, the inculcation of the most unquestioning acquiescence in the deeds of government, a lullaby of rest, security, confidence—the doctrine that the Law can do no wrong, a Te Deum in praise of the continuous encroachments of the powers of the general government upon the reserved rights of the States, shameless falsification of all acts of rebellion, to put the government in the right and the rebels in the wrong, pyrotechnic glorifications of union, power, and force, and a complete ignoring of the essential liberties to maintain which was the purpose of the revolutionists. The anti-Anarchist law of post-McKinley passage, a much worse law than the Alien and Sedition acts which roused the wrath of Kentucky and Virginia to the point of threatened rebellion, is exalted as a wise provision of our All-Seeing Father in Washington.

Such is the spirit of government-provided schools. Ask any child what he knows about Shays' rebellion, and he will answer, "Oh, some of the farmers couldn't pay their taxes, and Shays led a rebellion against the court-house at Worcester, so they could burn up the deeds; and when Washington heard of it he sent over an army quick and taught 'em a good lesson"—"And what was the result of it?" "The result? Why—why—the result was—Oh yes, I remember—the result was they saw the need of a strong federal government to collect the taxes and pay the debts." Ask if he knows what was said on the other side of the story, ask if he knows that the men who had given their goods and their health and their strength for the freeing of the country now found themselves cast into prison for debt, sick, disabled, and poor, facing a new tyranny for the old; that their demand was that the land should become the free communal possession of those who wished to work it, not subject to tribute, and the child will answer "No." Ask him if he ever read Jefferson's letter to Madison about it, in which he says:

"Societies exist under three forms, sufficiently distinguishable.

>Without government, as among our Indians.
>Under government wherein the will of every one has a just influence; as is the case in England in a slight degree, and in our States in a great one.
>Under government of force, as is the case in all other monarchies, and in most of the other republics.

To have an idea of the curse of existence in these last, they must be seen. It is a government of wolves over sheep. It is a problem not clear in my mind that the first condition is not the best. But I believe it to be inconsistent with any great degree of population. The second state has a great deal of good in it...It has its evils too, the principal of which is the turbulence to which it is subject...But even this evil is productive of good. It prevents the degeneracy of government, and nourishes a general attention to public affairs. I hold that a little rebellion now and then is a good thing."

Or to another correspondent:

>"God forbid that we should ever be twenty years without such a rebellion!...What country can preserve its liberties if its rulers are not warned from time to time that the people preserve the spirit of resistance? Let them take up arms...The tree of liberty must be refreshed from time to time with the blood of patriots and tyrants. It is its natural manure."

Ask any school child if he was ever taught that the author of the Declaration of Independence, one of the great founders of the common school, said these things, and he will look at you with open mouth and unbelieving eyes. Ask him if he ever heard that the man who sounded the bugle note in the darkest hour of the Crisis, who roused the courage of the soldiers when Washington saw only mutiny and despair ahead, ask him if he knows that this man also wrote, "Government at best is a necessary evil, at worst an intolerable one," and if he is a little better informed than the average he will answer, "Oh well, he [Tom Paine] was an infidel!" Catechize him about the merits of the Constitution which he has learned to repeat like a poll-parrot, and you will find his chief conception is not of the powers withheld from Congress, but of the powers granted.

Such are the fruits of government schools. We, the Anarchists, point to them and say: If the believers in liberty wish the principles of liberty taught, let them never entrust that instruction to any government; for the nature of government is to become a thing apart, an institution existing for its own sake, preying upon the people, and teaching whatever will tend to keep it secure in its seat. As the fathers said of the governments of Europe, so say we of this government also after a century and a quarter of independence: "The blood of the people has become its inheritance, and those who fatten on it will not relinquish it easily."

Public education, having to do with the intellect and spirit of a people, is probably the most subtle and far-reaching engine for molding the course of a nation; but commerce, dealing as it does with material things and producing immediate effects, was the force that bore down soonest upon the paper barriers of constitutional restriction, and shaped the government to its requirements. Here, indeed, we arrive at the point where we, looking over the hundred and twenty five years of independence, can see that the simple government conceived by the revolutionary republicans was a foredoomed failure. It was so because of:

> the essence of government itself;
> the essence of human nature
> the essence of Commerce and Manufacture.

Of the essence of government, I have already said, it is a thing apart, developing its own interests at the expense of what opposes it; all attempts to make it anything else fail. In this Anarchists agree with the traditional enemies of the Revolution, the monarchists, federalists, strong government believers, the Roosevelts of today, the Jays, Marshalls, and Hamiltons of then—that Hamilton, who, as Secretary of the Treasury, devised a financial system of which we are the unlucky heritors, and whose objects were twofold: To puzzle the people and make public finance obscure to those that paid for it; to serve as a machine for corrupting the legislatures; "for he avowed the opinion that man could be governed by two motives only, force or interest"; force being then out of the question, he laid hold of interest, the greed of the legislators, to set going an association of persons having an entirely separate welfare from the welfare of their electors, bound together by mutual corruption and mutual desire for plunder. The Anarchist agrees that Hamilton was logical, and understood the core of government; the difference is, that while strong governmentalists believe this is necessary and desirable, we choose the opposite conclusion, *No Government Whatsoever.*

As to the essence of human nature, what our national experience has made plain is this, that to remain in a continually exalted moral condition is not human nature. That has happened which was prophesied: we have gone down hill from the Revolution until now; we are absorbed in "mere money-getting." The desire for material ease long ago vanquished the spirit of '76. What was that spirit? The spirit that animated the people of Virginia, of the Carolinas, of Massachusetts, of New York, when they refused to import goods from England; when they preferred (and stood by it) to wear coarse, homespun cloth, to drink the brew of their own growths, to fit their appetites to the home supply, rather than submit to the taxation of the imperial ministry. Even within the lifetime of the revolutionists, the spirit decayed. The love of material ease has been, in the mass of men and permanently speaking, always greater than the love of liberty. Nine hundred and ninety nine women out of a thousand are more interested in the cut of a dress than in the independence of their sex; nine hundred and ninety nine men out of a thousand are more interested in drinking a glass of beer than in questioning the tax that is laid on it; how many children are not willing to trade the liberty to play for the promise of a new cap or a new dress? That it is which begets the complicated mechanism of society; that it is which, by multiplying the concerns of government, multiplies the strength of government and the corresponding weakness of the people; this it is which begets indifference to public concern, thus making the corruption of government easy.

As to the essence of Commerce and Manufacture, it is this: to establish bonds between every corner of the earth's surface and every other corner, to multiply the needs of mankind, and the desire for material possession and enjoyment.

The American tradition was the isolation of the States as far as possible. Said they: We have won our liberties by hard sacrifice and struggle unto death. We wish now to be let alone and to let others alone, that our principles may have time for trial; that we may become accustomed to the exercise of our rights; that we may be kept free from the contaminating influence of European gauds, pageants, distinctions. So richly did they esteem the absence of these that they could in all fervor write: "We shall see multiplied instances of Europeans coming to America, but no man living will ever seen an instance of an American removing to settle in Europe, and continuing there." Alas! In less than a hundred years the highest aim of a "Daughter of the Revolution" was, and is, to buy a castle, a title, and rotten lord, with the money wrung from American servitude! And the commercial interests of America are seeking a world empire!

In the earlier days of the revolt and subsequent independence, it appeared that the "manifest destiny" of America was to be an agricultural people, exchanging food stuffs and raw materials for manufactured articles. And in those days it was written: "We shall be virtuous as long as agriculture is our principal object, which will be the case as long as there remain vacant lands in any part of America. When we get piled upon one another in large cities, as in Europe, we shall become corrupt as in Europe, and go to eating one another as they do there." Which we are doing, because of the inevitable development of Commerce and Manufacture, and the concomitant development of strong government. And the parallel prophecy is likewise fulfilled: "If ever this vast country is brought under a single government, it will be one of the most extensive corruption, indifferent and incapable of a wholesome care over so wide a spread of surface." There is not upon the face of the earth today a government so utterly and shamelessly corrupt as that of the United States of America. There are others more cruel, more tyrannical, more devastating; there is none so utterly venal.

And yet even in the very days of the prophets, even with their own consent, the first concession to this later tyranny was made. It was made when the Constitution was made; and the Constitution was made chiefly because of the demands of Commerce. Thus it was at the outset a merchant's machine, which the other interests of the country, the land and labor interests, even then foreboded would destroy their liberties. In vain their jealousy of its central power made enact the first twelve amendments. In vain they endeavored to set bounds over which the federal power dare not trench. In vain they enacted into general law the freedom of speech, of the press, of assemblage and petition. All of these things we see ridden roughshod upon every day, and have so seen with more or less intermission since the beginning of the nineteenth century. At this day, every police lieutenant considers himself, and rightly so, as more powerful than the General Law of the Union; and that one who told Robert Hunter that he held in his fist something stronger than the Constitution, was perfectly correct. The right of assemblage is an American tradition which has gone out of fashion; the police club is now the mode. And it is so in virtue of the people's indifference to liberty, and the steady progress of constitutional interpretation towards the substance of imperial government.

It is an American tradition that a standing army is a standing menace to liberty; in Jefferson's presidency the army was reduced to 3,000 men. It is American tradition that we keep out of the affairs of other nations. It is American practice that we meddle with the affairs of everybody else from the West to the East Indies, from Russia to Japan; and to do it we have a standing army of 83,251 men.

It is American tradition that the financial affairs of a nation should be transacted on the same principles of simple honesty that an individual conducts his own business; viz., that debt is a bad thing, and a man's first surplus earning should be applied to his debts; that offices and office holders should be few. It is American practice that the general government should always have millions of debt, even if a panic or a war has to be forced to prevent its being paid off; and as to the application of its income office holders come first. And within the last administration it is reported that 99,000 offices have been created at an annual expense of 1663,000,000. Shades of Jefferson! "How are vacancies to be obtained? Those by deaths are few; by resignation none." Roosevelt cuts the knot by making 99,000 new ones! And few will die—and none resign. They will beget sons and daughters, and Taft will have to create 99,000 more! Verily a simple and a serviceable thing is our general government.

It is American tradition that the Judiciary shall act as a check upon the impetuosity of Legislatures, should these attempt to pass the bounds of constitutional limitation. It is American practice that the Judiciary justifies every law which trenches on the liberties of the people and nullifies every act of the Legislature by which the people seek to regain some measure of their freedom. Again, in the words of Jefferson: "The Constitution is a mere thing of wax in the hands of the Judiciary, which they may twist and shape in any form they please." Truly, if the men who fought the good fight for the triumph of simple, honest, free life in that day, were now to look upon the scene of their labors, they would cry out together with him who said:

> "I regret that I am now to die in the belief that the useless sacrifices of themselves by the generation of '76 to acquire self-government and happiness to their country, is to be thrown away by the unwise and unworthy passions of their sons, and that my only consolation is to be that I shall not live to see it."

And now, what has Anarchism to say to all this, this bankruptcy of republicanism, this modern empire that has grown up on the ruins of our early freedom? We say this, that the sin our fathers sinned was that they did not trust liberty wholly. They thought it possible to compromise between liberty and government, believing the latter to be "a necessary evil," and the moment the compromise was made, the whole misbegotten monster of our present tyranny began to grow. Instruments which are set up to safeguard rights become the very whip with which the free are struck.

Anarchism says, Make no laws whatever concerning speech, and speech will be free; so soon as you make a declaration on paper that speech shall be free, you will have a hundred lawyers proving that "freedom does not mean abuse, nor liberty license"; and they will define and define freedom out of existence. Let the guarantee of free speech be in every man's determination to use it, and we shall have no need of paper declarations. On the other hand, so long as the people do not care to exercise their freedom, those who wish to tyrannize will do so; for tyrants are active and ardent, and will devote themselves in the name of any number of gods, religious and otherwise, to put shackles upon sleeping men.

The problem then becomes, Is it possible to stir men from their indifference? We have said that the spirit of liberty was nurtured by colonial life; that the elements of colonial life were the desire for sectarian independence, and the jealous watchfulness incident thereto; the isolation of pioneer communities which threw each individual strongly on his own resources, and thus developed all-around men, yet at the same time made very strong such social bonds as did exist; and, lastly, the comparative simplicity of small communities.

All this has disappeared. As to sectarianism, it is only by dint of an occasional idiotic persecution that a sect becomes interesting; in the absence of this, outlandish sects play the fool's role, are anything but heroic, and have little to do with either the name or the substance of liberty. The old colonial religious parties have gradually become the "pillars of society," their animosities have died out, their offensive peculiarities have been effaced, they are as like one another as beans in a pod, they build churches—and sleep in them.

As to our communities, they are hopelessly and helplessly interdependent, as we ourselves are, save that continuously diminishing proportion engaged in all around farming; and even these are slaves to mortgages. For our cities, probably there is not one that is provisioned to last a week, and certainly there is none which would not be bankrupt with despair at the proposition that it produce its own food. In response to this condition and its correlative political tyranny, Anarchism affirms the economy of self-sustenance, the disintegration of the great communities, the use of the earth.

I am not ready to say that I see clearly that this will take place; but I see clearly that this *must* take place if ever again men are to be free. I am so well satisfied that the mass of mankind prefer material possessions to liberty, that I have no hope that they will ever, by means of intellectual or moral stirrings merely, throw off the yoke of oppression fastened on them by the present economic system, to institute free societies. My only hope is in the blind development of the economic system and political oppression itself. The great characteristic looming factor in this gigantic power is Manufacture. The tendency of each nation is to become more and more a manufacturing one, an exporter of fabrics, not an importer. If this tendency follows its own logic, it must eventually circle round to each community producing for itself. What then will become of the surplus product when the manufacturer shall have no foreign market? Why, then mankind must face the dilemma of sitting down and dying in the midst of it, or confiscating the goods.

Indeed, we are partially facing this problem even now; and so far we are sitting down and dying. I opine, however, that men will not do it forever, and when once by an act of general expropriation they have overcome the reverence and fear of property, and their awe of government, they may waken to the consciousness that things are to be used, and therefore men are greater than things. This may rouse the spirit of liberty.

If, on the other hand, the tendency of invention to simplify, enabling the advantages of machinery to be combined with smaller aggregations of workers, shall also follow its own logic, the great manufacturing plants will break up, population will go after the fragments, and there will be seen not indeed the hard, self-sustaining, isolated pioneer communities of early America, but thousands of small communities stretching along the lines of transportation, each producing very largely for its own needs, able to rely upon itself, and therefore able to be independent. For the same rule holds good for societies as for individuals—those may be free who are able to make their own living.

In regard to the breaking up of that vilest creation of tyranny, the standing army and navy, it is clear that so long as men desire to fight, they will have armed force in one form or another. Our fathers thought they had guarded against a standing army by providing for the voluntary militia. In our day we have lived to see this militia declared part of the regular military force of the United States, and subject to the same demands as the regulars. Within another generation we shall probably see its members in the regular pay of the general government. Since any embodiment of the fighting spirit, any military organization, inevitably follows the same line of centralization, the logic of Anarchism is that the least objectionable form of armed force is that which springs up voluntarily, like the minute men of Massachusetts, and disbands as soon as the occasion which called it into existence is past: that the really desirable thing is that all men—not Americans only—should be at peace; and that to reach this, all peaceful persons should withdraw their support from the army, and require that all who make war shall do so at their own cost and risk; that neither pay nor pensions are to be provided for those who choose to make man-killing a trade.

As to the American tradition of non-meddling, Anarchism asks that it be carried down to the individual himself. It demands no jealous barrier of isolation; it knows that such isolation is undesirable and impossible; but it teaches that by all men's strictly minding their own business, a fluid society, freely adapting itself to mutual needs, wherein all the world shall belong to all men, as much as each has need or desire, will result.

And when Modern Revolution has thus been carried to the heart of the whole world—if it ever shall be, as I hope it will—then may we hope to see a resurrection of that proud spirit of our fathers which put the simple dignity of Man above the gauds of wealth and class, and held that to, be an American was greater than to be a king.

In that day there shall be neither kings nor Americans—only Men; over the whole earth, *Men*.

Chapter 16

EMMA GOLDMAN
from
Anarchism and Other Essays (1910)

If anarchism believed in rulers then Emma Goldman would be the undisputed queen. The tiny woman took on the federal and state governments throughout most of her life, eventually challenging Woodrow Wilson and his Great War and getting deported for her radical views by a young J. Edgar Hoover. Once in the Soviet Union she lost very little time telling Lenin to his face what he was doing wrong. At various times the most hated woman in America and the face of assassination, "Red Emma"'s provocative life and ideas still radicalize people today.

MINORITIES VERSUS MAJORITIES

If I were to give a summary of the tendency of our times, I would say, Quantity. The multitude, the mass spirit, dominates everywhere, destroying quality. Our entire life—production, politics, and education—rests on quantity, on numbers. The worker who once took pride in the thoroughness and quality of his work, has been replaced by brainless, incompetent automatons, who turn out enormous quantities of things, valueless to themselves, and generally injurious to the rest of mankind. Thus quantity, instead of adding to life's comforts and peace, has merely increased man's burden.

In politics, naught but quantity counts. In proportion to its increase, however, principles, ideals, justice, and uprightness are completely swamped by the array of numbers. In the struggle for supremacy the various political parties outdo each other in trickery, deceit, cunning, and shady machinations, confident that the one who succeeds is sure to be hailed by the majority as the victor. That is the only god—Success. As to what expense, what terrible cost to character, is of no moment. We have not far to go in search of proof to verify this sad fact. Never before did the corruption, the complete rottenness of our government stand so thoroughly exposed; never before were the American people brought face to face with the Judas nature of that political body, which has claimed for years to be absolutely beyond reproach, as the mainstay of our institutions, the true protector of the rights and liberties of the people.

Yet when the crimes of that party became so brazen that even the blind could see them, it needed but to muster up its minions, and its supremacy was assured. Thus the very victims, duped, betrayed, outraged a hundred times, decided, not against, but in favor of the victor. Bewildered, the few asked how could the majority betray the traditions of American liberty? Where was its judgment, its reasoning capacity? That is just it, the majority cannot reason; it has no judgment. Lacking utterly in originality and moral courage, the majority has always placed its destiny in the hands of others. Incapable of standing responsibilities, it has followed its leaders even unto destruction. Dr. Stockman was right: "The most dangerous enemies of truth and justice in our midst are the compact majorities, the damned compact majority." Without ambition or initiative, the compact mass hates nothing so much as innovation. It has always opposed, condemned, and hounded the innovator, the pioneer of a new truth.

The oft repeated slogan of our time is, among all politicians, the Socialists included, that ours is an era of individualism, of the minority. Only those who do not probe beneath the surface might be led to entertain this view. Have not the few accumulated the wealth of the world? Are they not the masters, the absolute kings of the situation? Their success, however, is due not to individualism, but to the inertia, the cravenness, the utter submission of the mass. The latter wants but to be dominated, to be led, to be coerced. As to individualism, at no time in human history did it have less chance of expression, less opportunity to assert itself in a normal, healthy manner.

The individual educator imbued with honesty of purpose, the artist or writer of original ideas, the independent scientist or explorer, the non-compromising pioneers of social changes are daily pushed to the wall by men whose learning and creative ability have become decrepit with age.

Educators of Ferrer's type are nowhere tolerated, while the dietitians of predigested food, a la Professors Eliot and Butler, are the successful perpetuators of an age of nonentities, of automatons. In the literary and dramatic world, the Humphrey Wards and Clyde Fitches are the idols of the mass, while but few know or appreciate the beauty and genius of an Emerson, Thoreau, Whitman; an Ibsen, a Hauptmann, a Butler Yeats, or a Stephen Phillips. They are like solitary stars, far beyond the horizon of the multitude.

Publishers, theatrical managers, and critics ask not for the quality inherent in creative art, but will it meet with a good sale, will it suit the palate of the people? Alas, this palate is like a dumping ground; it relishes anything that needs no mental mastication. As a result, the mediocre, the ordinary, the commonplace represents the chief literary output.

Need I say that in art we are confronted with the same sad facts? One has but to inspect our parks and thoroughfares to realize the hideousness and vulgarity of the art manufacture. Certainly, none but a majority taste would tolerate such an outrage on art. False in conception and barbarous in execution, the statuary that infests American cities has as much relation to true art, as a totem to a Michael Angelo. Yet that is the only art that succeeds. The true artistic genius, who will not cater to accepted notions, who exercises originality, and strives to be true to life, leads an obscure and wretched existence. His work may some day become the fad of the mob, but not until his heart's blood had been exhausted; not until the pathfinder has ceased to be, and a throng of an idealless and visionless mob has done to death the heritage of the master.

It is said that the artist of today cannot create because Prometheus-like he is bound to the rock of economic necessity. This, however, is true of art in all ages. Michael Angelo was dependent on his patron saint, no less than the sculptor or painter of today, except that the art connoisseurs of those days were far away from the madding crowd. They felt honored to be permitted to worship at the shrine of the master.

The art protector of our time knows but one criterion, one value—the dollar. He is not concerned about the quality of any great work, but in the quantity of dollars his purchase implies. Thus the financier in Mirbeau's *Les Affaires sont les Affaires* points to some blurred arrangement in colors, saying: "See how great it is; it cost 50,000 francs." Just like our own parvenus. The fabulous figures paid for their great art discoveries must make up for the poverty of their taste.

The most unpardonable sin in society is independence of thought. That this should be so terribly apparent in a country whose symbol is democracy, is very significant of the tremendous power of the majority.

Wendell Phillips said fifty years ago: "In our country of absolute democratic equality, public opinion is not only omnipotent, it is omnipresent. There is no refuge from its tyranny, there is no hiding from its reach, and the result is that if you take the old Greek lantern and go about to seek among a hundred, you will not find a single American who has not, or who does not fancy at least he has, something to gain or lose in his ambition, his social life, or business, from the good opinion and the votes of those around him. And the consequence is that instead of being a mass of individuals, each one fearlessly blurting out his own conviction, as a nation compared to other nations we are a mass of cowards. More than any other people we are afraid of each other." Evidently we have not advanced very far from the condition that confronted Wendell Phillips.

Today, as then, public opinion is the omnipresent tyrant; today, as then, the majority represents a mass of cowards, willing to accept him who mirrors its own soul and mind poverty. That accounts for the unprecedented rise of a man like Roosevelt. He embodies the very worst element of mob psychology. A politician, he knows that the majority cares little for ideals or integrity. What it craves is display. It matters not whether that be a dog show, a prize fight, the lynching of a "nigger," the rounding up of some petty offender, the marriage exposition of an heiress, or the acrobatic stunts of an ex-president. The more hideous the mental contortions, the greater the delight and bravos of the mass. Thus, poor in ideals and vulgar of soul, Roosevelt continues to be the man of the hour.

On the other hand, men towering high above such political pygmies, men of refinement, of culture, of ability, are jeered into silence as mollycoddles. It is absurd to claim that ours is the era of individualism. Ours is merely a more poignant repetition of the phenomenon of all history: every effort for progress, for enlightenment, for science, for religious, political and economic liberty, emanates from the minority, and not from the mass. Today, as ever, the few are misunderstood, hounded, imprisoned, tortured, and killed.

The principle of brotherhood expounded by the agitator of Nazareth preserved the germ of life, of truth and justice, so long as it was the beacon light of the few. The moment the majority seized upon it, that great principle became a shibboleth and harbinger of blood and fire, spreading suffering and disaster. The attack on the omnipotence of Rome, led by the colossal figures of Huss, Calvin, and Luther, was like a sunrise amid the darkness of the night. But so soon as Luther and Calvin turned politicians and began catering to the small potentates, the nobility, and the mob spirit, they jeopardized the great possibilities of the Reformation. They won success and the majority, but that majority proved no less cruel and bloodthirsty in the persecution of thought and reason than was the Catholic monster. Woe to the heretics, to the minority, who would not bow to its dicta. After infinite zeal, endurance, and sacrifice, the human mind is at last free from the religious phantom; the minority has gone on in pursuit of new conquests, and the majority is lagging behind, handicapped by truth grown false with age.

Politically the human race should still be in the most absolute slavery, were it not for the John Balls, the Wat Tylers, the Tells, the innumerable individual giants who fought inch by inch against the power of kings and tyrants. But for individual pioneers the world would have never been shaken to its very roots by that tremendous wave, the French Revolution. Great events are usually preceded by apparently small things. Thus the eloquence and fire of Camille Desmoulins was like the trumpet before Jericho, razing to the ground that emblem of torture, of abuse, of horror, the Bastille.

Always, at every period, the few were the banner bearers of a great idea, of liberating effort. Not so the mass, the leaden weight of which does not let it move. The truth of this is borne out in Russia with greater force than elsewhere. Thousands of lives have already been consumed by that bloody regime, yet the monster on the throne is not appeased. How is such a thing possible when ideas, culture, literature, when the deepest and finest emotions groan under the iron yoke? The majority, that compact, immobile, drowsy mass, the Russian peasant, after a century of struggle, of sacrifice, of untold misery, still believes that the rope which strangles "the man with the white hands"[i] brings luck.

In the American struggle for liberty, the majority was no less of a stumbling block. Until this very day the ideas of Jefferson, of Patrick Henry, of Thomas Paine, are denied and sold by their posterity. The mass wants none of them. The greatness and courage worshipped in Lincoln have been forgotten in the men who created the background for the panorama of that time. The true patron saints of the black men were represented in that handful of fighters in Boston, Lloyd Garrison, Wendell Phillips, Thoreau, Margaret Fuller, and Theodore Parker, whose great courage and sturdiness culminated in that somber giant John Brown. Their untiring zeal, their eloquence and perseverance undermined the stronghold of the Southern lords. Lincoln and his minions followed only when abolition had become a practical issue, recognized as such by all.

About fifty years ago, a meteorlike idea made its appearance on the social horizon of the world, an idea so far-reaching, so revolutionary, so all-embracing as to spread terror in the hearts of tyrants everywhere. On the other hand, that idea was a harbinger of joy, of cheer, of hope to the millions. The pioneers knew the difficulties in their way, they knew the opposition, the persecution, the hardships that would meet them, but proud and unafraid they started on their march onward, ever onward. Now that idea has become a popular slogan. Almost everyone is a Socialist today: the rich man, as well as his poor victim; the upholders of law and authority, as well as their unfortunate culprits; the freethinker, as well as the perpetuator of religious falsehoods; the fashionable lady, as well as the shirtwaist girl. Why not? Now that the truth of fifty years ago has become a lie, now that it has been clipped of all its youthful imagination, and been robbed of its vigor, its strength, its revolutionary ideal—why not? Now that it is no longer a beautiful vision, but a "practical, workable scheme," resting on the will of the majority, why not? Political cunning ever sings the praise of the mass:

the poor majority, the outraged, the abused, the giant majority, if only it would follow us.

Who has not heard this litany before? Who does not know this never-varying refrain of all politicians? That the mass bleeds, that it is being robbed and exploited, I know as well as our vote-baiters. But I insist that not the handful of parasites, but the mass itself is responsible for this horrible state of affairs. It clings to its masters, loves the whip, and is the first to cry Crucify! the moment a protesting voice is raised against the sacredness of capitalistic authority or any other decayed institution. Yet how long would authority and private property exist, if not for the willingness of the mass to become soldiers, policemen, jailers, and hangmen. The Socialist demagogues know that as well as I, but they maintain the myth of the virtues of the majority, because their very scheme of life means the perpetuation of power. And how could the latter be acquired without numbers? Yes, authority, coercion. and dependence rest on the mass, but never freedom or the free unfoldment of the individual, never the birth of a free society.

Not because I do not feel with the oppressed, the disinherited of the earth; not because I do not know the shame, the horror, the indignity of the lives the people lead, do I repudiate the majority as a creative force for good. Oh, no, no! But because I know so well that as a compact mass it has never stood for justice or equality. It has suppressed the human voice, subdued the human spirit, chained the human body. As a mass its aim has always been to make life uniform, gray, and monotonous as the desert. As a mass it will always be the annihilator of individuality, of free initiative, of originality. I therefore believe with Emerson that "the masses are crude. lame, pernicious in their demands and influence, and need not to be flattered, but to be schooled. I wish not to concede anything to them, but to drill, divide, and break them up, and draw individuals out of them. Masses! The calamity are the masses. I do not wish any mass at all, but honest men only, lovely, sweet, accomplished women only."

In other words, the living, vital truth of social and economic well-being will become a reality only through the zeal, courage, the non-compromising determination of intelligent minorities, and not through the mass.

_____

i The intellectuals.

Chapter 17

CHARLES ROBERT PLUNKETT
Dynamite! (1914)

Emma Goldman's anarchist periodical Mother Earth *was a clearinghouse for many prominent names in leftist circles. In 1914 one issue was released without her supervision while she had been away on a lecture tour. Though Goldman was more bloodthirsty than her mentor Johann Most or her partner Alexander Berkman—even he thought the McKinley assassination was pointless and a shame—she still knew enough to be careful as to where and when to discuss political violence. As Goldman later wrote, "I had tried always to keep our magazine free from such language, and now the whole number was filled with prattle about force and dynamite. I was so furious that I wanted the entire issue thrown into the fire. But it was too late; the magazine had gone out to the subscribers." Here is the anarchist essay that so disquieted even Emma Goldman.*

It had to come. It was the logical culmination of events. The past five months have witnessed a period of Anarchist activity in New York City unequaled in this country since the stirring days of 1880 in Chicago. Also, and consequently, they have witnessed unexampled police brutality, court persecution, newspaper slander and popular prejudice. The end was inevitable.

It began in the stormy days of February with the Revolt of the

Unemployed—well-fed, pharisaical clergy-men and their smug, self-righteous congregations rudely awakened from their fatuous dreams of seventeenth-century theology by hordes of hungry men demanding food and shelter—mass-meetings and demonstrations, the greatest ever held in New York, at which thousands of workers listened to and applauded the speeches of avowed Anarchists—the Black Flag of Hunger borne by ragged, starving men through the residential street of the world's industrial potentates—the city stirred, the country aroused, the pillars of capitalist society shaken. Hunger had become articulate, Misery had found its voice! The authorities, deaf to the groans of Starvation, quickly gave ear to the first murmurs of Revolt. One hundred and ninety-two men arrested at once for seeking food; Frank Tanenbaum sentenced to practically two and a half years in jail for declaring that a hungry man has the right to eat; meetings forcibly broken up by the police, workingmen clubbed, arrested and jailed for expressing their opinions,—and they ask if we believe in violence!

Then came the massacre of Ludlow—two hundred men, women and children of the working class shot down or burned alive by the hired butchers of Standard Oil. Again it was the Anarchists who took up the fight of the workers, and brought home the responsibility where it belonged—to the oily murderer who teaches a Bible class on Sunday and roasts alive defenseless women on Monday. "My conscience acquits me," said young Rockefeller. We replaced his conscience; we became his Nemesis. His well-oiled conscience acquitted him; but we, the militant workers, have convicted him and passed judgment from his own Bible—"A life for a life."

Driven from his office at 26 Broadway, from his city home and his pet Sunday School,—the world's most potent monarch was forced to take refuge behind barred gates and armed guards at his Tarrytown estate. Having driven the rat into his hole, we followed him there. We went to Tarrytown. More clubs, more arrests, more jail, more persecution. A dozen men and women thrown into a filthy, stinking jail for speaking on the street, more arrested and clubbed the next day, jail sentences of thirty to ninety days punished the temerity of the rebels who dared invade Rockefeller's home town. Finally, finding his town police, his private guards and special deputies unable to cope with the situation, a hired "mob" was organized, which, inflamed with patriotism, rural bigotry and Rockefeller's whiskey, and gratuitously aided by the New York City authorities, attacked, stoned, and—had not their "Dutch courage" failed them—would have lynched the Anarchist speakers.

After this, the mask was off. Not content with legal violence, the ruling class itself had first appealed to extra-legal violence. None could suppose that the Anarchists would not accept the challenge.

This was the situation on the morning of July 4th. Then came the explosion, startling the country and striking terror into the hearts of the reaction. A large tenement house on Lexington Avenue was destroyed and three well-known Anarchists—Arthur Caron, Charles Berg and Carl Hanson—were killed. The ruin was evidently caused by a large quantity of dynamite exploding in the flat occupied by our comrades. These are the facts. More than this no one knows, and probably never will know.

Whatever may be the truth of the matter, the police and the capitalist press immediately assumed that the dynamite was being made into a bomb for use against Rockefeller or in Tarrytown. This was the story flashed over the country, and the moral effect of the explosion was as great as if our comrades had succeeded in their purpose, whatever it may have been.

As usual, many of the lip-revolutionists scurried to cover and hastened to "repudiate" violence, Anarchy, the dead men, and everything connected with them. The Anarchists, however, have stood their ground. Although we know nothing of the facts, we do not hesitate to admit the possibility, nor fear to face the accusation that our Comrades met their death in an attempt to retaliate upon the violence of the ruling classes in the only possible way—with violence.

If they did, we own them proudly, and we honor them for their intelligence, their initiative, and their courage. They did the only logical thing, the only courageous thing, the only revolutionary thing under the circumstances. When Free Speech is suppressed, when men are jailed for asking food, clubbed for assembling to discuss their grievances, and stoned for expressing their opinions, there is but one recourse—violence. The ruling class has guns, bullets, bayonets, police, jails, militia, armies and navies. To oppose all this the worker has only—dynamite.

All honor to the men who acted, while others talked. All honor to the men who were preparing to strike a blow of terror into the hearts of the enemy. They are dead—the last in the long list of martyrs to the cause of human liberty—but there are hundreds and thousands still alive who, inspired by their act, will follow their example—with better success.

Off with the mask! This is war. Violence can be met only with violence. "If they attack us with cannon, we will attack them with dynamite"—and, whenever possible, let us attack first. To oppression, to exploitation, to persecution, to police, jails, militia, armies and navies, there is but one answer—DYNAMITE!

Chapter 18

MORRIS AND LINDA TANNEHILL
from
The Market for Liberty (1970)

Though they never use the word "anarchism," the Tannehills' book was the first to lay out what a competitive market for policing would look like. What had been a completely fringe concept at the time has become a commonplace position on many pockets of the internet (though still far from mainstream). Here they lay out the question of what one school of anarchism would do in lieu of a government monopoly on policing.

DEALING WITH COERCION

Throughout history, the means of dealing with aggression (crime) has been punishment. Traditionally, it has been held that when a man commits a crime against society, the government, acting as the agent of society, must punish him. However, because punishment has not been based on the principle of righting the wrong but only of causing the criminal "to undergo pain, loss, or suffering," it has actually been revenge. This principle of vengeance is expressed by the old saying, "An eye for an eye, a tooth for a tooth," which means: "When you destroy a value of mine, I'll destroy a value of yours." Present day penology no longer makes such demands; instead of the eye or the tooth, it takes the criminal's life (via execution), or a part of his life (via imprisonment), and/or his possessions (via fines). As can be readily seen, the principle—vengeance—is the same, and it inevitably results in a compound loss of value, first the victim's, then the criminal's. Because destroying a value belonging to the criminal does nothing to compensate the innocent victim for his loss but only causes further destruction, the principle of vengeance ignores, and in fact opposes, justice.

When an aggressor causes the loss, damage, or destruction of an innocent man's values, justice demands that the aggressor pay for his crime, not by forfeiting a part of his life to "society," but *by repaying the victim* for his loss, plus all expenses directly occasioned by the aggression (such as the expense of apprehending the aggressor). By destroying the victim's values, the aggressor *has created a debt* which he owes to the victim and which the principle of justice demands must be paid. With the principle of justice in operation, there is only one loss of value; and, while this loss must initially be sustained by the victim, ultimately it is the aggressor—the one who caused the loss—who must pay for it.

There is a further fallacy in the belief that when a man commits a crime against society, the government, acting as the agent of society, must punish him. This fallacy is the assumption that society is a living entity and that, therefore, a crime *can be* committed against it. A society is no more than the sum of all the individual persons of which it is composed; it can have no existence apart from, or in contradistinction to, those individual persons. A crime is always committed against one or more persons; a crime cannot be committed against that amorphous non-entity known as "society." Even if some particular crime injured every member of a given society, the crime would still have been committed against individuals, not society, since it is only the individuals who are distinct, separate, independent, living entities. Since a crime can only be committed against individuals, a criminal cannot be rationally regarded as "owing a debt to society," nor can he "pay his debt to society:" the only debt he owes is to the injured individual(s).

Every dispute is between aggressor(s) and victim(s); neither society nor its members as a group have any direct interest in the matter. It is true that all honest members of a society have a general interest in seeing aggressors brought to justice in order to discourage further aggression. This interest, however, applies not to specific acts of aggression but to the total social structure which either encourages or discourages acts of aggression. An interest in maintaining a just social structure does not constitute a direct interest in the solution of any particular dispute involving aggression.

Because crimes cannot be committed against society, it is fallacious to regard government as an agent of society for the punishment of crime. Nor can government be considered to be the agent of the individual members of society, since these individuals have never signed a contract naming the government as their agent. There is, therefore, no valid reason for government officials to be designated the arbiters of disputes and rectifiers of injustice.

Granted, we are used to the governmental punishment-of-crime, so that to many people it seems "normal" and "reasonable," and any other means of dealing with aggression seems suspicious and strange; but an unbiased examination of the facts shows that this governmental system is actually traditional rather than rational.

Since neither "society" nor government can have any rational interest in bringing a specific aggressor to justice, who *is* interested? Obviously, the victim—and secondarily, those to whom the victim's welfare is a value, such as his family, friends, and business associates. According to the principle of justice, those who have suffered the loss from an aggresive act should be compensated (at the aggressor's expense), and, therefore, it is those who have suffered the loss who have an interest in seeing the aggressor brought to justice.

The steps which the victim may morally take to bring the aggressor to justice and exact reparations from him rest on the right to property, which, in turn, rests on the right to life. A man's property is his property, and this fact of ownership is not changed if the property comes into the possession of an aggressor by means of an act of force. The aggressor may be in possession of the property, but only the owner has a moral right to it. To illustrate: Suppose that as you come out of a building you see a stranger in the driver's seat of your car, preparing to drive it away. Would you have the moral right to push him out and thus regain possession of your car by force? Yes, since the thief's temporary possession does not alter the fact that it is your property. The thief used a substitute for initiated force when he attempted to steal your car, and you are morally justified in using retaliatory force to regain it.

Suppose that instead of catching the thief immediately you are forced to chase him and your car for two blocks and only catch up with him as he's stopped by a train. Do you still have the right to push him out and regain your car? Yes, since the passage of time does not erode your right to possess your property.

Suppose instead that the thief gets away, but that two months later you spot him downtown getting out of your car. You verify by serial number that it is, indeed, your car. Do you have the moral right to drive it away? Yes; again the passage of time makes no difference to your property rights.

Suppose that instead of yourself it is the detective you have hired to recover the car who spots the thief getting out of it. The detective, acting as your agent, has the right to repossess your car, just as you would.

You find that a front fender and headlight of your car are smashed in, due to the aggressor's careless driving. Repairs cost you $150. Do you have the right to collect this amount from the aggressor? Yes, you were the innocent victim of an act of aggression; it is the thief, not the victim, who is morally obligated to pay all costs occasioned by his aggression.

To summarize: the ownership of property is not changed if the property is stolen, nor is it eroded by the passage of time. The theft, damage, or destruction of another person's property constitutes an act of coercion, and the victim has a moral right to use retaliatory force to repossess his property. He also has a right to collect from the aggressor compensation for any costs occasioned by the aggression. If he wishes, the victim may hire an agent or agents to perform any of these actions in his place.

It should be noted that aggression often harms not only the victim but also those who are closely associated with him. For example, when a man is assaulted and seriously injured, his family may be caused expense, as well as anxiety. If he is a key man in his business, his employer or his partners and/or his company may suffer financial loss. All this destruction of value is a direct result of the irrational behavior of the aggressor and, since actions do have consequences, the aggressor has the responsibility of making reparations for these secondary losses, as well as for the primary loss suffered by the victim. There are practical limits to the amount of these secondary reparations. First, no one would bother to make such a claim unless the reparations he hoped to be paid were substantial enough to offset the expense, time, and inconvenience of making the claim. Second, the total amount of reparations which can be collected is limited by the aggressor's ability to pay, and first consideration goes to the victim. For the sake of simplicity, only the victim's loss will be dealt with here, but all the principles and considerations which apply to him apply as well to any others who have suffered a direct and serious loss as a result of the aggression.

In the process of collecting from the aggressor, the victim (or his agents) may not carelessly or viciously destroy values belonging to the aggressor or take more from him than the original property (or an equivalent value) plus costs occasioned by the aggression. If the victim does so, he puts himself in debt to the aggressor (unless, of course, the aggressor has made the destruction inevitable by refusing to give up the victim's property without a fight).

If the accused aggressor claims he is innocent or that the amount of reparations claimed by the victim is excessive, a situation of dispute exists between them which may require arbitration. The conditions of such arbitration, the forces impelling both parties to accept it as binding, and the market guarantees of its justice will now be examined.

In a laissez-faire society, insurance companies would sell policies covering the insured against loss of value by aggression (the cost of the policy based on the worth of the values covered and the amount of risk). Since aggressors would, in most instances, pay the major costs of their aggression, the insurance companies would lose only when the aggressor could not be identified and/or apprehended, when he died before making full reparations, or when the reparations were too great for him to be able to pay in his lifetime. Since the companies would recover most of their losses and since aggression would be much less common in a free-market society, costs of aggression insurance would be low, and almost all individuals could afford to be covered. For this reason, we shall deal primarily with the case of an insured individual who becomes the victim of aggression.

Upon suffering the aggression (assuming that immediate self-defense was either impossible or inappropriate), the victim would, as soon as possible, call his insurance company. The company would immediately send an investigator to determine the validity of his claim and the extent of the loss. When the amount was ascertained, the company would fully compensate the victim within the limits of the terms of the insurance policy. It would also act where feasible to minimize his inconvenience—e.g., lend him a car until his stolen one is recovered or replaced—in order to promote customer good will and increase sales (anyone ever heard of a government police department doing this?).

When the terms of the policy had been fulfilled, the insurance company, exercising its right of subrogation, would attempt to identify and apprehend the aggressor in order to recover its losses. At this point, the victim would be relieved of any further responsibilities in the case, except possibly appearing as a witness at any arbitration hearings.

If necessary, the insurance company would use detectives to apprehend the aggressor. Whether it used its own company detectives or hired an independent defense service would depend on which course was more feasible under the circumstances. Obviously, a competitive private enterprise defense agency, whether an auxiliary of a particular insurance company or an independent firm hired by several insurance companies (as are some claims adjusting companies today) would be far more efficient at the business of solving crimes and apprehending aggressors than are the present governmental police departments. In a free market, competition impels toward excellence!

Upon apprehending the aggressor, the insurance company's representatives would present him with a bill covering all damages and costs. Their first approach would be as peaceful as the situation permitted, since force is a nonproductive expenditure of energy and resources and is, therefore, avoided by the market whenever possible. First, the insurance company's representatives would attempt a voluntary settlement with the accused aggressor. If he was obviously guilty and the amount of reparations requested was just, it would be in his interest to agree to this settlement and avoid involving an arbitration agency, since the cost of any arbitration would be added on to his bill if he lost in his attempt to cheat justice.

If the accused aggressor claimed innocence or wished to contest the amount of the bill and he and the insurance company's representatives could come to no agreement, the matter would have to be submitted to binding arbitration, just as would a contractual dispute. Legislation forcing the parties to submit to binding arbitration would be unnecessary, since each party would find arbitration to be in his own self-interest. Nor would it be necessary to have legal protection for the rights of all involved, because the structure of the market situation would protect, them. For example, the insurance company would not dare to bring charges against a man unless it had very good evidence of his guilt, nor would it dare to ignore any request he made for arbitration. If the insurance company blundered in this manner, the accused, especially if he were innocent, could bring charges against the company, forcing it to drop its original charges and/or billing it for damages. Nor could it refuse to submit to arbitration on his charges against it, for it would do serious damage to its business reputation if it did; and in a free-market context, in which economic success is dependent on individual or corporate reputation, no company can afford to build a reputation of carelessness, unreliability, and unfairness.

It is worthy of note here that the notion of always presuming a man innocent until he is proved guilty by a jury trial can be irrational and sometimes downright ridiculous. For instance, when a man commits a political assassination in plain sight of several million television viewers, many of whom can positively identify him from the films of the incident, and is arrested on the spot with the gun still in his hand, it is foolish to attempt to ignore the facts and pretend he is innocent until a jury can rule on the matter. Though the burden of proof always rests on the accuser and the accused must always be given the benefit of the doubt, a man should be presumed neither innocent nor guilty until there is sufficient evidence to make a clear decision, and when the evidence is in he should be presumed to be whatever the facts indicate he is. An arbiter's decision is necessary only when the evidence is unclear and/or there is a dispute which cannot be resolved without the help of an unbiased third party.

The accused aggressor would desire arbitration if he wanted to prove his innocence or felt that he was being overcharged for his aggression, since without arbitration the charges against him would stand as made and he would have to pay the bill. By means of arbitration, he could prove his innocence and thus avoid paying reparations or if guilty he would have some say about the amount of reparations. If innocent, he would be especially eager for arbitration, not only to confirm his good reputation, but to collect damages from the insurance company for the trouble it had caused him (and thereby rectify the injustice against him).

A further guarantee against the possibility of an innocent man being railroaded is that every individual connected with his case would be fully responsible for his own actions, and none could hide behind legal immunity as do governmental police and jailers. If you knew that a prisoner put into your custody to work off his debt could, *if innocent*, demand and get reparations from you for holding him against his will, you would be very reluctant to accept any prisoners without being fully satisfied as to their guilt.

Thus, the unhampered market would, in this area as in any other, set up a situation in which irrationality and injustice were automatically discouraged and penalized without any resort to statutory law and government.

The insurance company and the accused aggressor, as disputing parties, would mutually choose an arbitration agency (or agencies, in case they wished to provide for an appeal) and contractually bind themselves to abide by its decision. In the event they were unable to agree on a single arbitration agency, each could designate his own agency preference and the two agencies would hear the case jointly, with the prior provision that if they disagreed on the decision they would submit the case to a third agency previously selected by both for final arbitration. Such a course might be more expensive.

The insurance company could order its defense agency to incarcerate the accused aggressor before and during arbitration (which would probably be only a matter of a few days, since the market is always more efficient than the bumbling government), but in doing so they would have to take two factors into consideration. First, if the accused were shown to be innocent, the insurance company and defense agency would owe him reparations for holding him against his will. Even if he were judged guilty, they would be responsible to make reparations if they had treated him with force in excess of what the situation warranted; not being government agents, they would have no legal immunity from the consequences of their actions. Second, holding a man is expensive—it requires room, board, and guards. For these reasons, the defense company would put the accused aggressor under no more restraint than was deemed necessary to keep him from running off and hiding.

It would be the job of the arbitration agency to ascertain the guilt or innocence of the accused and to determine the amount of reparations due. In settling the reparations payment, the arbiters would operate according to the principle that justice in a case of aggression consists of requiring the aggressor to compensate the victim for his loss *insofar as is humanly possible*. Since each case of aggression is unique—involving different people, actions, and circumstances, reparations payments would be based on the circumstances of each case, rather than on statutory law and legal precedent. Although cases of aggression vary widely, there are several expense factors which, in varying combinations, determine the amount of loss and, thus, the size of the reparations.

A basic expense factor is the cost of any property stolen, damaged, or destroyed. The aggressor would be required to return any stolen property still in his possession. If he had destroyed a replaceable item, such as a television set, he would have to pay the victim an amount of money equal to its value so that the victim could replace it. If the aggressor had destroyed an item which couldn't be replaced but which had a market value (for example, a famous art work like the Mona Lisa), he would still have to pay its market value, even though another one couldn't be bought. The principle here is that, even though the value can never be replaced, the victim should at least be left no worse off financially than if he had sold it instead of losing it to a thief. Justice requires the aggressor to compensate the victim *insofar as is humanly possible*, and replacing an irreplaceable value is impossible.

In addition to the basic expense of stolen and destroyed property, an act of aggression may cause several additional costs, for which the aggressor would be responsible to pay. An aggressor who stole a salesman's car might cause the salesman to lose quite a bit of business—an additional financial cost. A rapist who attacked and beat a woman would be responsible not only for paying medical bills for all injuries he had caused her and reparations for time she might lose from work, but he would also owe his victim compensation for her pain and suffering, both mental and physical. Besides all debts owed to the primary victim, the aggressor might also owe secondary reparations to others who had suffered indirectly because of his actions (for example, the victim's family). In addition to these expenses, occasioned by the aggression itself, the aggressor would also be responsible for any reasonable costs involved in apprehending him and for the cost of arbitration (which would probably be paid by the loser in any case).

Since the arbitration agency's service would be the rendering of just decisions, and since justice is the basis on which they would compete in the market, the arbiters would make every attempt to fix reparations at a fair level, in accordance with market values. For instance, if the defense company had run up an excessively high bill in apprehending the aggressor, the arbiters would refuse to charge the aggressor for the excessive expense. Thus, the defense company would be forced to pay for its own poor business practices instead of "passing the buck" to someone else.

In case the reparations amounted to more than the aggressor could possibly earn in his lifetime (for example, an unskilled laborer who set a million dollar fire), the insurance company and any other claimants would negotiate a settlement for whatever amount he could reasonably be expected to pay over time. This would be done because it would be no profit to them to set the reparations higher than the aggressor could ever hope to pay and thus discourage him from working to discharge his obligation. It is worth noting here that quite a large percentage of a worker's pay can be taken for a long period of time without totally removing his incentive to live and work—at present the average American pays out well over a third of his income in taxes and expects to do so for the rest of his life, yet those who go on the government "welfare" dole are still in the minority.

Many values which can be destroyed or damaged by aggression are not only irreplaceable, they are also non-exchangeable—that is, they can't be exchanged in the market, so no monetary value can be placed on them. Examples of non-exchangeable values are life, a hand or eye, the life of a loved one, the safety of a kidnapped child, etc. When confronted with the problem of fixing the amount of reparations for a non-exchangeable value, many people immediately ask, "But how can you set a price on a human life?" The answer is that when an arbitration agency sets the reparations for a loss of life it isn't trying to put a monetary price on that life, any more than is an insurance company when it sells a $20,000 life insurance policy. It is merely trying to compensate the victim (or his survivors) to the fullest extent possible under the circumstances.

The problem in fixing reparations for loss of life or limb is that the loss occured in one kind of value (non-exchangeable) and repayment must be made in another kind (money). These two kinds of values are incommensurable—neither can be measured in terms of the other. The value which has been destroyed not only can't be replaced with a similar value, it can't even be replaced with an equivalent sum of money, since there is no way to determine what *is* equivalent. And yet, monetary payment is the practical way to make reparations.

It is useful to remember here that justice consists of requiring the aggressor to compensate his victims for their losses *insofar as is humanly possible*, since no one can be expected to do the impossible. Even a destroyed item which has a market value can't always be replaced (e.g., the Mona Lisa). To demand that justice require the impossible is to make justice impossible. To reject the reparations system because it can't always replace the destroyed value with an equivalent value is like rejecting medicine because the patient can't always be restored to as good a state of health as he enjoyed before his illness. Justice, like medicine, must be contextual—it must not demand what is impossible in any given context. The question, then, is not how arbiters can set a price on life and limb; it is, rather, "How can they see that the victim is fairly compensated, insofar as is humanly possible, without doing injustice to the aggressor by requiring overcompensation?"

In attempting to reach a fair compensation figure, the arbitration agency would act, not as a judge handing down a sentence, but as a mediator resolving a conflict which the disputants can't settle themselves. The highest possible limit on the amount of reparations is, obviously, the aggressor's ability to pay, short of killing his incentive to live and earn. The lowest limit is the total amount of economic loss suffered (with no compensation for such non-exchangeables as anxiety, discomfort, and inconvenience). The reparations payment must be set somewhere in the broad range between these two extremes. The function of the arbitration agency would be to aid the disputants in reaching a reasonable figure between these extremes, not to achieve the impossible task of determining the monetary value of a non-exchangeable.

Although the limits within which the reparations payment for a non-exchangeable would be set are very broad, the arbitration agency could not capriciously set the amount of reparations at any figure it pleased. An arbitration agency would be a private business competing in a free market, and the action of the market itself would provide guidelines and controls regarding the "price" of aggression, just as it does with any other price. Any free-market business, including an arbitration agency, can survive and prosper only as customers choose to patronize it instead of its competitors. An arbitration agency must be chosen by both (or all) disputants in a case, which means that its record of settling previous disputes of a similar nature must be more satisfactory, to both complainant and defendant, than the records of its competitors. Any arbitration agency which consistently set reparations too high or too low in the opinion of the majority of its customers and potential customers would lose business rapidly. It would have to either adjust its payments to fit consumer demand...or go out of business. In this way, arbitration agencies whose levels of reparation displeased consumers would be weeded out (as would any other business which failed to satisfy customers). Arbitration agencies which wanted to stay in business would adjust reparation levels to meet consumer demand. In a relatively short time, reparations payments for various non-exchangeable losses would become pretty well standardized, just as are charges for various kinds and amounts of insurance protection.

The manner in which the amount of reparations for a non-exchangeable value would be set by the action of the free market is very similar to the way in which the market sets any price. No good or service has an intrinsic monetary value built into it by the nature of things. A commodity has a particular monetary value because that amount of money is what buyers are willing to give for it and sellers are willing to take for it. "Value" means *value to the people who trade that commodity in the market*. All the traders determine what the price will be. In a similar way, the people who bought the services of arbitration agencies would determine the levels of reparations payments—the levels they considered just and fair compensation for various kinds of losses. It is impossible for us to foresee, in advance of the actual market situation, just where these levels would be set. But we can see, from a knowledge of how a free market operates, that the market would determine them in accordance with consumer desires.

Each reparation claim would be a complex combination of compensations for losses of various kinds of exchangeable and non-exchangeable values. For example, if a hoodlum beat a man and stole $100 from him, the aggressor would be required not only to return the $100 but also to pay the victim's medical bills, his lost earnings, compensation for pain and suffering, and reparations for any permanent injuries sustained. If the victim were a key man in his business, the aggressor would also have to pay the business for the loss of his services. Each reparation claim is also a highly individual matter, because the destruction of the same thing may be a much greater loss to one man than to another. While the loss of a finger is tragic for anyone, it is a much more stunning blow to a professional concert pianist than to an accountant. Because of the complexity and individuality of reparations claims, only a system of competing free-market arbitration agencies can satisfactorily solve the problem of what constitutes just payment for losses caused by aggression.

Murder poses a special problem in that it constitutes an act of aggression which, by its very nature, renders the victim incapable of ever collecting the debt owed by the aggressor. Nevertheless, the aggressor did create a debt, and the death of the creditor (victim) does not cancel this debt or excuse him from making payment. This point can be easily seen by supposing that the aggressor did not kill, but only critically injured the victim, in which case the aggressor would owe reparations for injuries sustained, time lost from work, physical disability, etc. But if the victim then died from his injuries before the debt could be paid, the debtor obviously would not be thereby released from his obligation.

In this connection, it is useful to recall what a debt actually is. A debt is property which morally belongs to one person but which is in the actual or potential possession of another. Since the debt occasioned by the attack on the victim would have been his property had he survived that attack, his death places it, together with the rest of his property, in his estate to become the property of his heirs.

In addition to the primary debt owed to the estate of the victim, the aggressor also owes debts to all those whom the victim's death has caused a direct and major loss of value (such as his family), even though such people may also be his heirs. (Not to pay reparations to heirs simply because they will also inherit the reparations which would have been paid the victim had he survived, would be like refusing to pay them because they would inherit any other part of the victim's property.)

But suppose an aggressor murdered a grouchy old itinerant fruit picker who had neither family, friends, nor aggression insurance. Would the aggressor "get off scott free" just because his victim was of value to no one but himself and left no heirs to his property? No, the aggressor would still owe a debt to the fruit picker's estate, just as he would if there were an heir. The difference is that, without an heir, the estate (including the debt occasioned by the aggression) becomes unowned potential property. In our society, such unowned potential property is immediately expropriated by the government, as is much other unowned wealth. Such a practice can be justified only if one assumes that the government (or "the public") is the original and true owner of all property, and that individuals are merely permitted to hold property by the grace and at the pleasure of the government. In a free-market society, unowned wealth would belong to whatever person first went to the trouble of taking possession of it. In regard to the debt owed by an aggressor to the estate of his victim, this would mean that anyone who wished to go to the trouble and expense of finding the aggressor and, if necessary, proving him guilty before professional arbiters, would certainly deserve to collect the debt. This function could be performed by an individual, by an agency specially constituted for this purpose (though it seems unlikely that there would be enough situations of this nature to support such an agency), or by a defense agency or an insurance company. Insurance companies would be most likely to take care of this kind of aggression in order to deter violence and gain customer good will.

Before taking up the means by which an aggressor would be forced to pay reparations (if force were necessary), the position of an uninsured victim of aggression will be examined briefly. Whenever a demand for a service exists, the market moves to fill it. For this reason, a man who was uninsured would also have access to defense services and arbitration agencies. But, although he would have a similar recourse to justice, the uninsured man would find that his lack of foresight had put him at a disadvantage in several ways.

The uninsured victim would not receive immediate compensation but would have to wait until the aggressor paid reparations (which might involve a span of years if the aggressor didn't have the money to discharge the debt immediately and had to pay it off in instalments). Similarly, he would run the risk of being forced to forgo all or most of his compensation if the aggressor were not caught, died before being able to complete payment, or had incurred a debt too large to pay during his life. Also, the uninsured victim would have to bear all costs of apprehending the aggressor and, if necessary, of arbitration, until the aggressor was able to pay them back.

In addition to these monetary disadvantages, he would be put to extra inconvenience. If he wished to collect reparations, he would have to detect and apprehend the aggressor himself or (more likely) hire a defence agency to do it for him. He would also have to make his own arrangements for arbitration. Taking everything into consideration, a man would find aggression insurance well worth the expense, and there is little doubt that most people would have it.

RECTIFICATION OF INJUSTICE

Since aggression would be dealt with by forcing the aggressor to repay his victim for the damage caused (whenever the use of force was required), rather than by destroying values belonging to the aggressor, the free market would evolve a reparations-payment system vastly superior to and different from the present governmental prisons.

If the aggressor had the money to make his entire reparations payment immediately or could sell enough property to raise the money, he would do so and be free to go his way with no more than a heavy financial loss. Situations of this kind, however, would probably be very rare, because aggression is expensive. Even a small theft or destruction can quickly pile up a fairly large debt when related expenses, secondary payments to others who suffered because of the victim's loss, cost of defense and arbitration, etc., are taken into account. In a totally free society, men tend to be financially successful according to their merit. Few successful men would desire to commit aggression. Few unsuccessful men could afford to make immediate payment for it.

Assuming the aggressor could not make immediate payment of his entire debt, the method used to collect it would depend on the amount involved, the nature of the aggression, the aggressor's past record and present attitude, and any other pertinent variables. Several approaches suggest themselves.

If the aggression were not of a violent nature and the aggressor had a record of trustworthiness, it might be sufficient to leave him free and arrange a regular schedule of payments, just as would be done for any ordinary debt. If the aggressor could not be trusted to make regular payments, a voluntary arrangement could be made between the insurance company, the aggressor, and his employer, whereby the employer would be compensated for deducting the reparations payment from the aggressor's earnings each pay period.

If the aggressor were unable to find or hold a job because employers were unwilling to risk hiring him, he might have to seek employment from a company which made a practice of accepting untrustworthy workers at lower than market wages. (In an economy of full employment, some companies would be motivated to adopt such a practice in order to reach new sources of labor. Although the price of their product would remain close to that of their competitors, as prices are determined by supply and demand, the wages they paid would necessarily be lower to compensate for the extra risk involved in hiring employees of dubious character.)

If the facts indicated that the aggressor was of an untrustworthy and/or violent nature, he would have to work off his debt while under some degree of confinement. The confinement would be provided by rectification companies—firms specializing in this field, who would maintain debtors workhouses (use of the term "prison" is avoided here because of the connotations of value-destruction attached to it). The labor of the men confined would be furnished to any companies seeking assured sources of labor, either by locating the debtors workhouses adjacent to their plants or by transporting the debtors to work each day. The debtors would work on jobs for wages, just as would ordinary employees, but the largest part of their earnings would be used to make reparations payments, with most of the rest going for their room and board, maintenance of the premises, guards, etc. To insure against refusal to work, the reparations payment would be deducted from each pay before room and board costs, so that if a man refused to work he would not eat, or at most would eat only a very minimal diet.

There would be varying degrees of confinement to fit various cases. Many debtors workhouses might provide a very minimum amount of security, such as do a few present-day prison farms where inmates are told, "There are no fences to keep you here; however, if you run away, when you are caught you will not be allowed to come back here but will be sent to a regular prison instead." Such workhouses would give the debtor a weekly allowance out of his pay, with opportunities to buy small luxuries or, perhaps, to rent a better room. Weekend passes to visit family and friends, and even more extended vacations, might be arranged for those who had proved themselves sufficiently trustworthy.

Other workhouses would provide facilities of greater security, ranging up to a maximum security for individuals who had proved themselves extremely violent and dangerous. A man whose actions had forced his confinement in such a workhouse would find himself at a disadvantage in several ways. He would find he had less liberty, less luxuries, limited job opportunities, and a longer period of confinement because, with more of his earnings spent on guards and security facilities, it would take him longer to pay off his debt.

Since there will be cases of mental imbalance even in the most rational of cultures, it is probable that there will be an occasional individual who will refuse to work and to rehabilitate himself, regardless of the penalties and incentives built into the system. Such an individual would be acting in a self-destructive manner and could properly be classified as insane. Obviously, neither the rectification company, the defense service that brought him to justice, nor the insurance company or other creditor has any obligation to go to the expense of supporting him (as victims are forced through taxation to do today). Nor would they wish to turn him loose to cause further destruction. And if they allowed him to die, they would cut off all hope of recouping the financial loss he had caused. What, then, could they do?

One solution that suggests itself is to sell his services as a subject of study by medical and psychiatric doctors who are doing research on the causes and cures of insanity. This should provide enough money to pay for his upkeep, while at the same time advancing psychological knowledge and ultimately offering hope of help for this aggressor and his fellow sufferers. If such an arrangement were made, it would be in the interests of all concerned to see that the aggressor received no ill treatment. In a rational culture, severe mental illness would be much rarer than it is in ours, and the medical-psychiatric team would not wish to damage such a valuable specimen. The rectification company in charge of the aggressor would be even more eager to protect him from harm, since no arbitration agency could afford the reputation of sending aggressors to a debtors workhouse where there was ill treatment of the inmates.

This free-market system of debtors workhouses would have numerous practical advantages over the Dark Ages barbarity of the present governmental prison system. These advantages are a necessary consequence of the fact that the system would be run for profit—from the standpoint of both the insurance companies and the rectification companies operating the workhouses. In a laissez-faire economy, it is impossible to make consistent profits over a long-range period unless one acts with maximum rationality, which means: with maximum honesty and fairness.

A practical example of this principle can be seen in the results of the insurance company's desire to recoup its loss quickly. Because it would be in the insurance company's interest to have the aggressor's reparations instalments as large as possible, it would have him confined to no greater degree than his own actions made necessary, since closer confinement means greater expense, which means less money left for reparations payments. Thus, it would be the aggressor himself who would determine, by his character and his past and present behavior, the amount of freedom he would lose while repaying his debt and, to a certain degree, the length of time it would take him to pay it. Furthermore, at any time during his confinement, should the aggressor-debtor show himself to be a good enough risk, the insurance company would find it in their interest to gradually decrease his confinement—an excellent incentive to rational behavior.

Because both the insurance companies and the rectification companies would want to run their businesses profitably, it would be in their interest to have debtors be as productive as possible. In an industrialized society, a laborer's productivity depends not on his muscles but on his mind, his skills. So the debtor would be allowed to work in an area as close to the field of his aptitudes as possible and encouraged to develop further productive skills by on-the-job training, night school courses, etc. All this would help prepare him for a productive and honest life once his debt was paid. Thus, the application of free-market principles to the problem of aggression provides a built-in rehabilitation system. This is in sharp contrast to government-run prisons, which are little more than "schools for crime," where young first offenders are caged with hardened criminals and there is no incentive or opportunity for rehabilitation.

A system of monetary repayment for acts of aggression would remove a great deal of the "profit" incentive for aggressors. A thief would know that if he were caught he would have to part with all his loot (and probably quite a bit of his own money, too). He could never just stash the booty, wait out a five year prison term, and come out a rich man.

The insurance company's desire for speedy repayment would be the aggressor-debtor's best guarantee against mistreatment. Earning power depends on productivity, and productivity depends on the use of the mind. But a man who is physically mistreated or mentally abused will be unwilling and even unable to use his mind effectively. A mistreated man is good for little more than brute physical labor—a situation of prohibitively low productivity.

Another strong guarantee of good treatment for the aggressor-debtor is that, in a laissez-faire society, every man would be fully responsible for his own actions. No guard in a debtors workhouse could beat a debtor and get away with it. The mistreated debtor could complain to a defense service agent or to the insurance company to whom he was making reparations. If he could prove his assertion of mistreatment, the guilty guard would soon find himself paying a debt to his former prisoner. Furthermore, the guard's employers would never dare to support their guard if the debtor had a good case, because if they knowingly permitted the guard's sadism the debtor could bring charges against them, too.

A guard in a government prison can treat the prisoners as less than animals and never be brought to account for it, because he is protected by his status as part of the policing arm of the government. But a guard in a debtors workhouse couldn't hide behind the skirts of the rectification company which employed him, the way the prison guard hides behind the skirts of the government. The debtors workhouse guard would be recognized as an individual, responsible for his own actions. If he mistreated a debtor in his custody, he would be held personally responsible, and he couldn't wriggle out of it by putting the blame on "the system."

A free-market system of dealing with aggression would operate with a maximum of justice precisely because it was based on the principle of self-interest. The entirety of a man's self-interest consists of rational thought and action and the rewards of such behavior; the irrational is never in man's self-interest. As long as a man is behaving rationally, he cannot intentionally harm any other non-coercive person. One of the reasons for the success of a laissez-faire society is that the free-market system impels men to act in their own rational self-interest to the extent that they wish to successfully participate in it. It thus rewards honesty and justice and penalizes dishonesty and the initiation of force. This principle would work just as well if the market were free to deal with the problem of aggression as it does when the market deals with the supply of food or the building of computers.

There have been several questions and objections raised concerning the proposal that payment for aggression be made in monetary terms. For instance, it has been objected that a thief could "get off the hook" simply by voluntarily returning the stolen item. But this is to overlook two important facts—additional expenses and loss of reputation. First, as long as the thief held the item in his possession he would be causing its owner inconvenience and expense, plus the ever-mounting cost involved in the owner's attempt to recover the item, all of which would be part of the debt created by the thief's act of aggression. In aggressive acts of any seriousness at all, it would be almost impossible for the aggressor to return the stolen item quickly enough to avoid incurring additional costs. For example, suppose a man stole $20,000 at gunpoint from a bank, but, regretting his action a few minutes later, came back and returned the money. Could he get by without paying any further reparations? No, because his irrational actions interrupted the bank's business and may have caused a financial loss, for which he is directly responsible. In order to get the money, he had to threaten force against the teller and possibly other bank employees and customers, so he would owe them reparations for endangering their lives and safety. Also, as soon as he left the bank, the teller undoubtedly tripped an alarm, summoning the bank's defense agency, so the aggressor is responsible for paying the cost of the defense agency's coming to answer the call, plus any other related expenses.

But the second factor, loss of reputation, would be even more damaging to the aggressor. Just as specialized companies would keep central files, listing poor contractual risks, they would also list aggressors so that anyone wishing to do business with a man could first check his record. Insurance companies in particular would make use of this service. So our bank robber would find insurance companies listing him as a very poor risk and other firms reluctant to enter into contracts with him. Thus, if a man were foolish enough to engage in such a whim-motivated action as this bank robbery, he would find that he had caused himself considerable expense and loss of valuable reputation but had gained absolutely nothing.

In a similar vein, it has been objected that a very rich man could afford to commit any number of coercive acts, since all he would lose would be a little of his vast fortune. It is a bit difficult to imagine such a mentally ill person being able to continue existing uncured and unchallenged in a predominantly rational culture, but, assuming that he did, he would immediately find that money was hardly the only loss his actions cost him. As soon as his career of aggression was recognized for what it was, no honest man would take the chance of having anything to do with him. The only individuals who would not avoid him like The Plague would be those who felt they were tougher or craftier than he, and their only purpose in risking an association with him would be to part him from as large a share of his money as possible. Furthermore, he would run an immense risk of being killed by some victim acting in self-defense. Considering his reputation for aggression, a man would probably be justified in shooting him for any threatening gesture. So, in spite of his ability to pay, his life would be miserable and precarious, and his fortune would probably dwindle rapidly.

Again, it has been said that if a man confined himself to thefts so petty that the recoverable amount would be smaller than the cost of recovering it, thus making prosecution of the case economically unfeasible, he could get away with a career of aggression (of sorts). But such a "bubblegum thief" would lose much more than he could possibly gain, because he would lose his good reputation as his acts of aggression were discovered and recorded.

In each of these incidents, it is obvious that the aggressor's loss of reputation would be at least as damaging as his financial loss and that his lost reputation could not be regained unless he made reparations for his aggressive act and showed a determination to behave more reasonably in the future. He might shrug off the financial loss, but the loss of a good reputation would force him to live a substandard life, cut off from insurance protection, credit, reputable business dealings, and the friendship of all honest persons.

All the foregoing objections to a monetary payment assume that it would not be sufficiently costly to deter aggression, or, in other words, that it is severity of punishment which deters aggression. The untruth of this assumption should be evident from an examination of such historical eras as Elizabethan England, in which punishments of extreme severity prevailed, including physical mutilation and hanging for petty theft. Yet in spite of the great loss of value imposed on criminals, crime rates were very high. The reason for this is that it is not severity, but justice, which deters aggression. To punish the aggressor with more severity than his actions warrant—that is, to impose on him a greater loss of value than that which is necessary for him to make reasonable reparations to the victim—is to commit an injustice against him. Injustice cannot be a deterrent to injustice. The aggressor who is treated with such excessive severity feels, quite rightly, that he has been victimized. Seeing little or no justice in his punishment, he feels a vast resentment, and often forms a resolve to "get even with society" as soon as possible. Thus, in dealing with aggression, excessive severity, as much as excessive laxity, can provoke further aggressive acts. The only valid answer to injustice, is justice! Justice cannot be served by excessive severity or by taking revenge against the aggressor, or by pacifism, but only by requiring the aggressor to pay the debt which he has created by his coercive action.

Dealing with a man justly helps him to improve himself and his life by inducing him to act in his own self-interest. In the case of an aggressor, justice induces him to want to, and be able to, live a productive, honest, non-coercive life, both while he is paying the debt he owes to his victim, and afterwards. Justice helps a man get on the right track by sending him the right signals. It penalizes him for his misdeeds—but only as much as he actually deserves. It also rewards him when he does the right thing. Injustice sends out incorrect signals which lead men astray. The injustice of letting an aggressor get away without paying for his aggressions teaches him to believe that "crime pays," which induces him to commit more and bigger crimes. The injustice of punishing an aggressor by making him pay more than he really owes the victim teaches the aggressor that he can't expect justice from others, so there's little point in his trying to treat them justly. He concludes that this is a dog-eat-dog world and that his best course is to "do it unto others before they do it unto him." Only justice sends the aggressor the right signals, so only justice can be a satisfactory deterrent to aggression.

It may be objected that some men will attempt to take advantage of a free-market system of dealing with aggression. This is true, as it is true of any other social system. But the big advantage of any action of the free market is that errors and injustices are self-correcting. Because competition creates a need for excellence on the part of each business, a free-market institution must correct its errors in order to survive. Government, on the other hand, survives not by excellence but by coercion; so an error or flaw in a governmental institution can (and usually will) perpetuate itself almost indefinitely, with its errors usually being "corrected" by further errors. Private enterprise must, therefore, always be superior to government in any field, including that of dealing with aggressors.

WARRING DEFENSE AGENCIES AND ORGANIZED CRIME

Some opponents of a laissez-faire society have contended that, because a governmentless society would have no single, society-wide institution able to legitimately wield superior force to prevent aggression, a state of gang warfare between defense agencies would arise. Then (as they argue), brute force, rather than justice, would prevail and society would collapse in internecine conflict. This contention assumes that private defense service entrepreneurs would find it to their advantage, at least in some circumstances, to use coercive, rather than market, means to achieve their ends. There is a further, unstated assumption that governmental officials would not only prevent coercion but would themselves consistently refrain from initiating force (or that the force they initiated would be somehow preferable to the chaos it is feared would result from an unhampered market).

The second of these assumptions is obviously groundless, since government is a coercive monopoly which must initiate force in order to survive, and which cannot be kept limited. But what of the first assumption? Would a free market system of value-protection lead to gang warfare between the competing defense companies?

The "gang warfare" objection has been raised in regard to theories advocating a system of competing governments. When applied to any type of governments, the objection is a valid one. A government, being a coercive monopoly, is always in the position of initiating force simply by the fact of its existence, so it is not surprising that conflicts between governments frequently take the form of war. Since a government is a coercive *monopoly*, the notion of more than one government occupying the same area at the same time is ridiculous. But a laissez-faire society would involve, not governments, but private businesses operating in a free market.

All actions have specific consequences, and the nature of these consequences is determined by the nature of the action and by the context in which it takes place. What would be the consequences for a free-market defense company which committed an act of aggression in a laissez-faire society?

Suppose, for example, that the Old Reliable Defense Company, acting on behalf of a client who had been robbed of his wallet, sent its agents to break into and search every house in the client's neighborhood. Suppose further that the agents shot the first man who offered resistance, taking his resistance as proof of guilt.

The most immediate consequence of the aggression is that the defense company either does or does not realize its objective (in this case, the return of the wallet, together with damages), depending on the circumstances and the amount of counter-force it meets with. But this is only the first of several important consequences springing directly from the aggression.

Not only has Old Reliable's action put it in the precarious position of being a target of retaliatory force, it has also made the company the subject of severe business ostracism. All honest and productive individuals and businesses will immediately dissociate themselves from Old Reliable, because they will fear that any disagreement which may arise in their business dealings with it may turn its aggressive force against them. Further, they will realize that, even if they manage to remain on good terms with Old Reliable, they are in danger of becoming accidental casualties when retaliatory force is exercised by some indignant victim of Old Reliable's aggressions.

But there is an even stronger reason which will persuade Old Reliable's customers and business associates to quickly sever all relations with it. In a laissez-faire society, as has been pointed out, a good reputation is the most valuable asset any business or individual can have. In a free society, a man with a bad reputation would have a hard time getting customers, business associates, or credit and insurance at rates he could afford. Knowing this, no one would wish to risk his personal reputation or the business reputation of his firm by having any dealings with a known aggressor.

Insurance companies, a very important sector of any totally free economy, would have a special incentive to dissociate themselves from any aggressor and, in addition, to bring all their considerable business influence to bear against him. *Aggressive violence causes value loss*, and the insurance industry would suffer the major cost in most such value losses. An unrestrained aggressor is a walking liability, and no insurance company, however remotely removed from his original aggression, would wish to sustain the risk that he might aggress against one of its own clients next. Besides, aggressors and those who associate with them are more likely to be involved in situations of violence and are, thus, bad insurance risks. An insurance company would probably refuse coverage to such people out of a foresighted desire to minimize any future losses which their aggressions might cause. But even if the company were not motivated by such foresight, it would still be forced to rate their premiums up drastically or cancel their coverage altogether in order to avoid carrying the extra risk involved in their inclination to violence. In a competitive economy, no insurance company could afford to continue covering aggressors and those who had dealings with aggressors and simply pass the cost on to its honest customers; it would soon lose these customers to more reputable firms which could afford to charge less for their insurance coverage.

What would loss of insurance coverage mean in a free economy? Even if the Old Reliable Defense Company (or any other business or individual) could generate enough force to protect itself against any aggressive or retaliatory force brought against it by any factor or combination of factors, it would still have to go completely without several economic necessities. It could not purchase insurance protection against auto accidents, natural disasters, or contractual disputes. It would have no protection against damage suits resulting from accidents occurring on its property. It is very possible that Old Reliable would even have to do without the services of a fire extinguishing company, since such companies are natural outgrowths of the fire insurance business.

In addition to the terrific penalties imposed by the business ostracism which would naturally follow its aggressive act, Old Reliable would have trouble with its employees. Government employees are legally protected from suffering any personal consequences as a result of all but the most blatant of the aggressive acts which they perpetrate "in the line of duty." Such functionaries as police officials, judges, and Internal Revenue and narcotics agents can initiate force with immunity simply by taking protection under such clichés as "I don't write the law; I just enforce it," or "That's a matter for a jury to decide," or "This statute was passed by the duly elected representatives of the people." But employees of a free-market defense company would have no such legal immunity from retaliatory force; they would have to assume responsibility for their own actions. If a defense service agent carried out an order which involved the intentional initiation of force, both the agent and the entrepreneur or manager who gave him the order, as well as any other employees knowledge-ably involved, would be liable for any damages caused. Since he could not take refuge in "the system," no honest defense service employee would carry out an order which involved the initiation of force (nor would an honest employer give such an order or sanction such action on the part of his employee). Thus, if Old Reliable managed to keep any employees at all, or to hire any new ones to replace those who had left, it would have to settle for people who were either terribly stupid or desperate enough to believe they had nothing to lose by being associated with aggression—in other words, simpletons and hoodlums.

In a laissez-faire society, a defense company which committed aggression, unless it acted speedily to rectify the injustices, would be left with no customers, associates, or employees except for undesirables. This raises the question of whether the criminal element in a laissez-faire society would, or even could, support their own "Mafia" defense company for the purpose of defending them against the retaliatory force of their victims.

Only a man who was willing to be openly identified as an aggressor would buy the services of such a "Mafia" defense agency, since the nature of the activities and clients of such a defense agency could not be kept hidden. This open aggressor would have to support himself entirely by aggression, because no honest man would take the chance of having business dealings with him. Furthermore, he would have to be existing very well financially, since the cost of protecting a man continually involved in acts of violence would be extremely high.

It is reasonable to conclude, therefore, that the only clients of such a "Mafia" defense company would be highly successful, big time, open aggressors. Since an aggressor could hardly hope to obtain that much money all by himself, the existence of such men presupposes the existence of a fairly extensive, well organized network of lesser hoodlums working for the "big operators." In other words, organized criminal gangs would be required to provide sufficient support for a "Mafia" defense company.

Although such an organized criminal gang may enter into many fields, organized crime finds its basic support in black market activities. A black market is any area of the market which is legally prohibited. If left unprohibited, it would be an area of trade involving peaceful, willing exchanges between sellers and buyers. But when government initiates force by forbidding this area of trade to honest men, it throws it open to men who are willing to take the risk of violating bureaucratic dictates and the statutory laws of the politicians. The violence and fraud associated with any black market do not spring from the nature of the good or service being sold; they are a direct result of the fact that entrepreneurs have been legally forbidden to deal in this area of the market, leaving it open to men who dare to ignore prohibitions and who are willing to resort to violence in order to do business without getting caught. Unless prohibited, every market activity is operated on the basis of willing exchange, without the initiation of force, because this is the only way a business can be operated successfully, as *force is a nonproductive expenditure of energy.*

An excellent example of a black market occurred during the Prohibition era of the 1920s. When government prohibited the manufacture and sale of liquor, an area of the market was arbitrarily closed to anyone who wished to remain law-abiding. Since there was still a market demand for liquor, hosts of criminals were attracted and created to fill the vacuum. Numerous gangs, including the Mafia, were founded and/or grew into organizations of immense power on the basis of the black market afforded by the Prohibition Amendment of the U. S. Constitution. Many of these organized criminal gangs are still with us; although they lost a great deal of their base with the repeal of Prohibition, they were able to survive by shifting the major part of their activities to other governmentally forbidden areas, such as gambling and prostitution. (It is interesting to note that the two organizations which fought hardest against the repeal of Prohibition were the Women's Christian Temperance Union and the Mafia!)

There is a compelling reason why organized crime must base its support in black market activities. Wealth does not exist in nature but must be created. The only means of creating wealth is value-production and free exchange—the manufacture and trade of some desired good or service. One may obtain wealth directly, by productive work, or one may obtain it indirectly, by looting it from a producer, but the wealth must be created by production in the first place in order to exist at all. The looter is a parasite who will not create his own wealth and its consequent power but is dependent on some producer to furnish it. This means that looting cannot be a profitable business in the long run (to the extent that producers are not disarmed by a false ideology—such as pacifism—or by being legally prohibited from acting in their own defense). *Producers* are the ones who hold the source of wealth and power, and in any long-range contest between looters and non-disarmed producers the weight of wealth and power must be on the side of the producers.

This is the reason that an organized hoodlum gang cannot support its large size and relatively complex structure by acts of aggression alone; the risk inevitably outweighs the profit (and this would be particularly true in a society where value-protection was a service sold in a competitive, free market). Such a gang can only support itself by obtaining its wealth directly, through production and trade in some black market. Thus, *organized* crime depends for its existence on black markets...*which are the result of government prohibitions.* Without *government-caused* black markets, criminals would have to operate singly or in small groups because they would have no area of production and trade to furnish support for large and complex organizations. So it is clear that the criminal element in a laissez-faire society couldn't possibly support a "Mafia" defense company.

It is also worth noting that much of the success of organized crime in our present society is due to the alliances which crime bosses are able to make with government officials on nearly all levels. From the $50 pay-off to the local cop, clear up to the $10,000 contribution to the senator's campaign fund, organized crime regularly protects itself by buying off governmental opposition. In a laissez-faire society, aggressors would not only be scattered, weak, and unorganized, they would find it next to impossible to buy off free-market protection and arbitration agencies. The customers of a defense company don't have to keep patronizing it if they find out that some of its employees have been accepting payoffs from aggressors. They are free to do what citizens can never do—find some other agency to protect them. A free-market agency, unlike a government, couldn't afford to have underworld connections, even with the small and unimportant "underworld" of a free society. When the news media revealed its shady dealings, its customers would all desert it, and the aggressors wouldn't be able to keep it in business...for the simple reason that the criminal element in a laissez-faire society would be too small and weak to support a "Mafia" defense company.

But even though a "Mafia" defense company could not exist in a free-market society, wouldn't it be possible for some respectable defense agency to attain a position of monopoly and then begin exercising its powers in a tyrannical manner? Of course there is some possibility that any social structure can be subverted—anything which some men can build, other men can find a way to destroy. What obstacles would a would-be tyrant (or group of tyrants) have to overcome in order to gain control of a free society?

First, the would-be tyrant would have to gain control of the defense company he intended to use, and it would have to be one which controlled a fairly strong army or had the means to build one. Even if he inherited the business lock, stock, and bankroll, he would still not control it in the same way that a government controls its bureaucrats and armies, because he would have no way of guaranteeing his employees immunity from retaliation if they committed coercive acts for him. Nor would he be able to hold his employees (as a government can with its conscript soldiers) if they objected to his orders or feared to carry them out.

But if this would-be tyrant were clever and subtle enough either to gain the loyalty of his employees or to keep them from realizing what he was about, he would still have only begun his task. In order to have sufficient power to carry out his schemes, he would have to gain monopoly or near-monopoly status. He could only do this by becoming the most efficient and excellent entrepreneur in his field; and he would have to continue this excellence, even after he had gained monopoly status, to prevent other large businesses from diversifying into his field to reap the benefits of higher profit margins. This means that our would-be tyrant couldn't charge his customers high prices in order to amass a fortune to buy weapons and hire soldiers to further his schemes of conquest.

In fact, the would-be tyrant's customers would probably be more of an obstacle to his ambitions than his employees would. He couldn't extract taxes from them, as a government does, and, at least until he reached the stage of full power, he couldn't even force them to buy his service and support his company at all. A market relationship is a free relationship, and if a customer doesn't like a company's service or mistrusts its goals, he is free to take his business elsewhere, or to start his own competitive company, or to do without the service altogether and just provide for himself. Furthermore, customers aren't imbued with the citizens' spirit of patriotic fervor and obedience and are, thus, much harder to lure into foolish collectivistic endeavors (such as "national unity"). Free men aren't in the habit of leaping like fools and sheep to "defend the Flag" or to "sacrifice for the Cause." In these vitally important respects, the free-market system differs fundamentally and completely from a government system of any sort.

The would-be tyrant might try to build his forces in complete secrecy until he was ready to make his coup, but he would find this far from easy. Imagine amassing the cash to buy guns, tanks, airplanes, ships, missiles, and all the other paraphernalia of modern warfare. Imagine finding such items and making deals to purchase them or have them manufactured. Imagine hiring and equipping a large force of soldiers and training them for months. Then imagine doing all this in complete secrecy while alert members of the news media were continually nosing around for a big story! If you can imagine such a thing, your ability at fantasizing is remarkable, indeed.

The fear of a tyrant is a very real one, and, in the light of history, it is well justified. But, as can be seen from the foregoing examination, it applies to a governmentally run society rather than to a free society. *The objection that a tyrant might take over is actually a devastating argument against government.*

Chapter 19

DAVID FRIEDMAN
from
The Machinery of Freedom (1973, 2014)

Economist David Friedman comes to anarcho-capitalism from a largely utilitarian perspective, as opposed to the natural-rights perspective preferred by most ancaps. His The Machinery of Freedom *is a collection of essays that includes attempts to resolve issues that make people squirmy about fully hoisting the black flag. Here he addresses two very common critique of the ideology: that anarchism is inherently unstable and will resolve to a state anyway, and that an anarchist society would be incapable of defending itself from an aggressive foreign government.*

THE STABILITY PROBLEM

Anyone with a little imagination can dream up a radical new structure for society, anarcho-capitalist or otherwise. The question is, will it work? Most people, when they hear my description of anarcho-capitalism for the first time, immediately explain to me two or three reasons why it won't. Most of their arguments can be reduced to two: The system will be at the mercy of the Mafia, which can establish its own agency or take over existing ones and convert them into protection rackets. Or else the agencies will realize that theft is more profitable than business, get together, and become a government.

The main defensive weapon of organized crime is bribery. It works because policemen have no real stake in doing their job well and the taxpayers have no standard of comparison to tell them if they are getting their money's worth. What is the cost to the chief of a police department of letting his men accept bribes to permit crime? In most cases, nothing. The higher crime rate might even persuade the voters to vote more money and higher salaries to the police department.

If employees of a rights enforcement agency accept such bribes, the situation is rather different. The worse the job the agency does, the lower the fee it can charge. If the customers of one agency find they lose, on average, ten dollars a year more to thieves than the customers of another, they will continue to do business with the inferior agency only if it is at least ten dollars a year cheaper. So every dollar stolen from the customer comes, indirectly, out of the revenue of the agency. If the agency is one that guarantees performance by insuring its customers against losses, the connection is more direct. Either way, it is very much in the interest of the men running a rights enforcement agencies to see that their employees do not take bribes. The only bribe it would pay the agency to take would be one for more than the value of the goods stolen—a poor deal for the thief.

This does not mean that employees of rights enforcement agencies will never take bribes. The interests of the employee and of the agency are not identical. It does mean that the men running the agencies will do their best to keep their men honest. That is more than you can say for a police force. Organized crime, if it continues to exist under anarcho-capitalism, should be in a much weaker position than it now is. In addition, as I shall argue later, most of the things that organized crime now makes money on would be legal in an anarcho-capitalist society. Thus both its size and its popularity would be greatly reduced.

What about the possibility of the Mafia getting its own agency? In order for such a firm to provide its clients with the service they want—protection against the consequences of their crimes—it must either get the other agencies to agree to arbitration by a court that approves of crime or refuse to go to arbitration at all. In order to do the first, it must offer the other agencies terms so good that their customers are willing to be stolen from; as in the previous case, this reduces to the thief bribing the victim by more than the amount stolen, which is improbable. If it refuses to accept arbitration, the Mafia's agency finds itself constantly in conflict with the other agencies. The victims of theft will be willing to pay more to be protected than the thieves will pay to be able to steal, since stolen goods are worth less to the thief than to the victim. Therefore the noncriminal agencies will find it profitable to spend more to defeat the criminal agency than the criminal agency could spend to defeat them. In effect, the criminals fight a hopeless war with the rest of society and are destroyed.

Another and related argument against anarcho-capitalism is that the strongest agency will always win, the big fish will eat the little fish, and the justice you get will depend on the military strength of the agency you patronize.

This is a fine description of governments, but rights enforcement agencies are not territorial sovereigns. One which settles its disputes on the battlefield has already lost, however many battles it wins. Battles are expensive—also dangerous for clients whose front yards get turned into free-fire zones. The clients will find a less flamboyant protector. No clients means no money to pay the troops.

Perhaps the best way to see why anarcho-capitalism would be so much more peaceful than our present system is by analogy. Consider our world as it would be if the cost of moving from one country to another were zero. Everyone lives in a house trailer and speaks the same language. One day the president of France announces that because of troubles with neighboring countries, new military taxes are being levied and conscription will begin shortly. The next morning he finds himself ruling a peaceful but empty landscape, the population having been reduced to himself, three generals, and twenty-seven war correspondents.

We do not all live in house trailers. But if we buy our protection from a private firm instead of from a government, we can buy it from a different firm as soon as we think we can get a better deal. We can change protectors without changing countries.

The risk of private agencies throwing their weight—and lead— around is not great, provided there are lots of them. Which brings us to the second and far more serious argument against anarcho-capitalism.

The rights enforcement agencies will have a large fraction of the armed might of the society. What can prevent them from getting together and using that might to set themselves up as a government?

In some ultimate sense, nothing can prevent that save a populace possessing arms and willing, if necessary, to use them. That is one reason I am against gun-control legislation.

But there are safeguards less ultimate than armed resistance. After all, our present police departments, national guard, and armed forces already possess most of the armed might. Why have they not combined to run the country for their own benefit? Neither soldiers nor policemen are especially well paid; surely they could impose a better settlement at gunpoint.

The complete answer to that question comprises nearly the whole of political science. A brief answer is that people act according to what they perceive as right, proper, and practical. The restraints which prevent a military coup are essentially restraints interior to the men with guns.

We must ask, not whether an anarcho-capitalist society would be safe from a power grab by the men with the guns (safety is not an available option), but whether it would be safer than our society is from a comparable seizure of power by the men with the guns. I think the answer is yes. In our society, the men who must engineer such a coup are politicians, military officers, and policemen, men selected precisely for the characteristic of desiring power and being good at using it. They are men who already believe that they have a right to push other men around—that is their job. They are particularly well qualified for the job of seizing power. Under anarcho-capitalism the men in control of the agencies are selected for their ability to run an efficient business and please their customers. It is always possible that some will turn out to be secret power freaks as well, but it is surely less likely than under a system where the corresponding jobs are labeled 'non-power freaks need not apply'.

In addition to the temperament of potential conspirators, there is another relevant factor: the number of agencies. If there are only two or three in the entire area now covered by the United States, a conspiracy among them may be practical. If there are a thousand, then when any group of them start acting like a government their customers will hire someone else to protect them against their protectors.

How many agencies there are depends on what size agency does the most efficient job of protecting its clients. My own guess is that the number will be nearer a thousand than three. If the performance of present-day police forces is any indication, an agency protecting as many as one million people is far above optimum size.

My conclusion is one of guarded optimism. Once anarcho-capitalist institutions are established with widespread acceptance over a large area, they should be reasonably stable against internal threats.

Are such institutions truly anarchist? Are the private agencies I have described actually governments in disguise? No. Under my definition of government—which comes closer than any other, I think, to describing why people call some things governments and not others—they are not governments. They have no rights which individuals do not have and they therefore cannot engage in legitimized coercion.

Most people, myself included, believe that an individual has the right to use force to prevent another from violating his rights—stealing from him, say, or murdering him. Most agree that the victim has a right to take back what the thief has stolen and to use force to do so. Social contract theories start from the premise that individuals have these rights and delegate them to the government. In order for such a government to be legitimate, it must be established by unanimous consent, otherwise it has no special rights over those who refuse to sign the 'social contract'. Under a system of private rights enforcement agencies the actual agencies, like the ideal government, are acting as agents for willing clients who have employed them to enforce their own rights. They claim no rights over non-clients other than the right to defend their clients against coercion—the same right every individual has. They do nothing that a private individual cannot do.

This does not mean that they will never coerce anyone. A rights enforcement agency, like a government, can make a mistake and arrest the wrong man. In exactly the same way, a private citizen can shoot at what he thinks is a prowler and bag the postman instead. In each case, coercion occurs, but it occurs by accident and the coercer is liable for the consequences of his acts. The citizen can be indicted for postman-slaughter and the agency sued for false arrest. Once the facts that make an act coercive are known, it is no longer regarded as having been legitimate.

This is not true of government actions. In order to sue a policeman for false arrest I must prove not merely that I was innocent but that the policeman had no reason to suspect me. If I am locked up for twenty years and then proven innocent, I have no legal claim against the government for my lost time and mental anguish. It is recognized that the government made a mistake, but the government is allowed to make mistakes and need not, like the rest of us, pay for them. If, knowing that I am innocent, I try to escape arrest and a policeman shoots me down, he is entirely within his rights and I am the criminal. If, to keep him from shooting me, I shoot him in self-defense, I am guilty of murder even after it is proved that I was innocent of the theft and so doing no more than defending myself against the government's (unintentional) coercion.

This difference between the rights claimed by a private rights enforcement agency and those claimed by a government affects more than the semantic question of what is or is not anarchy. It is one of the crucial reasons why a government, however limited, can more easily grow into a tyranny than can a system of private agencies. Even the most limited government has the sort of special rights I have described; everything I said in the previous paragraph was true of this country in its earliest and (for white males) freest days.

Such special rights allow a government to kill its opponents and then apologize for the mistake. Unless the evidence of criminal intent is very clear, the murderers are immune from punishment. Even when the evidence is overwhelming, as in the case of the 1969 Chicago Black Panther raid[i], there is no question of trying those responsible for their actual crime. The Cook County state attorney responsible for the raid, in which two men were killed, and the police officers who executed it, were eventually charged not with conspiracy to commit murder but with obstruction of justice—not, in other words, with killing people but with lying about it afterwards.

This is not an isolated instance of the miscarriage of justice. It is the natural result of a system under which the government has certain special rights above and beyond the rights of ordinary individuals—among them the right not to be held responsible for its mistakes. When these rights are taken away, when the agent of government is reduced to the status of a private citizen and has the same rights and responsibilities as his neighbors, what remains is no longer a government.

> ...a policeman...is protected by the legislative and judicial arms in the peculiar rights and prerogatives that go with his high office, including especially the right to jug the laity at his will, to sweat and mug them, and to subdue their resistance by beating out their brains.

H.L. MENCKEN, *PREJUDICES*

NATIONAL DEFENSE: THE HARD PROBLEM

National defense has traditionally been regarded, even by believers in a severely limited state, as a fundamental function of government. To understand why, one must first understand the economic concept of a public good and the difficulties of financing a public good without coercion.

A public good is an economic good which, by its nature, cannot be provided separately to each individual but must be provided, or not provided, to all members of a pre-existing group. A simple example is the control of a river whose flooding injures the land of many farmers in the valley below. There is no way that an entrepreneur who proposes to build a dam can protect only those farmers who agree to pay part of the cost of the dam. An individual farmer may refuse to pay, reasoning that if the others all pay he will be protected anyway and if they do not his contribution will not be enough to build the dam. The small probability that his contribution will make the difference between the dam being built and not being built, multiplied by the value to him of the dam, is not enough to justify the expenditure.

This is the traditional problem of the public good. It is a problem because if there are enough farmers like this, each acting rationally on a correct calculation of his own self-interest, the dam will not be built even if the combined value to all the farmers is more than the cost of building the dam.

In our society the usual solution is to use government force, taxation, to make those benefited (and others) pay for the dam. One problem with this solution is that the dam may be produced even when its total value is less than its cost. The government has no market mechanism for measuring the total value of the dam to the farmers. And since government decisions are made on political grounds, the government may choose to ignore cost and value entirely. In practice, public dams are often built even when the return on the capital spent building them, including a generous estimate of nonmonetary benefits, is far below the market rate of return on other investments.

There are several market solutions to the problem of providing a public good. For instance, the entrepreneur might estimate how much the dam is worth to each farmer, draw up a contract obligating each farmer to pay that amount if and only if every other farmer agrees to pay his share, and circulate it. Each farmer knows that if he refuses to sign the dam will not be built, since the contract has to be unanimous. It is therefore in his interest to sign.

In order for this to work, the entrepreneur must estimate correctly the value of the dam to each farmer. If he sets the price for one farmer too high, the dam will not be built. His job is made more difficult by those farmers who realize that it is in their interest to pretend that they think the dam of little value in order to have only a small part of the cost assigned to them.

A farmer interested in raising rice, for instance, might find occasional floods a useful supplement to his irrigation and have no interest in paying for flood control. The entrepreneur would have to remove such a farmer's name from the contract in order to have any chance at all of getting it signed. That is fair enough; there is no reason for the farmer to pay for something that is worthless to him. But as soon as word spreads, other farmers realize that an interest in growing rice can save them a lot of money. *The Rice Growers' Gazette* acquires new subscribers, all of whom are careful to leave their copies in prominent places around the house when the dam entrepreneur comes to call. Talk at the general store shifts from mowing hay to the relative virtues of different strains of rice. The entrepreneur is faced with the problem of figuring out which farmers are really interested in growing rice and which are only interested in being interested in growing rice, with the objective of growing wheat and getting flood control without paying for it. If he guesses wrong and puts a real rice farmer on his unanimous contract, it does not get signed. If he plays safe and takes everyone who pretends to be interested in rice off the contract, he may not be able to raise enough money.

The larger the public for a given public good, the harder it is to arrange such a unanimous contract successfully. The larger the difference between the value of the good and its price, on the other hand, the easier the entrepreneur's job. He can leave a generous margin for error by only listing the farmers of whom he is sure and charging each of them less than the dam is probably worth to him, yet still raise enough money.

Another way to provide a public good without coercion is by temporarily converting it into a private good. The entrepreneur could do this by purchasing most of the land in the valley before telling anyone that he is thinking of building a dam. He then builds the dam and resells the land at a higher price, since the dam raises the land's value. The increase in the value of the land measures the total benefit from the dam. If it is much larger than the cost of the dam, the entrepreneur makes a profit. There may be a few farmers who refuse to sell, but as long as the entrepreneur owns most of the land he receives most of the benefit.

Here again, the entrepreneur's job is harder the more people are involved. It becomes difficult to buy all the land before the owners realize what is happening and raise their price. Here also, the job is easier the bigger the difference between cost and benefit. If the benefit is more than twice the cost of building the dam, the entrepreneur makes a profit even if he can only buy half the land.

In both cases the transactions themselves have a cost and thus increase the effective cost of building the dam. Gathering the information needed to draw up a successful unanimous contract may be expensive. Buying up all the land in the valley involves substantial brokerage fees. Farmers who were not planning to sell must be paid more than the market price to compensate for their inconvenience. A clever entrepreneur, buying not the land but merely an option to buy at a predetermined price, can reduce such costs but not eliminate them.

How does this apply to national defense? Is it a public good? Can it be financed without coercion?

Some contemporary anarchists argue that national defense can be provided or not provided for each individual or at least each small group. One form of this argument is the assertion that national defense is unnecessary in an anarchist society, since there is no nation to defend. Unfortunately, there will still be nations to defend against, unless we postpone the abolition of our government until anarchy is universal. Defense against nations, in the present state of military technology, is a public good. It is all very well to fantasize about fighting the invader village by village, commune by commune, or corporation by corporation, according to the dreamer's particular brand of anarchy. A serious invader would inform each unit that if it resisted or failed to pay tribute it would be destroyed by a nuclear weapon. After the invader proved that he meant business, the citizens of the surviving communities would be eager to create the institutions, voluntary or otherwise, necessary to give the invader what he wanted.

Pending major technological change, defense against nations must be provided on a large enough scale to support retaliatory, and perhaps also defensive, nuclear forces. This makes it difficult to sell national defense on the free market. An ABM fired at a missile a thousand miles from its target cannot distinguish warheads aimed at those who have paid for defense from warheads aimed at those who have not. Even if defense is retaliatory and even if the retaliatory system is secure enough to hold its fire until it knows whether its customers have been hit, the problem remains. The citizens of New York, having paid their share of defense costs, can hardly look with equanimity on the H-bombing of Philadelphia, which has contributed not a penny. Not, at least, if the wind is blowing the wrong way.

So national defense—defense against nations—must defend areas of national size, whether or not they contain nations. It is thus a public good, and one with a very large public.

Can this public good be financed by some variant of one of the noncoercive methods I have discussed? It is not obvious how. The size of the public is so enormous that a unanimous contract is virtually impossible, especially since one secret supporter of a foreign power could prevent the whole deal. Buying up most of the land affected by national defense might be less difficult than negotiating a unanimous contract among 200 million people, but hardly easy, since the land must be purchased before sellers realize what is going on and increase their price. Raising enough money to buy the United States would be a hard project to keep secret. In addition, the transaction costs would be substantial—about $100 billion in realtor commissions for all the fixed property in the United States.

There is one favorable factor to help offset these difficulties. I estimate the cost of a minimal national defense at about $20 billion to $40 billion a year.[ii] The value to those protected is several hundred billion dollars a year. National defense is thus a public good worth about ten times what it costs; this may make it easier, although not easy, to devise some noncoercive way of financing it.

The problem would be simpler if it could be subdivided. Groups much smaller than our present population might be able to create defense organizations and finance them voluntarily. It would be in their interest to do so if such groups could defend themselves. Once such organizations existed, hundreds of them could combine, via unanimous contracts, to defend areas of national or even continental size. One could imagine an alternate history in which, as military technology developed, such voluntary arrangements evolved, just as coercive governments evolved in our history.

But in the present world small groups cannot defend themselves. They therefore have no incentive to develop voluntary arrangements to finance defense.

A solution to the problem of developing institutions that provide defense without the state, paradoxically enough, might be provided by the state itself. Suppose that over the next fifty or a hundred years private institutions gradually take over all governmental functions except defense. The state, without control of local institutions, might find the cost of collecting taxes substantial and be tempted to raise money in the manner of the French monarchy, by selling tax exemptions. It could offer to exempt any community from taxation in exchange for either a capital sum or an annual payment. Such a tax exemption would itself be a public good (defense, via bribery, from one's own state) for the community. Since the collection costs of taxation are high, the value of a tax exemption is greater than its cost. The members of the community might therefore find it in their interest to set up an organization designed to pay off the state. It could be financed voluntarily by one of the ways of financing public goods that I have described. It would probably pay an annual fee instead of a lump sum in order to make sure the state stayed bought.

Over a period of time, many or most communities develop such institutions. There then exists a group of organizations, voluntarily funded either by the interest on a capital endowment or by contractual agreements to pay on the part of members of the community and charged with the task of defending their communities. These organizations could then contract with each other to take over from the existing state the job of financing and providing national defense.

So one solution to the problem of national defense might be the development for some related purpose of local defense organizations. These must be organizations permanently endowed for the purpose of providing defense; they cannot be simply local firms with an interest in the protection of their territory, since such firms, having agreed to pay part of the cost of national defense, would be driven out of business by new competitors who had not. This is the problem with Morris and Linda Tannehill's idea of financing national defense through an insurance company or companies which would insure customers against injury by foreign states and finance national defense out of the money saved by defending their customers. Such an insurance company, in order to pay the cost of defense, would have to charge rates substantially higher than the real risk, given the existence of its defense system, justified. Since people living in the geographical area defended would be protected whether or not they were insured by that particular company, it would be in their interest either not to be insured or to be insured by a company that did not have to bear the burden of paying for defense and could therefore charge lower rates. The national defense insurance company would lose all its customers and go bankrupt, just as it would if it were simply selling national defense directly to individual customers who would be defended whether or not they paid.

The same difficulty occurs with Ayn Rand's suggestion of financing national defense by having the government charge for the use of its courts. In order to raise money for defense, such a government must either charge more than competing private court systems or provide a worse product. Such private courts, if permitted, would therefore drive the government out of the court business, depriving it of its source of income.

Miss Rand apparently expects her government to have a monopoly of the court (and protection) business. But if the government does not use coercion to keep out competitors there is no obvious reason why the sorts of institutions described earlier in this section should not arise. If the government does claim special rights that it does not give to private courts and rights enforcement agencies—for instance, the right of policemen to make mistakes and not be responsible for the damage done or the right of government courts to subpoena witnesses—then it becomes a government in my sense of the term (Miss Rand uses a different definition), an agency of legitimized coercion. Either the things the government does but forbids its competitors from doing are coercion, in which case it is coercing private citizens, or they are not coercion, in which case it coerces the private rights enforcement agencies by forbidding them to do the same (noncoercive) things. Either way, Rand's government must be coercive in order to work, so it is not a solution to the libertarian's problem of providing national defense without coercion.

Although local defense organizations must be endowed, they might evolve in ways other than those I have described. For instance, existing insurance companies would receive a capital windfall at the time an adequate national protection system was first constructed, since outstanding policies that had been sold at high rates under high risk conditions could be paid off under low risk conditions. They could use this windfall, which comes only from policies already written and thus represents only that small part of the benefit of defense which accrues in the near future to those already insured, to endow national defense. Such an endowment would not be sufficient to pay all the costs of national defense, unless it becomes far cheaper than it now is, but it might cover some of them.

There are other ways that part of the cost might be paid. Charities exist for the purpose of financing public goods. They currently collect billions of dollars a year. There is no reason why national defense should not be partly financed by charitable contributions. Historically it has been; in time of war people often donate money, labor, and weapons and purchase war bonds for more than their market value.

There is another common way of financing public goods that is intermediate between normal economic methods and charity. The best example is the institution of tipping. Customers at a restaurant leave a tip even if they have no intention of eating there again and therefore no personal interest in rewarding good service. The rewarding of good service is a public good; if everyone does it, everyone will benefit by the improved service, but if I do it at a restaurant where I rarely eat most of the benefit goes to the other people who use the restaurant. I tip partly because I realize this and view good restaurant service as a desirable goal—in effect, a worthy object of charity. A more important reason is that I feel I ought to tip; an internal feeling of obligation or external social pressure make me act according to a sort of implicit contract, an obligation to reward the waiter if he does a good job, even though I know that there is nothing forcing me to do so and that I will suffer no material loss if I do not. Similarly, if national defense were financed voluntarily, people would give money not as a matter of charity but because they felt that they were receiving something and *ought* to pay for it. As with tipping, the amount received might have some connection with how good a job they thought was being done. And, like tipping, people might feel obligated to give something even if the job were only barely satisfactory; however bad the service, few of us have the temerity to leave no tip at all.

How much are people willing to pay on such a basis? I do not know, but one way of getting a rough idea is by seeing how much they pay in tips under circumstances where they receive no direct benefit by tipping well. This is usually the case with taxis, since few of us expect to get the same driver twice, but only sometimes with restaurants, since many customers go to the same restaurant regularly. Taxi tips total about $150 million a year; all sorts of tips combined total about $2 billion. Such figures suggest that individual feelings of obligation, reinforced by social pressure, might provide a substantial fraction of the cost of defending against foreign enemies—a service most of us regard as more important than keeping up the quality of restaurant service.

Although national defense is primarily a public good, there are parts of it which can be sold separately to individuals or groups. Foreign states would probably treat a national defense agency as a government with respect to such matters as passports and extradition treaties. It could get some income by selling passports, arranging to extradite criminals from foreign countries at the request of local rights enforcement agencies, and similar enterprises.

In addition, there would be some areas which a national defense agency would have the option of defending or not defending. Hawaii, to take an extreme example, could be excluded from the nuclear umbrella covering the mainland. Communities on the edges of the defended area, although necessarily protected from nuclear attack by any national defense system, could be defended or not defended against conventional attack. A national defense agency could go into these areas and inform those individuals and corporations who had the most to gain by being defended (large landholders, insurance agencies, and the like) that they would have to pay a price for defense.

In all of these ways a national defense agency might raise enough money to finance national defense without taxation. Obviously, a system that depends on local agencies evolved for a different purpose or a ramshackle system financed by charity, passport sales, and threats to Hawaiian insurance companies is economically very imperfect. So is a system financed by coercion and run by government.

These arguments suggest that it may be possible to defend against foreign nations by voluntary means. They do not prove that it will be; I am only balancing one imperfect system against another and trying to guess which will work better. What if the balance goes the other way? What will I do if, when all other functions of our government have been abolished, I conclude that there is no effective way to defend against aggressive foreign governments save by national defense financed by taxes—financed, in other words, by money taken by force from the taxpayers?

In such a situation I would not try to abolish that last vestige of government. I do not like paying taxes, but I would rather pay them to Washington than to Moscow—the rates are lower. I would still regard the government as a criminal organization, but one which was, by a freak of fate, temporarily useful. It would be like a gang of bandits who, while occasionally robbing the villages in their territory, served to keep off other and more rapacious gangs. I do not approve of any government, but I will tolerate one so long as the only other choice is another and worse government. Meanwhile, I would do my best to develop voluntary institutions that might eventually take over the business of defense. That is what I meant when I said, near the beginning of this book, that I thought all government functions were divided into two classes, those we could do away with today and those we hope to be able to do away with tomorrow.

THE HARD PROBLEM: PART II

"A well regulated Militia being necessary to the security of a free State, the right of the people to keep and bear Arms, shall not be infringed." *(U.S. Constitution, Second Amendment)*

When I wrote ["National Defense: The Hard Problem"], more than forty years ago, I described national defense as the hard problem. Its logic has not changed and it is still hard, although less hard now that the Soviet Union no longer exists as a threat. But I have had additional thoughts since then of ways in which it might be solved. They are based on an odd variety of sources: the Second Amendment to the U.S. Constitution, paintball, the Society for Creative Anachronism, the Open Source movement, and a short story by Rudyard Kipling. I will start with the Second Amendment.

As I interpret the relevant history, the Second Amendment was intended as a solution to a problem strikingly demonstrated in the previous century. Oliver Cromwell, in winning the first English Civil War, had shown that a professional army could beat an amateur army, which was a good reason to have one. By winning the second English Civil War he demonstrated something else a professional army could do—and ruled for five years, until his death, as Lord Protector of the Commonwealth of England, aka military dictator.[iii] That was a good reason not to have a professional army. Damned if you did, damned if you didn't.

The solution hit upon by the founders was a compromise, a kludge. Combine a small professional army with a vast amateur militia consisting of all adult men of suitable age. In peacetime, give Congress and the professionals the job of producing enough coordination so that, in time of war, the state militias and the regulars could function tolerably well together:

> "The Congress shall have Power...To provide for organizing, arming, and disciplining the Militia, and for governing such Part of them as may be employed in the Service of the United States, reserving to the States respectively, the Appointment of the Officers, and the Authority of training the Militia according to the discipline prescribed by Congress;"

(Article I, Section 8)

If the professionals tried to seize power, they would be outnumbered by about three hundred to one. In case of war, the large size of the militia combined with the skills of the regulars would, with luck, make up for the militia's low quality. It was an ingenious solution and one that worked, judged by the nonexistence so far of either foreign conquest or military coup.

A similar solution might work for a stateless society. It too requires some way of dealing with foreign aggressors. It too faces the risk that a military sufficiently formidable to defend it might be formidable enough to seize power. It, unlike a state, faces the additional problem of funding a military without tax revenues. Amateurs are cheaper than professionals. Cutting your cost per soldier in half does not solve the problem of paying for the military if you need more than twice as many soldiers, but reducing it to zero does. Which brings in the next element of my plan.

I know quite a lot of people who not only train to fight without being paid, but pay the cost of their own equipment to do so; for many years I was one of them. It is true that our equipment, consisting of swords, shields, and armor, would be of little use in modern warfare—or medieval warfare, given that the swords are made out of rattan, not steel. But if the same resources of time, energy, and money were put into similar training with more up to date equipment, the result would be an amateur army, a militia numbering ten thousand or so, a first small step towards an adequate military.

The Society for Creative Anachronism, which fields armies of upwards of a thousand fighters a side for its annual Pennsic war, is one part of a much larger picture, people who engage in military exercises for fun. The sport of paintball, in which I have not participated, is another. The weaponry and skills are much closer to those relevant to modern warfare; paintball is sometimes used by the U.S. military for training. The number of people involved is also somewhat larger; according to industry estimates, more than ten million people in the U.S. played paintball at least once in 2006 and almost two million played at least fifteen times a year. Expenditures for equipment came to about four hundred million dollars. That is getting towards the numbers required for an adequate militia.

Paintball and SCA combat are fun and exciting. They could be even more fun if there was more of a point to them, if the participants believed that in addition to playing a game, they were also training to protect themselves, their loved ones, the society they lived in. Structure the institutions right and you have the labor for your militia and at least part of the gear for free. Not that different from the militia contemplated by the Constitution.

Which gets me to one of Rudyard Kipling's odder stories: "The Army of a Dream." The narrator has just returned to England after an extended absence. An old friend, a military officer, explains the changes to him.

The central one is very simple. War games, the kind you play in field or forest at a scale of an inch to an inch, have replaced football and cricket as England's most popular sport. Public schools compete with each other in fake battles refereed by volunteers from the military, with bets on the outcome.

'I should say it was,' said Pigeon suddenly. 'I was roped in the other day as an Adjustment Committee by the Kemptown Board School. I was riding under the Brighton racecourse, and I heard the whistle goin' for umpire——the regulation, two longs and two shorts. I didn't take any notice till an infant about a yard high jumped up from a furze-patch and shouted: "Guard! Guard! Come 'ere! I want you per-fessionally. Alf says 'e ain't outflanked. Ain't 'e a liar? Come an' look 'ow I've posted my men." You bet I looked! The young demon trotted by my stirrup and showed me his whole army (twenty of 'em) laid out under cover as nicely as you please round a cowhouse in a hollow. He kept on shouting: "I've drew Alf into there. 'Is persition ain't tenable. Say it ain't tenable, Guard!" I rode round the position, and Alf with his army came out of his cowhouse an' sat on the roof and protested like a——like a Militia Colonel; but the facts were in favour of my friend and I umpired according. Well, Alf abode by my decision. I explained it to him at length, and he solemnly paid up his head-money——farthing points if you please!'

Kipling is not describing an anarchist society—the initial training is compulsory and the system is elaborately interwoven with the professional military. But a central part of his vision is a society where learning military skills is something people want to do, enjoy doing, and get social as well as governmental rewards for doing.

'We're a free people. We get up and slay the man who says we aren't. But as a little detail we never mention, if we don't volunteer in some corps or another—as combatants if we're fit, as non-combatants if we ain't—till we're thirty-five—we don't vote, and we don't get poor-relief, and the women don't love us.'

The result is a society that can field an enormous army if needed but does not have to spend an enormous amount to create and maintain it. It is, of course, the army of a dream:

Then it came upon me, with no horror, but a certain mild wonder, that we had waited, Vee and I, that night for the body of Boy Bayley; and that Vee himself had died of typhoid in the spring of 1902. The rustling of the papers continued, but Bayley, shifting slightly, revealed to me the three-day-old wound on his left side that had soaked the ground about him.

Combine Kipling's imagined picture with the observation that millions of people already engage in military games and military training for fun. Add in the institutions of open source software,[iv] the system that produced Linux, the third most popular desktop operating system, as well as the Apache software that a majority of web servers run on. Open source software is developed by volunteers, mostly unpaid, for a mix of non-pecuniary reasons: to get the programs they want, to get prestige with their peers, to demonstrate their coding ability to potential employers. It provides a striking example of how sophisticated voluntary production in a non-market context can be.

Individual military equipment may be paid for by the individual hobbyist, but not many enthusiasts can afford a tank, an artillery piece, or whatever the equivalent will be in the military technology of the future. Companies, on the other hand...

Every April 15th, the platoon fielded by Apple Computer marches in the Liberty Day parade led by a robot tank flying Apple's banner—clear evidence that Apple is a responsible and patriotic company whose computers (and phones and tablets and watches) you should buy. Microsoft tries to do them one better, parading its larger platoon, also employee volunteers, under a swarm of armed robot drones.

I have offered a rough blueprint for fielding a very large militia at a very low cost. There remains the problem of coordination, of how to get millions of volunteers divided into thousands of independent units to work together. For that we require professionals—funded, as many functions are funded already, by charity. It should not take too much charity, since we do not need very many of them.

We are back with the military structure of the Second Amendment, a large militia of amateurs, a small cadre of professionals. In peacetime the professionals provide services to the amateurs, possibly for pay, making sure that all their communication devices can talk to each other, refereeing their mock combats, encouraging some degree of standardization of parts and ammunition. In war, if there is a war, the professionals make up the top cadre of officers.

I do not want to overstate my argument; when trying to analyze how imaginary institutions would work, certainty is in short supply. I have sketched one way in which a stateless society might defend itself. How well it, or other alternatives that have not occurred to me, worked would depend in part on how serious the threat was. When I wrote ["National Defense: The Hard Problem"], the threat was a Soviet Union allied to China, both equipped with arsenals of nuclear weapons. That was one of the reasons I was not at all sure that a future American anarchy could defend itself. Today the situation is rather different. Before the first Gulf War I added up the GNPs of the two sides. The odds were just about a hundred to one. Currently, the nearest thing the U.S. has to a serious enemy is Iran. Its GNP is about one fiftieth that of the U.S. and it is a long distance away. Mexico and Canada are closer, but neither seems likely to invade us. In that respect, the situation has sharply improved.

A second factor, one hard to predict, is the culture of the stateless society. The mechanism I described assumes a society most of whose inhabitants approve of it, want to defend it. Without that condition, it might work much less well.

On the other hand, that mechanism shares with the original system of the Constitution one important advantage over a more centralized system: The army it creates is poorly suited to pull off a military coup. The militia is made up of a multitude of different groups with different views and loyalties and it outnumbers the professionals a hundred, perhaps a thousand, to one.

---

i State attorney Hanrahan and his codefendants were eventually acquitted, but in 1982, thirteen years after the raid, a civil case by the survivors and the mothers of the two men who were killed was settled for $1.85 million, paid by the city, county and federal governments.

ii All numbers as of about 1970, when this chapter was written.

iii "King, Lords and Commons, land-lords and merchants, the City and the countryside, bishops and presbyters, the Scottish army, the Welsh people and the English Fleet, all now turned against the New Model Army. The Army beat the lot." (Winston Churchill, History of the English Speaking Peoples)

iv For a good summary account and analysis, see Eric Raymond, The Cathedral and the Bazaar.

Chapter 20

MURRAY ROTHBARD
Anatomy of the State (1974)

Murray Rothbard is popularly regarded as the godfather of anarcho-capitalism. Throughout his very long career, the economist, philosopher and historian covered an enormous swath of issues from the perspective of individual rights. His article "Anatomy of the State" is commonly cited as the one which gets readers to take a radically different perspective on the nature of the state from what they had been taught in school, and makes them realize just how malevolent government really is.

WHAT THE STATE IS NOT

The State is almost universally considered an institution of social service. Some theorists venerate the State as the apotheosis of society; others regard it as an amiable, though often inefficient, organization for achieving social ends; but almost all regard it as a necessary means for achieving the goals of mankind, a means to be ranged against the "private sector" and often winning in this competition of resources. With the rise of democracy, the identification of the State with society has been redoubled, until it is common to hear sentiments expressed which violate virtually every tenet of reason and common sense such as, "we are the government." The useful collective term "we" has enabled an ideological camouflage to be thrown over the reality of political life.

If "we are the government," then anything a government does to an individual is not only just and untyrannical but also "voluntary" on the part of the individual concerned. If the government has incurred a huge public debt which must be paid by taxing one group for the benefit of another, this reality of burden is obscured by saying that "we owe it to ourselves"; if the government conscripts a man, or throws him into jail for dissident opinion, then he is "doing it to himself" and, therefore, nothing untoward has occurred. Under this reasoning, any Jews murdered by the Nazi government were not murdered; instead, they must have "committed suicide," since they were the government (which was democratically chosen), and, therefore, anything the government did to them was voluntary on their part. One would not think it necessary to belabor this point, and yet the overwhelming bulk of the people hold this fallacy to a greater or lesser degree.

We must, therefore, emphasize that "we" are not the government; the government is not "us." The government does not in any accurate sense "represent" the majority of the people.[i] But, even if it did, even if 70 percent of the people decided to murder the remaining 30 percent, this would still be murder and would not be voluntary suicide on the part of the slaughtered minority.[ii] No organicist metaphor, no irrelevant bromide that "we are all part of one another," must be permitted to obscure this basic fact.

If, then, the State is not "us," if it is not "the human family" getting together to decide mutual problems, if it is not a lodge meeting or country club, what is it? Briefly, the State is that organization in society which attempts to maintain a monopoly of the use of force and violence in a given territorial area; in particular, it is the only organization in society that obtains its revenue not by voluntary contribution or payment for services rendered but by coercion. While other individuals or institutions obtain their income by production of goods and services and by the peaceful and voluntary sale of these goods and services to others, the State obtains its revenue by the use of compulsion; that is, by the use and the threat of the jailhouse and the bayonet.[iii] Having used force and violence to obtain its revenue, the State generally goes on to regulate and dictate the other actions of its individual subjects. One would think that simple observation of all States through history and over the globe would be proof enough of this assertion; but the miasma of myth has lain so long over State activity that elaboration is necessary.

WHAT THE STATE IS

Man is born naked into the world, and needing to use his mind to learn how to take the resources given him by nature, and to transform them (for example, by investment in "capital") into shapes and forms and places where the resources can be used for the satisfaction of his wants and the advancement of his standard of living. The only way by which man can do this is by the use of his mind and energy to transform resources ("production") and to exchange these products for products created by others. Man has found that, through the process of voluntary, mutual exchange, the productivity and hence, the living standards of all participants in exchange may increase enormously. The only "natural" course for man to survive and to attain wealth, therefore, is by using his mind and energy to engage in the production-and-exchange process. He does this, first, by finding natural resources, and then by transforming them (by "mixing his labor" with them, as Locke puts it), to make them his individual *property*, and then by exchanging this property for the similarly obtained property of others. The social path dictated by the requirements of man's nature, therefore, is the path of "property rights" and the "free market" of gift or exchange of such rights. Through this path, men have learned how to avoid the "jungle" methods of fighting over scarce resources so that A can only acquire them at the expense of B and, instead, to multiply those resources enormously in peaceful and harmonious production and exchange.

The great German sociologist Franz Oppenheimer pointed out that there are two mutually exclusive ways of acquiring wealth; one, the above way of production and exchange, he called the "economic means." The other way is simpler in that it does not require productivity; it is the way of seizure of another's goods or services by the use of force and violence. This is the method of one-sided confiscation, of theft of the property of others. This is the method which Oppenheimer termed "the political means" to wealth. It should be clear that the peaceful use of reason and energy in production is the "natural" path for man: the means for his survival and prosperity on this earth. It should be equally clear that the coercive, exploitative means is contrary to natural law; it is parasitic, for instead of adding to production, it subtracts from it. The "political means" siphons production off to a parasitic and destructive individual or group; and this siphoning not only subtracts from the number producing, but also lowers the producer's incentive to produce beyond his own subsistence. In the long run, the robber destroys his own subsistence by dwindling or eliminating the source of his own supply. But not only that; even in the short-run, the predator is acting contrary to his own true nature as a man.

We are now in a position to answer more fully the question: what is the *State*? The State, in the words of Oppenheimer, is the "organization of the political means"; it is the systematization of the predatory process over a given territory.[iv] For crime, at best, is sporadic and uncertain; the parasitism is ephemeral, and the coercive, parasitic lifeline may be cut off at any time by the resistance of the victims. The State provides a legal, orderly, systematic channel for the predation of private property; it renders certain, secure, and relatively "peaceful" the lifeline of the parasitic caste in society.[v] Since production must always precede predation, the free market is anterior to the State. The State has never been created by a "social contract"; it has always been born in conquest and exploitation. The classic paradigm was a conquering tribe pausing in its time-honored method of looting and murdering a conquered tribe, to realize that the time-span of plunder would be longer and more secure, and the situation more pleasant, if the conquered tribe were allowed to live and produce, with the conquerors settling among them as rulers exacting a steady annual tribute.[vi] One method of the birth of a State may be illustrated as follows: in the hills of southern "Ruritania," a bandit group manages to obtain physical control over the territory, and finally the bandit chieftain proclaims himself "King of the sovereign and independent government of South Ruritania"; and, if he and his men have the force to maintain this rule for a while, lo and behold! a new State has joined the "family of nations," and the former bandit leaders have been transformed into the lawful nobility of the realm.

HOW THE STATE PRESERVES ITSELF

Once a State has been established, the problem of the ruling group or "caste" is how to maintain their rule.[vii] While force is their *modus operandi*, their basic and long-run problem is ideological. For in order to continue in office, *any* government (not simply a "democratic" government) must have the support of the majority of its subjects. This support, it must be noted, need not be active enthusiasm; it may well be passive resignation as if to an inevitable law of nature. But support in the sense of acceptance of some sort it must be; else the minority of State rulers would eventually be outweighed by the active resistance of the majority of the public. Since predation must be supported out of the surplus of production, it is necessarily true that the class constituting the State—the full-time bureaucracy (and nobility)—must be a rather small minority in the land, although it may, of course, purchase allies among important groups in the population. Therefore, the chief task of the rulers is always to secure the active or resigned acceptance of the majority of the citizens.[viii] [ix]

Of course, one method of securing support is through the creation of vested economic interests. Therefore, the King alone cannot rule; he must have a sizable group of followers who enjoy the prerequisites of rule, for example, the members of the State apparatus, such as the full-time bureaucracy or the established nobility.[x] But this still secures only a minority of eager supporters, and even the essential purchasing of support by subsidies and other grants of privilege still does not obtain the consent of the majority. For this essential acceptance, the majority must be persuaded by *ideology* that their government is good, wise and, at least, inevitable, and certainly better than other conceivable alternatives. Promoting this ideology among the people is the vital social task of the "intellectuals." For the masses of men do not create their own ideas, or indeed think through these ideas independently; they follow passively the ideas adopted and disseminated by the body of intellectuals. The intellectuals are, therefore, the "opinion-molders" in society. And since it is precisely a molding of opinion that the State most desperately needs, the basis for age-old alliance between the State and the intellectuals becomes clear.

It is evident that the State needs the intellectuals; it is not so evident why intellectuals need the State. Put simply, we may state that the intellectual's livelihood in the free market is never too secure; for the intellectual must depend on the values and choices of the masses of his fellow men, and it is precisely characteristic of the masses that they are generally uninterested in intellectual matters. The State, on the other hand, is willing to offer the intellectuals a secure and permanent berth in the State apparatus; and thus a secure income and the panoply of prestige. For the intellectuals will be handsomely rewarded for the important function they perform for the State rulers, of which group they now become a part.[xi]

The alliance between the State and the intellectuals was symbolized in the eager desire of professors at the University of Berlin in the nineteenth century to form the "intellectual bodyguard of the House of Hohenzollern." In the present day, let us note the revealing comment of an eminent Marxist scholar concerning Professor Wittfogel's critical study of ancient Oriental despotism: "The civilization which Professor Wittfogel is so bitterly attacking was one which could make poets and scholars into officials."[xii] Of innumerable examples, we may cite the recent development of the "science" of strategy, in the service of the government's main violence-wielding arm, the military.[xiii] A venerable institution, furthermore, is the official or "court" historian, dedicated to purveying the rulers' views of their own and their predecessors' actions.[xiv]

Many and varied have been the arguments by which the State and its intellectuals have induced their subjects to support their rule. Basically, the strands of argument may be summed up as follows: (a) the State rulers are great and wise men (they "rule by divine right," they are the "aristocracy" of men, they are the "scientific experts"), much greater and wiser than the good but rather simple subjects, and (b) rule by the extent government is inevitable, absolutely necessary, and far better, than the indescribable evils that would ensue upon its downfall. The union of Church and State was one of the oldest and most successful of these ideological devices. The ruler was either anointed by God or, in the case of the absolute rule of many Oriental despotisms, was himself God; hence, any resistance to his rule would be blasphemy. The States' priestcraft performed the basic intellectual function of obtaining popular support and even worship for the rulers.[xv]

Another successful device was to instill fear of any alternative systems of rule or nonrule. The present rulers, it was maintained, supply to the citizens an essential service for which they should be most grateful: protection against sporadic criminals and marauders. For the State, to preserve its own monopoly of predation, did indeed see to it that private and unsystematic crime was kept to a minimum; the State has always been jealous of its own preserve. Especially has the State been successful in recent centuries in instilling fear of *other* State rulers. Since the land area of the globe has been parceled out among particular States, one of the basic doctrines of the State was to identify itself with the territory it governed. Since most men tend to love their homeland, the identification of that land and its people with the State was a means of making natural patriotism work to the State's advantage. If "Ruritania" was being attacked by "Walldavia," the first task of the State and its intellectuals was to convince the people of Ruritania that the attack was really upon *them* and not simply upon the ruling caste. In this way, a war between *rulers* was converted into a war between *peoples*, with each people coming to the defense of its rulers in the erroneous belief that the rulers were defending *them*. This device of "nationalism" has only been successful, in Western civilization, in recent centuries; it was not too long ago that the mass of subjects regarded wars as irrelevant battles between various sets of nobles.

Many and subtle are the ideological weapons that the State has wielded through the centuries. One excellent weapon has been tradition. The longer that the rule of a State has been able to preserve itself, the more powerful this weapon; for then, the X Dynasty or the Y State has the seeming weight of centuries of tradition behind it.[xvi] Worship of one's ancestors, then, becomes a none too subtle means of worship of one's ancient rulers. The greatest danger to the State is independent intellectual criticism; there is no better way to stifle that criticism than to attack any isolated voice, any raiser of new doubts, as a profane violator of the wisdom of his ancestors. Another potent ideological force is to deprecate the individual and exalt the collectivity of society. For since any given rule implies majority acceptance, any ideological danger to that rule can only start from one or a few independently-thinking individuals. The new idea, much less the new critical idea, must needs begin as a small minority opinion; therefore, the State must nip the view in the bud by ridiculing any view that defies the opinions of the mass. "Listen only to your brothers" or "adjust to society" thus become ideological weapons for crushing individual dissent.[xvii] By such measures, the masses will never learn of the nonexistence of their Emperor's clothes.[xviii] It is also important for the State to make its rule seem inevitable; even if its reign is disliked, it will then be met with passive resignation, as witness the familiar coupling of "death and taxes." One method is to induce historiographical determinism, as opposed to individual freedom of will. If the X Dynasty rules us, this is because the Inexorable Laws of History (or the Divine Will, or the Absolute, or the Material Productive Forces) have so decreed and nothing any puny individuals may do can change this inevitable decree. It is also important for the State to inculcate in its subjects an aversion to any "conspiracy theory of history;" for a search for "conspiracies" means a search for motives and an attribution of responsibility for historical misdeeds. If, however, any tyranny imposed by the State, or venality, or aggressive war, was caused *not* by the State rulers but by mysterious and arcane "social forces," or by the imperfect state of the world or, if in some way, *everyone* was responsible ("We Are All Murderers," proclaims one slogan), then there is no point to the people becoming indignant or rising up against such misdeeds. Furthermore, an attack on "conspiracy theories" means that the subjects will become more gullible in believing the "general welfare" reasons that are always put forth by the State for engaging in any of its despotic actions. A "conspiracy theory" can unsettle the system by causing the public to doubt the State's ideological propaganda.

Another tried and true method for bending subjects to the State's will is inducing guilt. Any increase in private well-being can be attacked as "unconscionable greed," "materialism," or "excessive affluence," profit-making can be attacked as "exploitation" and "usury," mutually beneficial exchanges denounced as "selfishness," and somehow with the conclusion always being drawn that more resources should be siphoned from the private to the "public sector." The induced guilt makes the public more ready to do just that. For while individual persons tend to indulge in "selfish greed," the failure of the State's rulers to engage in exchanges is supposed to signify their devotion to higher and nobler causes—parasitic predation being apparently morally and esthetically lofty as compared to peaceful and productive work.

In the present more secular age, the divine right of the State has been supplemented by the invocation of a new god, Science. State rule is now proclaimed as being ultrascientific, as constituting planning by experts. But while "reason" is invoked more than in previous centuries, this is not the true reason of the individual and his exercise of free will; it is still collectivist and determinist, still implying holistic aggregates and coercive manipulation of passive subjects by their rulers.

The increasing use of scientific jargon has permitted the State's intellectuals to weave obscurantist apologia for State rule that would have only met with derision by the populace of a simpler age. A robber who justified his theft by saying that he really helped his victims, by his spending giving a boost to retail trade, would find few converts; but when this theory is clothed in Keynesian equations and impressive references to the "multiplier effect," it unfortunately carries more conviction. And so the assault on common sense proceeds, each age performing the task in its own ways.

Thus, ideological support being vital to the State, it must unceasingly try to impress the public with its "legitimacy," to distinguish its activities from those of mere brigands. The unremitting determination of its assaults on common sense is no accident, for as Mencken vividly maintained:

> The average man, whatever his errors otherwise, at least sees clearly that government is something lying outside him and outside the generality of his fellow men—that it is a separate, independent, and hostile power, only partly under his control, and capable of doing him great harm. Is it a fact of no significance that robbing the government is everywhere regarded as a crime of less magnitude than robbing an individual, or even a corporation? . . . What lies behind all this, I believe, is a deep sense of the fundamental antagonism between the government and the people it governs. It is apprehended, not as a committee of citizens chosen to carry on the communal business of the whole population, but as a separate and autonomous corporation, mainly devoted to exploiting the population for the benefit of its own members. . . . When a private citizen is robbed, a worthy man is deprived of the fruits of his industry and thrift; when the government is robbed, the worst that happens is that certain rogues and loafers have less money to play with than they had before. The notion that they have earned that money is never entertained; to most sensible men it would seem ludicrous.[xix]

HOW THE STATE TRANSCENDS ITS LIMITS

As Bertrand de Jouvenel has sagely pointed out, through the centuries men have formed concepts designed to check and limit the exercise of State rule; and, one after another, the State, using its intellectual allies, has been able to transform these concepts into intellectual rubber stamps of legitimacy and virtue to attach to its decrees and actions. Originally, in Western Europe, the concept of divine sovereignty held that the kings may rule only according to divine law; the kings turned the concept into a rubber stamp of divine approval for any of the kings' actions. The concept of parliamentary democracy began as a popular check upon absolute monarchical rule; it ended with parliament being the essential part of the State and its every act totally sovereign. As de Jouvenel concludes:

> Many writers on theories of sovereignty have worked out one . . . of these restrictive devices. But in the end every single such theory has, sooner or later, lost its original purpose, and come to act merely as a springboard to Power, by providing it with the powerful aid of an invisible sovereign with whom it could in time successfully identify itself.[xx]

Similarly with more specific doctrines: the "natural rights" of the individual enshrined in John Locke and the Bill of Rights, became a statist "right to a job"; utilitarianism turned from arguments for liberty to arguments against resisting the State's invasions of liberty, etc.

Certainly the most ambitious attempt to impose limits on the State has been the Bill of Rights and other restrictive parts of the American Constitution, in which written limits on government became the fundamental law to be interpreted by a judiciary supposedly independent of the other branches of government. All Americans are familiar with the process by which the construction of limits in the Constitution has been inexorably broadened over the last century. But few have been as keen as Professor Charles Black to see that the State has, in the process, largely transformed judicial review itself from a limiting device to yet another instrument for furnishing ideological legitimacy to the government's actions. For if a judicial decree of "unconstitutional" is a mighty check to government power, an implicit or explicit verdict of "constitutional" is a mighty weapon for fostering public acceptance of ever-greater government power.

Professor Black begins his analysis by pointing out the crucial necessity of "legitimacy" for any government to endure, this legitimation signifying basic majority acceptance of the government and its actions.[xxi] Acceptance of legitimacy becomes a particular problem in a country such as the United States, where "substantive limitations are built into the theory on which the government rests." What is needed, adds Black, is a means by which the government can assure the public that its increasing powers are, indeed, "constitutional." And this, he concludes, has been the major historic function of judicial review.

Let Black illustrate the problem:

> The supreme risk [to the government] is that of disaffection and a feeling of outrage widely disseminated throughout the population, and loss of moral authority by the government as such, however long it may be propped up by force or inertia or the lack of an appealing and immediately available alternative. Almost everybody living under a government of limited powers, must sooner or later be subjected to some governmental action which as a matter of private opinion he regards as outside the power of government or positively forbidden to government. A man is drafted, though he finds nothing in the Constitution about being drafted. . . . A farmer is told how much wheat he can raise; he believes, and he discovers that some respectable lawyers believe with him, that the government has no more right to tell him how much wheat he can grow than it has to tell his daughter whom she can marry. A man goes to the federal penitentiary for saying what he wants to, and he paces his cell reciting . . . "Congress shall make no laws abridging the freedom of speech.". . . A businessman is told what he can ask, and must ask, for buttermilk.

The danger is real enough that each of these people (and who is not of their number?) will confront the concept of governmental limitation with the reality (as he sees it) of the flagrant overstepping of actual limits, and draw the obvious conclusion as to the status of his government with respect to legitimacy.[xxii]

This danger is averted by the State's propounding the doctrine that one agency must have the ultimate decision on constitutionality and that this agency, in the last analysis, must be part of the federal government.[xxiii] For while the seeming independence of the federal judiciary has played a vital part in making its actions virtual Holy Writ for the bulk of the people, it is also and ever true that the judiciary is part and parcel of the government apparatus and appointed by the executive and legislative branches. Black admits that this means that the State has set itself up as a judge in its own cause, thus violating a basic juridical principle for aiming at just decisions. He brusquely denies the possibility of any alternative.[xxiv]

Black adds:

> The problem, then, is to devise such governmental means of deciding as will [hopefully] reduce to a tolerable minimum the intensity of the objection that government is judge in its own cause. Having done this, you can only hope that this objection, *though theoretically still tenable* [italics mine], will practically lose enough of its force that the legitimating work of the deciding institution can win acceptance.[xxv]

In the last analysis, Black finds the achievement of justice and legitimacy from the State's perpetual judging of its own cause as "something of a miracle."[xxvi]

Applying his thesis to the famous conflict between the Supreme Court and the New Deal, Professor Black keenly chides his fellow pro-New Deal colleagues for their shortsightedness in denouncing judicial obstruction:

> [t]he standard version of the story of the New Deal and the Court, though accurate in its way, displaces the emphasis. . . . It concentrates on the difficulties; it almost forgets how the whole thing turned out. The upshot of the matter was [and this is what I like to emphasize] that after some twenty-four months of balking . . . the Supreme Court, without a single change in the law of its composition, or, indeed, in its actual manning, *placed the affirmative stamp of legitimacy on the New Deal, and on the whole new conception of government in America.*[xxvii]

In this way, the Supreme Court was able to put the quietus on the large body of Americans who had had strong constitutional objections to the New Deal:

> Of course, not everyone was satisfied. The Bonnie Prince Charlie of constitutionally commanded laissez-faire still stirs the hearts of a few zealots in the Highlands of choleric unreality. But there is no longer any significant or dangerous public doubt as to the constitutional power of Congress to deal as it does with the national economy...

We had no means, other than the Supreme Court, for imparting legitimacy to the New Deal.[xxviii]

As Black recognizes, one major political theorist who recognized—and largely in advance—the glaring loophole in a constitutional limit on government of placing the ultimate interpreting power in the Supreme Court was John C. Calhoun. Calhoun was not content with the "miracle," but instead proceeded to a profound analysis of the constitutional problem. In his *Disquisition*, Calhoun demonstrated the inherent tendency of the State to break through the limits of such a constitution:

> A written constitution certainly has many and considerable advantages, but it is a great mistake to suppose that the mere insertion of provisions to restrict and limit the power of the government, *without investing those for whose protection they are inserted with the means of enforcing their observance* [my italics] will be sufficient to prevent the major and dominant party from abusing its powers. Being the party in possession of the government, they will, from the same constitution of man which makes government necessary to protect society, be in favor of the powers granted by the constitution and opposed to the restrictions intended to limit them. . . . The minor or weaker party, on the contrary, would take the opposite direction and regard them [the restrictions] as essential to their protection against the dominant party. . . . But where there are no means by which they could compel the major party to observe the restrictions, the only resort left them would

be a strict construction of the constitution. . . . To this the major party would oppose a liberal construction. . . . It would be construction against construction—the one to contract and the other to enlarge the powers of the government to the utmost. But of what possible avail could the strict construction of the minor party be, against the liberal construction of the major, when the one would have all the power of the government to carry its construction into effect and the other be deprived of all means of enforcing its construction? In a contest so unequal, the result would not be doubtful. The party in favor of the restrictions would be overpowered. . . . The end of the contest would be the subversion of the constitution . . . the restrictions would ultimately be annulled and the government be converted into one of unlimited powers.[xxix]

One of the few political scientists who appreciated Calhoun's analysis of the Constitution was Professor J. Allen Smith. Smith noted that the Constitution was designed with checks and balances to limit any one governmental power and yet had then developed a Supreme Court with the monopoly of ultimate interpreting power. If the Federal Government was created to check invasions of individual liberty by the separate states, who was to check the Federal power? Smith maintained that implicit in the check-and-balance idea of the Constitution was the concomitant view that no one branch of government may be conceded the ultimate power of interpretation: "It was assumed by the people that the new government could not be permitted to determine the limits of its own authority, since this would make it, and not the Constitution, supreme."[xxx]

The solution advanced by Calhoun (and seconded, in this century, by such writers as Smith) was, of course, the famous doctrine of the "concurrent majority." If any substantial minority interest in the country, specifically a state government, believed that the Federal Government was exceeding its powers and encroaching on that minority, the minority would have the right to veto this exercise of power as unconstitutional. Applied to state governments, this theory implied the right of "nullification" of a Federal law or ruling within a state's jurisdiction.

In theory, the ensuing constitutional system would assure that the Federal Government check any state invasion of individual rights, while the states would check excessive Federal power over the individual. And yet, while limitations would undoubtedly be more effective than at present, there are many difficulties and problems in the Calhoun solution. If, indeed, a subordinate interest should rightfully have a veto over matters concerning it, then why stop with the states? Why not place veto power in counties, cities, wards? Furthermore, interests are not only sectional, they are also occupational, social, etc. What of bakers or taxi drivers or any other occupation? Should *they* not be permitted a veto power over their own lives? This brings us to the important point that the nullification theory confines its checks to *agencies of government* itself. Let us not forget that federal and state governments, and their respective branches, are still states, are still guided by their own state interests rather than by the interests of the private citizens. What is to prevent the Calhoun system from working in reverse, with states tyrannizing over their citizens and only vetoing the federal government when it tries to intervene to *stop* that state tyranny? Or for states to acquiesce in federal tyranny? What is to prevent federal and state governments from forming mutually profitable alliances for the joint exploitation of the citizenry? And even if the private occupational groupings were to be given some form of "functional" representation in government, what is to prevent them from using the State to gain subsidies and other special privileges for themselves or from imposing compulsory cartels on their own members?

In short, Calhoun does not push his pathbreaking theory on concurrence far enough: he does not push it down to the *individual* himself. If the individual, after all, is the one whose rights are to be protected, then a consistent theory of concurrence would imply veto power by every individual; that is, some form of "unanimity principle." When Calhoun wrote that it should be "impossible to put or to keep it [the government] in action without the concurrent consent of all," he was, perhaps unwittingly, implying just such a conclusion.[xxxi] But such speculation begins to take us away from our subject, for down this path lie political systems which could hardly be called "States" at all.[xxxii] For one thing, just as the right of nullification for a state logically implies its right of *secession*, so a right of individual nullification would imply the right of any individual to "secede" from the State under which he lives.[xxxiii]

Thus, the State has invariably shown a striking talent for the expansion of its powers beyond any limits that might be imposed upon it. Since the State necessarily lives by the compulsory confiscation of private capital, and since its expansion necessarily involves ever-greater incursions on private individuals and private enterprise, we must assert that the State is profoundly and inherently *anti*capitalist. In a sense, our position is the reverse of the Marxist dictum that the State is the "executive committee" of the ruling class in the present day, supposedly the capitalists. Instead, the State—the organization of the political means—constitutes, and is the source of, the "ruling class" (rather, ruling caste), and is in permanent opposition to *genuinely* private capital. We may, therefore, say with de Jouvenel:

> Only those who know nothing of any time but their own, who are completely in the dark as to the manner of Power's behaving through thousands of years, would regard these proceedings [nationalization, the income tax, etc.] as the fruit of a particular set of doctrines. They are in fact the normal manifestations of Power, and differ not at all in their nature from Henry VIII's confiscation of the monasteries. The same principle is at work; the hunger for authority, the thirst for resources; and in all of these operations the same characteristics are present, including the rapid elevation of the dividers of the spoils. Whether it is Socialist or whether it is not, Power must always be at war with the capitalist authorities and despoil the capitalists of their accumulated wealth; in doing so it obeys the law of its nature.[xxxiv]

WHAT THE STATE FEARS

What the State fears above all, of course, is any fundamental threat to its own power and its own existence. The death of a State can come about in two major ways: (a) through conquest by another State, or (b) through revolutionary overthrow by its own subjects—in short, by war or revolution. War and revolution, as the two basic threats, invariably arouse in the State rulers their maximum efforts and maximum propaganda among the people. As stated above, any way must always be used to mobilize the people to come to the State's defense in the belief that they are defending themselves. The fallacy of the idea becomes evident when conscription is wielded against those who refuse to "defend" themselves and are, therefore, forced into joining the State's military band: needless to add, no "defense" is permitted them against this act of "their own" State.

In war, State power is pushed to its ultimate, and, under the slogans of "defense" and "emergency," it can impose a tyranny upon the public such as might be openly resisted in time of peace. War thus provides many benefits to a State, and indeed every modern war has brought to the warring peoples a permanent legacy of increased State burdens upon society. War, moreover, provides to a State tempting opportunities for conquest of land areas over which it may exercise its monopoly of force. Randolph Bourne was certainly correct when he wrote that "war is the health of the State," but to any particular State a war may spell either health or grave injury.[xxxv]

We may test the hypothesis that the State is largely interested in protecting *itself* rather than its subjects by asking: which category of crimes does the State pursue and punish most intensely—those against private citizens or those against *itself*? The gravest crimes in the State's lexicon are almost invariably not invasions of private person or property, but dangers to its *own* contentment, for example, treason, desertion of a soldier to the enemy, failure to register for the draft, subversion and subversive conspiracy, assassination of rulers and such economic crimes against the State as counterfeiting its money or evasion of its income tax. Or compare the degree of zeal devoted to pursuing the man who assaults a policeman, with the attention that the State pays to the assault of an ordinary citizen. Yet, curiously, the State's openly assigned priority to its *own* defense against the public strikes few people as inconsistent with its presumed *raison d'etre*.[xxxvi]

HOW STATES RELATE TO ONE ANOTHER

Since the territorial area of the earth is divided among different States, inter-State relations must occupy much of a State's time and energy. The natural tendency of a State is to expand its power, and externally such expansion takes place by conquest of a territorial area. Unless a territory is stateless or uninhabited, any such expansion involves an inherent conflict of interest between one set of State rulers and another. Only one set of rulers can obtain a monopoly of coercion over any given territorial area at any one time: complete power over a territory by State X can only be obtained by the expulsion of State Y. War, while risky, will be an ever-present tendency of States, punctuated by periods of peace and by shifting alliances and coalitions between States.

We have seen that the "internal" or "domestic" attempt to limit the State, in the seventeenth through nineteenth centuries, reached its most notable form in constitutionalism. Its "external," or "foreign affairs," counterpart was the development of "international law," especially such forms as the "laws of war" and "neutrals' rights."[xxxvii] Parts of international law were originally purely private, growing out of the need of merchants and traders everywhere to protect their property and adjudicate disputes. Examples are admiralty law and the law merchant. But even the governmental rules emerged voluntarily and were not imposed by any international super-State. The object of the "laws of war" was to limit inter-State *destruction to the State apparatus itself*, thereby preserving the innocent "civilian" public from the slaughter and devastation of war. The object of the development of neutrals' rights was to preserve private civilian international commerce, even with "enemy" countries, from seizure by one of the warring parties. The overriding aim, then, was to limit the extent of any war, and, particularly to limit its destructive impact on the private citizens of the neutral and even the warring countries.

The jurist F.J.P. Veale charmingly describes such "civilized warfare" as it briefly flourished in fifteenth-century Italy:

> the rich burghers and merchants of medieval Italy were too busy making money and enjoying life to undertake the hardships and dangers of soldiering themselves. So they adopted the practice of hiring mercenaries to do their fighting for them, and, being thrifty, businesslike folk, they dismissed their mercenaries immediately after their services could be dispensed with. Wars were, therefore, fought by armies hired for each campaign. . . . For the first time, soldiering became a reasonable and comparatively harmless profession. The generals of that period maneuvered against each other, often with consummate skill, but when one had won the advantage, his opponent generally either retreated or surrendered. It

was a recognized rule that a town could only be sacked if it offered resistance: immunity could always be purchased by paying a ransom. . . . As one natural consequence, no town ever resisted, it being obvious that a government too weak to defend its citizens had forfeited their allegiance. Civilians had little to fear from the dangers of war which were the concern only of professional soldiers.[xxxviii]

The well-nigh absolute separation of the private civilian from the State's wars in eighteenth-century Europe is highlighted by Nef:

Even postal communications were not successfully restricted for long in wartime. Letters circulated without censorship, with a freedom that astonishes the twentieth-century mind. . . . The subjects of two warring nations talked to each other if they met, and when they could not meet, corresponded, not as enemies but as friends. The modern notion hardly existed that . . . subjects of any enemy country are partly accountable for the belligerent acts of their rulers. Nor had the warring rulers any firm disposition to stop communications with subjects of the enemy. The old inquisitorial practices of espionage in connection with religious worship and belief were disappearing, and no comparable inquisition in connection with political or economic communications was even contemplated. Passports were originally created to provide safe conduct in time of war. During most of the eighteenth century it seldom occurred to Europeans to abandon their travels in a foreign country which their own was fighting.[xxxix]

And trade being increasingly recognized as beneficial to both parties; eighteenth-century warfare also counterbalances a considerable amount of "trading with the enemy."[xl]

How far States have transcended rules of civilized warfare in this century needs no elaboration here. In the modern era of total war, combined with the technology of total destruction, the very idea of keeping war limited to the State *apparati* seems even more quaint and obsolete than the original Constitution of the United States.

When States are not at war, agreements are often necessary to keep frictions at a minimum. One doctrine that has gained curiously wide acceptance is the alleged "sanctity of treaties." This concept is treated as the counterpart of the "sanctity of contract." But a treaty and a genuine contract have nothing in common. A contract transfers, in a precise manner, titles to private property. Since a government does not, in any proper sense, "own" its territorial area, any agreements that it concludes do not confer titles to property. If, for example, Mr. Jones sells or gives his land to Mr. Smith, Jones's heir cannot legitimately descend upon Smith's heir and claim the land as rightfully his. The property title has already been transferred. Old Jones's contract is automatically binding upon young Jones, because the former had already transferred the property; young Jones, therefore, has no property claim. Young Jones can only claim that which he has inherited from old Jones, and old Jones can only bequeath property which he still owns. But if, at a certain date, the government of, say, Ruritania is coerced or even bribed by the government of Waldavia into giving up some of its territory, it is absurd to claim that the governments or inhabitants of the two countries are forever barred from a claim to reunification of Ruritania on the grounds of the sanctity of a treaty. Neither the people nor the land of northwest Ruritania are owned by either of the two governments. As a corollary, one government can certainly not bind, by the dead hand of the past, a later government through treaty. A revolutionary government which overthrew the king of Ruritania could, similarly, hardly be called to account for the king's actions or debts, for a government is not, as is a child, a true "heir" to its predecessor's property.

HISTORY AS A RACE BETWEEN STATE POWER AND SOCIAL POWER

Just as the two basic and mutually exclusive interrelations between men are peaceful cooperation or coercive exploitation, production or predation, so the history of mankind, particularly its economic history, may be considered as a contest between these two principles. On the one hand, there is creative productivity, peaceful exchange and cooperation; on the other, coercive dictation and predation over those social relations. Albert Jay Nock happily termed these contesting forces: "social power" and "State power."[xli] Social power is man's power over nature, his cooperative transformation of nature's resources and insight into nature's laws, for the benefit of all participating individuals. Social power is the *power over nature*, the living standards achieved by men in mutual exchange. State power, as we have seen, is the coercive and parasitic seizure of this production—a draining of the fruits of society for the benefit of nonproductive (actually antiproductive) rulers. While social power is over nature, State power is *power over man*. Through history, man's productive and creative forces have, time and again, carved out new ways of transforming nature for man's benefit. These have been the times when social power has spurted ahead of State power, and when the degree of State encroachment over society has considerably lessened. But always, after a greater or smaller time lag, the State has moved into these new areas, to cripple and confiscate social power once more.[xlii] If the seventeenth through the nineteenth centuries were, in many countries of the West, times of accelerating social power, and a corollary increase in freedom, peace, and material welfare, the twentieth century has been primarily an age in which State power has been catching up—with a consequent reversion to slavery, war, and destruction.[xliii]

In this century, the human race faces, once again, the virulent reign of the State—of the State now armed with the fruits of man's creative powers, confiscated and perverted to its own aims. The last few centuries were times when men tried to place constitutional and other limits on the State, only to find that such limits, as with all other attempts, have failed. Of all the numerous forms that governments have taken over the centuries, of all the concepts and institutions that have been tried, none has succeeded in keeping the State in check. The problem of the State is evidently as far from solution as ever. Perhaps new paths of inquiry must be explored, if the successful, final solution of the State question is ever to be attained.[xliv]

---

[i] *We cannot, in this chapter, develop the many problems and fallacies of "democracy." Suffice it to say here that an individual's true agent or "representative" is always subject to that individual's orders, can be dismissed at any time and cannot act contrary to the interests or wishes of his principal. Clearly, the "representative" in a democracy can never fulfill such agency functions, the only ones consonant with a libertarian society.*

[ii] *Social democrats often retort that democracy—majority choice of rulers—logically implies that the majority must leave certain freedoms to the minority, for the minority might one day become the majority. Apart from other flaws, this argument obviously does*

not hold where the minority cannot become the majority, for example, when the minority is of a different racial or ethnic group from the majority.

[iii] *Joseph A. Schumpeter, Capitalism, Socialism, and Democracy (New York: Harper and Bros., 1942), p. 198.*

> *The friction or antagonism between the private and the public sphere was intensified from the first by the fact that...the State has been living on a revenue which was being produced in the private sphere for private purposes and had to be deflected from these purposes by political force. The theory which construes taxes on the analogy of club dues or of the purchase of the service of, say, a doctor only proves how far removed this part of the social sciences is from scientific habits of mind.*

Also see Murray N. Rothbard, "The Fallacy of the 'Public Sector,'" New Individualist Review (Summer, 1961): 3ff.

[iv] *Franz Oppenheimer, The State (New York: Vanguard Press, 1926) pp. 24-27:*

> *There are two fundamentally opposed means whereby man, requiring sustenance, is impelled to obtain the necessary means for satisfying his desires. These are work and robbery, one's own labor and the forcible appropriation of the labor of others...I propose in the following discussion to call one's own labor and the equivalent exchange of one's own labor for the labor of others, the "economic means" for the satisfaction of need while the unrequited appropriation of the labor of others will be called the "political means".....The State is an organization of the political means. No State, therefore, can come into being until the economic means has created a definite number of objects for the satisfaction of needs, which objects may be taken away or appropriated by warlike robbery.*

[v] *Albert Jay Nock wrote vividly that*

> *the State claims and exercises the monopoly of crime...It forbids private murder, but itself organizes murder on a colossal scale. It punishes private theft, but itself lays unscrupulous hands on anything it wants, whether the property of citizen or of alien.*

Nock, On Doing the Right Thing, and Other Essays (New York: Harper and Bros., 1929), p. 143; quoted in Jack Schwartzman, "Albert Jay Nock—A Superfluous Man," Faith and Freedom (December, 1953): 11.

[vi] *Oppenheimer, The State, p. 15:*

> *What, then, is the State as a sociological concept? The State, completely in its genesis...is a social institution, forced by a victorious group of men on a defeated group, with the sole purpose of regulating the dominion of the victorious group of men on a defeated group, and securing itself against revolt from within and attacks from abroad. Teleologically, this dominion had no other purpose than the economic exploitation of the vanquished by the victors.*

And de Jouvenel has written:

> *"the State is in essence the result of the successes achieved by a band of brigands who superimpose themselves on small, distinct societies." Bertrand de Jouvenel, On Power (New York: Viking Press, 1949), pp. 100-01.*

vii On the crucial distinction between "caste," a group with privileges or burdens coercively granted or imposed by the State and the Marxian concept of "class" in society, see Ludwig von Mises, Theory and History (New Haven, Conn.: Yale University Press, 1957), pp. 112ff.

viii Such acceptance does not, of course, imply that the State rule has become "voluntary"; for even if the majority support be active and eager, this support is not unanimous by every individual.

ix That every government, no matter how "dictatorial" over individuals, must secure such support has been demonstrated by such acute political theorists as Étienne de la Boétie, David Hume, and Ludwig von Mises. Thus, cf. David Hume, "Of the First Principles of Government," in Essays, Literary, Moral and Political (London: Ward, Locke, and Taylor, n.d.), p. 23; Etienne de la Boétie, Anti-Dictator (New York: Columbia University Press, 1942), pp. 8-9; Ludwig von Mises, Human Action (Auburn, Ala.: Mises Institute, 1998), pp. 188ff. For more on the contribution to the analysis of the State by la Boétie, see Oscar Jaszi and John D. Lewis, Against the Tyrant (Glencoe, Ill.: The Free Press, 1957), pp. 55-57.

x La Boétie, Anti-Dictator, pp. 43-44.

> Whenever a ruler makes himself dictator . . . all those who are corrupted by burning ambition or extraordinary avarice, these gather around him and support him in order to have a share in the booty and to constitute themselves petty chiefs under the big tyrant.

xi This by no means implies that all intellectuals ally themselves with the State. On aspects of the alliance of intellectuals and the State, cf. Bertrand de Jouvenel, "The Attitude of the Intellectuals to the Market Society," The Owl (January, 1951): 19-27; idem, "The Treatment of Capitalism by Continental Intellectuals," in F.A. Hayek, ed., Capitalism and the Historians (Chicago: University of Chicago Press, 1954), pp. 93-123; reprinted in George B. de Huszar, The Intellectuals (Glencoe, Ill.: The Free Press, 1960), pp. 385-99; and Schumpeter, Imperialism and Social Classes (New York: Meridian Books, 1975), pp. 143-55.

xii Wittfogel notes the Confucian doctrine that the glory of the ruling class rested on its gentleman scholar-bureaucrat officials, destined to be professional rulers dictating to the mass of the populace. Karl A. Wittfogel, Oriental Despotism (New Haven, Conn.: Yale University Press, 1957), pp. 320-21 and passim. For an attitude contrasting to Needham's, cf. John Lukacs, "Intellectual Class or Intellectual Profession?" in de Huszar, The Intellectuals, pp. 521-22.

xiii Jeanne Ribs, "The War Plotters," Liberation (August, 1961): 13. "[s]trategists insist that their occupation deserves the 'dignity of the academic counterpart of the military profession.'" Also see Marcus Raskin, "The Megadeath Intellectuals," New York Review of Books (November 14, 1963): 6-7.

xiv Thus the historian Conyers Read, in his presidential address, advocated the suppression of historical fact in the service of "democratic" and national values. Read proclaimed that "total war, whether it is hot or cold, enlists everyone and calls upon *everyone to play his part. The historian is not freer from this obligation than the physicist." Read, "The Social Responsibilities of the Historian," American Historical Review (1951): 283ff. For a critique of Read and other aspects of court history, see Howard K. Beale, "The Professional Historian: His Theory and Practice," The Pacific Historical Review (August, 1953): 227-55. Also cf. Herbert Butterfield, "Official History: Its Pitfalls and Criteria," History and Human Relations (New York: Macmillan, 1952), pp. 182-224; and Harry Elmer Barnes, The Court Historians Versus Revisionism (n.d.), pp. 2ff.*

[xv] *Cf. Wittfogel, Oriental Despotism, pp. 87-100. On the contrasting roles of religion vis-à-vis the State in ancient China and Japan, see Norman Jacobs, The Origin of Modern Capitalism and Eastern Asia (Hong Kong: Hong Kong University Press, 1958), pp. 161-94.*

[xvi] *De Jouvenel, On Power, p. 22:*

> *The essential reason for obedience is that it has become a habit of the species... Power is for us a fact of nature. From the earliest days of recorded history it has always presided over human destinies...the authorities which ruled [societies] in former times did not disappear without bequeathing to their successors their privilege nor without leaving in men's minds imprints which are cumulative in their effect. The succession of governments which, in the course of centuries, rule the same society may be looked on as one underlying government which takes on continuous accretions.*

[xvii] *On such uses of the religion of China, see Norman Jacobs, passim.*

[xviii] *H.L. Mencken, A Mencken Chrestomathy (New York: Knopf, 1949), p. 145:*

> *All [government] can see in an original idea is potential change, and hence an invasion of its prerogatives. The most dangerous man, to any government, is the man who is able to think things out for himself, without regard to the prevailing superstitions and taboos. Almost inevitably he comes to the conclusion that the government he lives under is dishonest, insane and intolerable, and so, if he is romantic, he tries to change it. And even if he is not romantic personally he is very apt to spread discontent among those who are.*

[xix] *Ibid., pp. 146-47.*

[xx] *De Jouvenel, On Power, pp. 27ff.*

[xxi] *Charles L. Black. Jr., The People and the Court (New York: Macmillan, 1960), pp. 35ff.*

[xxii] *Ibid., pp. 42-43.*

[xxiii] *Ibid., p. 52:*

> *The prime and most necessary function of the [Supreme] Court has been that of validation, not that of invalidation. What a government of limited powers needs, at the beginning and forever, is some means of satisfying the people that it has taken all steps humanly possible to stay within its powers. This is the condition of its legitimacy, and its legitimacy, in the long run, is the condition of its life. And the Court, through its history, has acted as the legitimation of the government.*

xxiv *To Black, this "solution," while paradoxical, is blithely self-evident:*

the final power of the State...must stop where the law stops it. And who shall set the limit, and who shall enforce the stopping, against the mightiest power? Why, the State itself, of course, through its judges and its laws. Who controls the temperate? Who teaches the wise? (Ibid., pp. 32-33)

And:

Where the questions concern governmental power in a sovereign nation, it is not possible to select an umpire who is outside government. Every national government, so long as it is a government, must have the final say on its own power. (Ibid., pp. 48-49)

xxv *Ibid., p. 49.*

xxvi *This ascription of the miraculous to government is reminiscent of James Burnham's justification of government by mysticism and irrationality:*

In ancient times, before the illusions of science had corrupted traditional wisdom, the founders of cities were known to be gods or demigods...Neither the source nor the justification of government can be put in wholly rational terms... why should I accept the hereditary or democratic or any other principle of legitimacy? Why should a principle justify the rule of that man over me?...I accept the principle, well...because I do, because that is the way it is and has been.

James Burnham, Congress and the American Tradition (Chicago: Regnery, 1959), pp. 3-8. But what if one does not accept the principle? What will "the way" be then?

xxvii *Black, The People and the Court, p. 64.*

xxviii *Ibid., p. 65.*

xxix *John C. Calhoun, A Disquisition on Government (New York: Liberal Arts Press, 1953), pp. 25-27. Also cf. Murray N. Rothbard, "Conservatism and Freedom: A Libertarian Comment," Modern Age (Spring, 1961): 219.*

xxx *J. Allen Smith, The Growth and Decadence of Constitutional Government (New York: Henry Holt, 1930), p. 88. Smith added:*

it was obvious that where a provision of the Constitution was designed to limit the powers of a governmental organ, it could be effectively nullified if its interpretation and enforcement are left to the authorities as it designed to restrain. Clearly, common sense required that no organ of the government should be able to determine its own powers. Clearly, common sense and "miracles" dictate very different views of government (p. 87).

xxxi *Calhoun, A Disquisition on Government, pp. 20-21.*

xxxii *In recent years, the unanimity principle has experienced a highly diluted revival, particularly in the writings of Professor James Buchanan. Injecting unanimity into the present situation, however, and applying it only to changes in the status quo and not to existing laws, can only result in another transformation of a limiting concept into a rubber stamp for the State. If the unanimity principle is to be applied only to changes in laws and edicts, the nature of the initial "point of origin" then makes all the difference.*

Cf. James Buchanan and Gordon Tullock, The Calculus of Consent (Ann Arbor: University of Michigan Press, 1962), passim.

xxxiii *Cf. Herbert Spencer, "The Right to Ignore the State," in Social Statics (New York: D. Appleton, 1890), pp. 229-39.*

xxxiv *De Jouvenel, On Power, p. 171.*

xxxv *We have seen that essential to the State is support by the intellectuals, and this includes support against their two acute threats. Thus, on the role of American intellectuals in America's entry into World War I, see Randolph Bourne, "The War and the Intellectuals," in The History of a Literary Radical and Other Papers (New York: S.A. Russell, 1956), pp. 205-22. As Bourne states, a common device of intellectuals in winning support for State actions, is to channel any discussion within the limits of basic State policy and to discourage any fundamental or total critique of this basic framework.*

xxxvi *As Mencken puts it in his inimitable fashion:*

This gang ("the exploiters constituting the government") is well nigh immune to punishment. Its worst extortions, even when they are baldly for private profit, carry no certain penalties under our laws. Since the first days of the Republic, less than a few dozen of its members have been impeached, and only a few obscure understrappers have ever been put into prison. The number of men sitting at Atlanta and Leavenworth for revolting against the extortions of the government is always ten times as great as the number of government officials condemned for oppressing the taxpayers to their own gain. (Mencken, A Mencken Chrestomathy, pp. 147-48)

For a vivid and entertaining description of the lack of protection for the individual against incursion of his liberty by his "protectors," see H.L. Mencken, "The Nature of Liberty," in Prejudices: A Selection (New York: Vintage Books, 1958), pp. 138-43.

xxxvii *This is to be distinguished from modern international law, with its stress on maximizing the extent of war through such concepts as "collective security."*

xxxviii *F.J.P. Veale, Advance to Barbarism (Appleton, Wis.: C.C. Nelson, 1953), p. 63. Similarly, Professor Nef writes of the War of Don Carlos waged in Italy between France, Spain, and Sardinia against Austria, in the eighteenth century:*

at the siege of Milan by the allies and several weeks later at Parma . . . the rival armies met in a fierce battle outside the town. In neither place were the sympathies of the inhabitants seriously moved by one side or the other. Their only fear as that the troops of either army should get within the gates and pillage. The fear proved groundless. At Parma the citizens ran to the town walls to watch the battle in the open country beyond. (John U. Nef, War and Human Progress [Cambridge, Mass.: Harvard University Press, 1950], p. 158.

Also cf. Hoffman Nickerson, Can We Limit War? [New York: Frederick A. Stoke, 1934])

xxxix *Nef, War and Human Progress, p. 162.*

---

xl *Ibid., p. 161. On advocacy of trading with the enemy by leaders of the American Revolution, see Joseph Dorfman, The Economic Mind in American Civilization (New York: Viking Press, 1946), vol. 1, pp. 210-11.*

xli *On the concepts of State power and social power, see Albert J. Nock, Our Enemy the State (Caldwell, Idaho: Caxton Printers, 1946). Also see Nock, Memoirs of a Superfluous Man (New York: Harpers, 1943), and Frank Chodorov, The Rise and Fall of Society (New York: Devin-Adair, 1959).*

xlii *Amidst the flux of expansion or contraction, the State always makes sure that it seizes and retains certain crucial "command posts" of the economy and society. Among these command posts are a monopoly of violence, monopoly of the ultimate judicial power, the channels of communication and transportation (post office, roads, rivers, air routes), irrigated water in Oriental despotisms, and education—to mold the opinions of its future citizens. In the modern economy, money is the critical command post.*

xliii *This parasitic process of "catching up" has been almost openly proclaimed by Karl Marx, who conceded that socialism must be established through seizure of capital previously accumulated under capitalism.*

xliv *Certainly, one indispensable ingredient of such a solution must be the sundering of the alliance of intellectual and State, through the creation of centers of intellectual inquiry and education, which will be independent of State power. Christopher Dawson notes that the great intellectual movements of the Renaissance and the Enlightenment were achieved by working outside of, and sometimes against, the entrenched universities. These academia of the new ideas were established by independent patrons. See Christopher Dawson, The Crisis of Western Education (New York: Sheed and Ward, 1961).*

Chapter 21

JOHN HASNAS
The Myth of the Rule of Law (1995)

It is taken as a given that a society without an objective monopoly of law via the state is the definition of chaos. Georgetown University law professor John Hasnas demonstrates that it is the precise opposite that is true: Namely, that "objective" law is both an incoherent concept and a utopian fantasy impossible to put into practice. For those minarchists holding on to their ideal of the smallest state possible, here is the anarchist rebuttal.

I

Stop! Before reading this article, please take the following quiz.

The First Amendment to the Constitution of the United States provides, in part: *"Congress shall make no law . . . abridging the freedom of speech, or of the press; . . . ."*[x]

On the basis of your personal understanding of this sentence's meaning (not your knowledge of constitutional law), please indicate whether you believe the following sentences to be true or false.

> *1) In time of war, a federal statute may be passed prohibiting citizens from revealing military secrets to the enemy.*

311

2) The President may issue an executive order prohibiting public criticism of his administration.
3) Congress may pass a law prohibiting museums from exhibiting photographs and paintings depicting homosexual activity.
4) A federal statute may be passed prohibiting a citizen from falsely shouting "fire" in a crowded theater.
5) Congress may pass a law prohibiting dancing to rock and roll music.
6) The Internal Revenue Service may issue a regulation prohibiting the publication of a book explaining how to cheat on your taxes and get away with it.
7) Congress may pass a statute prohibiting flag burning.

Thank you. You may now read on.

In his novel *1984*, George Orwell created a nightmare vision of the future in which an all-powerful Party exerts totalitarian control over society by forcing the citizens to master the technique of "doublethink," which requires them "to hold simultaneously two opinions which cancel[] out, knowing them to be contradictory and believing in both of them."[ii] Orwell's doublethink is usually regarded as a wonderful literary device, but, of course, one with no referent in reality since it is obviously impossible to believe both halves of a contradiction. In my opinion, this assessment is quite mistaken. Not only is it possible for people to believe both halves of a contradiction, it is something they do every day with no apparent difficulty. Consider, for example, people's beliefs about the legal system. They are obviously aware that the law is inherently political. The common complaint that members of Congress are corrupt, or are legislating for their own political benefit or for that of special interest groups demonstrates that citizens understand that the laws under which they live are a product of political forces rather than the embodiment of the ideal of justice. Further, as evidenced by the political battles fought over the recent nominations of Robert Bork and Clarence Thomas to the Supreme Court, the public obviously believes that the ideology of the people who serve as judges influences the way the law is interpreted.

This, however, in no way prevents people from simultaneously regarding the law as a body of definite, politically neutral rules amenable to an impartial application which all citizens have a moral obligation to obey. Thus, they seem both surprised and dismayed to learn that the Clean Air Act might have been written, not to produce the cleanest air possible, but to favor the economic interests of the miners of dirty-burning West Virginia coal (West Virginia coincidentally being the home of Robert Byrd, who was then chairman of the Senate Appropriations Committee) over those of the miners of cleaner-burning western coal.[iii] And, when the Supreme Court hands down a controversial ruling on a subject such as abortion, civil rights, or capital punishment, then, like Louis in *Casablanca*, the public is shocked, shocked to find that the Court may have let political considerations influence its decision. The frequent condemnation of the judiciary for "undemocratic judicial activism" or "unprincipled social engineering" is merely a reflection of the public's belief that the law consists of a set of definite and consistent "neutral principles"[iv] which the judge is obligated to apply in an objective manner, free from the influence of his or her personal political and moral beliefs.

I believe that, much as Orwell suggested, it is the public's ability to engage in this type of doublethink, to be aware that the law is inherently political in character and yet believe it to be an objective embodiment of justice, that accounts for the amazing degree to which the federal government is able to exert its control over a supposedly free people. I would argue that this ability to maintain the belief that the law is a body of consistent, politically neutral rules that can be objectively applied by judges in the face of overwhelming evidence to the contrary, goes a long way toward explaining citizens' acquiescence in the steady erosion of their fundamental freedoms. To show that this is, in fact, the case, I would like to direct your attention to the fiction which resides at the heart of this incongruity and allows the public to engage in the requisite doublethink without cognitive discomfort: the myth of the rule of law.

I refer to the myth of the rule of law because, to the extent this phrase suggests a society in which all are governed by neutral rules that are objectively applied by judges, there is no such thing. As a myth, however, the concept of the rule of law is both powerful and dangerous. Its power derives from its great emotive appeal. The rule of law suggests an absence of arbitrariness, an absence of the worst abuses of tyranny. The image presented by the slogan "America is a

government of laws and not people" is one of fair and impartial rule
rather than subjugation to human whim. This is an image that can
command both the allegiance and affection of the citizenry. After all,
who wouldn't be in favor of the rule of law if the only alternative
were arbitrary rule? But this image is also the source of the myth's
danger. For if citizens really believe that they are being governed by
fair and impartial rules and that the only alternative is subjection to
personal rule, they will be much more likely to support the state as it
progressively curtails their freedom.

In this article, I will argue that this is a false dichotomy.
Specifically, I intend to establish three points:

> *1) there is no such thing as a government of law and not
> people,*
> *2) the belief that there is serves to maintain public
> support for society's power structure, and*
> *3) the establishment of a truly free society requires the
> abandonment of the myth of the rule of law.*

II

Imagine the following scene. A first-year contracts course is being
taught at the prestigious Harvard Law School. The professor is a
distinguished scholar with a national reputation as one of the leading
experts on Anglo-American contract law. Let's call him Professor
Kingsfield. He instructs his class to research the following
hypothetical for the next day.

> *A woman living in a rural setting becomes ill and calls
> her family physician, who is also the only local doctor,
> for help. However, it is Wednesday, the doctor's day off
> and because she has a golf date, she does not respond.
> The woman's condition worsens and because no other
> physician can be procured in time, she dies. Her estate
> then sues the doctor for not coming to her aid. Is the
> doctor liable?*

Two of the students, Arnie Becker and Ann Kelsey, resolve to
make a good impression on Kingsfield should they be called on to
discuss the case. Arnie is a somewhat conservative, considerably
egocentric individual. He believes that doctors are human beings,

who like anyone else, are entitled to a day off, and that it would be unfair to require them to be at the beck and call of their patients. For this reason, his initial impression of the solution to the hypothetical is that the doctor should not be liable. Through his research, he discovers the case of *Hurley v. Eddingfield*,ᵛ which establishes the rule that in the absence of an explicit contract, i.e., when there has been no actual meeting of the minds, there can be no liability. In the hypothetical, there was clearly no meeting of the minds. Therefore, Arnie concludes that his initial impression was correct and that the doctor is not legally liable. Since he has found a valid rule of law which clearly applies to the facts of the case, he is confident that he is prepared for tomorrow's class.

Ann Kelsey is politically liberal and considers herself to be a caring individual. She believes that when doctors take the Hippocratic oath, they accept a special obligation to care for the sick, and that it would be wrong and set a terrible example for doctors to ignore the needs of regular patients who depend on them. For this reason, her initial impression of the solution to the hypothetical is that the doctor should be liable. Through her research, she discovers the case of *Cotnam v. Wisdom*,ᵛⁱ which establishes the rule that in the absence of an explicit contract, the law will imply a contractual relationship where such is necessary to avoid injustice. She believes that under the facts of the hypothetical, the failure to imply a contractual relationship would be obviously unjust. Therefore, she concludes that her initial impression was correct and that the doctor is legally liable. Since she has found a valid rule of law which clearly applies to the facts of the case, she is confident that she is prepared for tomorrow's class.

The following day, Arnie is called upon and presents his analysis. Ann, who knows she has found a sound legal argument for exactly the opposite outcome, concludes that Arnie is a typical privileged white male conservative with no sense of compassion, who has obviously missed the point of the hypothetical. She volunteers, and when called upon by Kingsfield criticizes Arnie's analysis of the case and presents her own. Arnie, who knows he has found a sound legal argument for his position, concludes that Ann is a typical female bleeding-heart liberal, whose emotionalism has caused her to miss the point of the hypothetical. Each expects Kingsfield to confirm his or her analysis and dismiss the other's as the misguided bit of illogic it so obviously is. Much to their chagrin, however, when a third student asks, "But who is right, Professor?," Kingsfield gruffly responds, "When you turn that mush between your ears into something useful and begin to think like a lawyer, you will be able to answer that question for yourself" and moves on to another subject.

What Professor Kingsfield knows but will never reveal to the students is that both Arnie's and Ann's analyses are correct. How can this be?

III

What Professor Kingsfield knows is that the legal world is not like the real world and the type of reasoning appropriate to it is distinct from that which human beings ordinarily employ. In the real world, people usually attempt to solve problems by forming hypotheses and then testing them against the facts as they know them. When the facts confirm the hypotheses, they are accepted as true, although subject to reevaluation as new evidence is discovered. This is a successful method of reasoning about scientific and other empirical matters because the physical world has a definite, unique structure. It works because the laws of nature are consistent. In the real world, it is entirely appropriate to assume that once you have confirmed your hypothesis, all other hypotheses inconsistent with it are incorrect.

In the legal world, however, this assumption does not hold. This is because unlike the laws of nature, political laws are not consistent. The law human beings create to regulate their conduct is made up of incompatible, contradictory rules and principles; and, as anyone who has studied a little logic can demonstrate, any conclusion can be validly derived from a set of contradictory premises. This means that a logically sound argument can be found for any legal conclusion.

When human beings engage in legal reasoning, they usually proceed in the same manner as they do when engaged in empirical reasoning. They begin with a hypothesis as to how a case should be decided and test it by searching for a sound supporting argument. After all, no one can "reason" directly to an unimagined conclusion. Without some end in view, there is no way of knowing what premises to employ or what direction the argument should take. When a sound argument is found, then, as in the case of empirical reasoning, one naturally concludes that one's legal hypothesis has been shown to be correct, and further, that all competing hypotheses are therefore incorrect.

This is the fallacy of legal reasoning. Because the legal world is comprised of contradictory rules, there will be sound legal arguments available not only for the hypothesis one is investigating, but for other, competing hypotheses as well. The assumption that there is a unique, correct resolution, which serves so well in empirical investigations, leads one astray when dealing with legal matters. Kingsfield, who is well aware of this, knows that Arnie and Ann have both produced legitimate legal arguments for their competing conclusions. He does not reveal this knowledge to the class, however, because the fact that this is possible is precisely what his students must discover for themselves if they are ever to learn to "think like a lawyer."

IV

Imagine that Arnie and Ann have completed their first year at Harvard and coincidentally find themselves in the same second-year class on employment discrimination law. During the portion of the course that focuses on Title VII of the Civil Rights Act of 1964[vii], the class is asked to determine whether § 2000e-2(a)(1), which makes it unlawful "to fail or refuse to hire or to discharge any individual, or otherwise to discriminate against any individual with respect to his compensation, terms, conditions, or privileges of employment, because of such individual's race, color, religion, sex, or national origin," permits an employer to voluntarily institute an affirmative action program giving preferential treatment to African-Americans. Perhaps unsurprisingly, Arnie strongly believes that affirmative action programs are morally wrong and that what the country needs are color-blind, merit-based employment practices. In researching the problem, he encounters the following principle of statutory construction: When the words are plain, courts may not enter speculative fields in search of a different meaning, and the language must be regarded as the final expression of legislative intent and not added to or subtracted from on the basis of any extraneous source[viii]. In Arnie's opinion, this principle clearly applies to this case. Section 2000e-2(a)(1) prohibits discrimination against any individual because of his race. What wording could be more plain? Since giving preferential treatment to African-Americans discriminates against whites because of their race, Arnie concludes that § 2000e-2(a)(1) prohibits employers from voluntarily instituting affirmative action plans.

Perhaps equally unsurprisingly, Ann has a strong belief that affirmative action is moral and is absolutely necessary to bring about a racially just society. In the course of her research, she encounters the following principle of statutory construction: "It is a familiar rule, that a thing may be within the letter of [a] statute and yet not within the statute because not within its spirit, nor within the intention of its makers";[ix] and that an interpretation which would bring about an end at variance with the purpose of the statute must be rejected.[x] Upon checking the legislative history, Ann learns that the purpose of Title VII of the Civil Rights Act is to relieve "the plight of the Negro in our economy" and "open employment opportunities for Negroes in occupations which have been traditionally closed to them."[xi] Since it would obviously contradict this purpose to interpret § 2000e-2 to make it illegal for employers to voluntarily institute affirmative action plans designed to economically benefit African-Americans by opening traditionally closed employment opportunities, Ann concludes that § 2000e-2 does not prohibit such plans.

The next day, Arnie presents his argument for the illegality of affirmative action in class. Since Ann has found a sound legal argument for precisely the opposite conclusion, she knows that Arnie's position is untenable. However, having gotten to know Arnie over the last year, this does not surprise her in the least. She regards him as an inveterate reactionary who is completely unprincipled in pursuit of his conservative (and probably racist) agenda. She believes that he is advancing an absurdly narrow reading of the Civil Rights Act for the purely political end of undermining the purpose of the statute. Accordingly, she volunteers, and when called upon, makes this point and presents her own argument demonstrating that affirmative action is legal. Arnie, who has found a sound legal argument for his conclusion, knows that Ann's position is untenable. However, he expected as much. Over the past year he has come to know Ann as a knee-jerk liberal who is willing to do anything to advance her mushy-headed, left-wing agenda. He believes that she is perversely manipulating the patently clear language of the statute for the purely political end of extending the statute beyond its legitimate purpose.

Both Arnie and Ann know that they have found a logically sound argument for their conclusion. But both have also committed the fallacy of legal reasoning by assuming that under the law there is a uniquely correct resolution of the case. Because of this assumption, both believe that their argument demonstrates that they have found the objectively correct answer, and that therefore, the other is simply playing politics with the law.

The truth is, of course, that both are engaging in politics. Because the law is made up of contradictory rules that can generate any conclusion, what conclusion one finds will be determined by what conclusion one looks for, i.e., by the hypothesis one decides to test. This will invariably be the one that intuitively "feels" right, the one that is most congruent with one's antecedent, underlying political and moral beliefs. Thus, legal conclusions are always determined by the normative assumptions of the decisionmaker. The knowledge that Kingsfield possesses and Arnie and Ann have not yet discovered is that the law is never neutral and objective.

V

I have suggested that because the law consists of contradictory rules and principles, sound legal arguments will be available for all legal conclusions, and hence, the normative predispositions of the decisionmakers, rather than the law itself, determine the outcome of cases. It should be noted, however, that this vastly understates the degree to which the law is indeterminate. For even if the law were consistent, the individual rules and principles are expressed in such vague and general language that the decisionmaker is able to interpret them as broadly or as narrowly as necessary to achieve any desired result. To see that this is the case, imagine that Arnie and Ann have graduated from Harvard Law School, gone on to distinguished careers as attorneys, and later in life find, to their amazement and despair, that they have both been appointed as judges to the same appellate court. The first case to come before them involves the following facts:

> *A bankrupt was auctioning off his personal possessions to raise money to cover his debts. One of the items put up for auction was a painting that had been in his family for years. A buyer attending the auction purchased the painting for a bid of $100. When the buyer had the*

painting appraised, it turned out to be a lost masterpiece worth millions. Upon learning of this, the seller sued to rescind the contract of sale. The trial court granted the rescission. The question on appeal is whether this judgment is legally correct.

Counsel for both the plaintiff seller and defendant buyer agree that the rule of law governing this case holds that a contract of sale may be rescinded when there has been a mutual mistake concerning a fact that was material to the agreement. The seller claims that in the instant case there has been such a mistake, citing as precedent the case of *Sherwood v. Walker.*[xii] In *Sherwood*, one farmer sold another farmer a cow which both farmers believed to be sterile. When the cow turned out to be fertile, the seller was granted rescission of the contract of sale on the ground of mutual mistake.[xiii] The seller argues that Sherwood is exactly analogous to the present controversy. Both he and the buyer believed the contract of sale was for an inexpensive painting. Thus, both were mistaken as to the true nature of the object being sold. Since this was obviously material to the agreement, the seller claims that the trial court was correct in granting rescission.

The buyer claims that the instant case is not one of mutual mistake, citing as precedent the case of *Wood v. Boynton.*[xiv] In *Wood*, a woman sold a small stone she had found to a jeweler for one dollar. At the time of the sale, neither party knew what type of stone it was. When it subsequently turned out to be an uncut diamond worth $700, the seller sued for rescission claiming mutual mistake. The court upheld the contract, finding that since both parties knew that they were bargaining over a stone of unknown value, there was no mistake.[xv] The buyer argues that this is exactly analogous to the present controversy. Both the seller and the buyer knew that the painting being sold was a work of unknown value. This is precisely what is to be expected at an auction. Thus, the buyer claims that this is not a case of mutual mistake and the contract should be upheld.

Following oral argument, Arnie, Ann, and the third judge on the court, Bennie Stolwitz, a non-lawyer appointed to the bench predominantly because the governor is his uncle, retire to consider their ruling. Arnie believes that one of the essential purposes of contract law is to encourage people to be self-reliant and careful in their transactions, since with the freedom to enter into binding arrangements comes the responsibility for doing so. He regards as crucial to his decision the facts that the seller had the opportunity to have the painting appraised and that by exercising due care he could have discovered its true value. Hence, he regards the contract in this case as one for a painting of unknown value and votes to overturn the trial court and uphold the contract. On the other hand, Ann believes that the essential purpose of contract law is to ensure that all parties receive a fair bargain. She regards as crucial to her decision the fact that the buyer in this case is receiving a massive windfall at the expense of the unfortunate seller. Hence, she regards the contract as one for an inexpensive painting and votes to uphold the trial court's decision and grant rescission. This leaves the deciding vote up to Bennie, who has no idea what the purpose of contract law is, but thinks that it just doesn't seem right for the bankrupt guy to lose out, and votes for rescission.

Both Arnie and Ann can see that the present situation bodes ill for their judicial tenure. Each believes that the other's unprincipled political manipulations of the law will leave Bennie, who is not even a lawyer, with control of the court. As a result, they hold a meeting to discuss the situation. At this meeting, they both promise to put politics aside and decide all future cases strictly on the basis of the law. Relieved, they return to court to confront the next case on the docket, which involves the following facts:

A philosophy professor who supplements her academic salary during the summer by giving lectures on political philosophy had contracted to deliver a lecture on the rule of law to the Future Republicans of America (FRA) on July 20, for $500. She was subsequently contacted by the Young Socialists of America, who offered her $1000 for a lecture to be delivered on the same day. She thereupon called the FRA, informing them of her desire to accept the better offer. The FRA then agreed to pay $1000 for her lecture. After the professor delivered the lecture, the FRA paid only the originally stipulated $500. The professor sued and the trial court ruled she was entitled to the additional $500. The question on appeal is whether this judgment is legally correct.

Counsel for both the plaintiff professor and defendant FRA agree that the rule of law governing this case holds that a promise to pay more for services one is already contractually bound to perform is not enforceable, but if an existing contract is rescinded by both parties and a new one is negotiated, the promise is enforceable. The FRA claims that in the instant case, it had promised to pay more for a service the professor was already contractually bound to perform, citing *Davis & Co. V. Morgan*[xvi] as precedent. In *Davis*, a laborer employed for a year at $40 per month was offered $65 per month by another company. The employer then promised to pay the employee an additional $120 at the end of the year if he stayed with the firm. At the end of the year, the employer failed to pay the $120, and when the employee sued, the court held that because he was already obligated to work for $40 per month for the year, there was no consideration for the employer's promise; hence, it was unenforceable[xvii]. The FRA argues that this is exactly analogous to the present controversy. The professor was already obligated to deliver the lecture for $500. Therefore, there was no consideration for the FRA's promise to pay an additional $500 and the promise is unenforceable.

The professor claims that in the instant case, the original contract was rescinded and a new one negotiated, citing *Schwartzreich v. Bauman-Basch, Inc.*[xviii] as precedent. In *Schwartzreich*, a clothing designer who had contracted for a year's work at $90 per week was subsequently offered $115 per week by another company. When the designer informed his employer of his intention to leave, the employer offered the designer $100 per week if he would stay and the designer agreed. When the designer sued for the additional compensation, the court held that since the parties had simultaneously rescinded the original contract by mutual consent and entered into a new one for the higher salary, the promise to pay was enforceable.[xix] The professor argues that this is exactly analogous to the present controversy. When the FRA offered to pay her an additional $500 to give the lecture, they were obviously offering to rescind the former contract and enter a new one on different terms. Hence, the promise to pay the extra $500 is enforceable.

Following oral argument, the judges retire to consider their ruling. Arnie, mindful of his agreement with Ann, is scrupulously careful not to let political considerations enter into his analysis of the case. Thus, he begins by asking himself why society needs contract law in the first place. He decides that the objective, nonpolitical answer is obviously that society needs some mechanism to ensure that individuals honor their voluntarily undertaken commitments. From this perspective, the resolution of the present case is clear. Since the professor is obviously threatening to go back on her voluntarily undertaken commitment in order to extort more money from the FRA, Arnie characterizes the case as one in which a promise has been made to pay more for services which the professor is already contractually bound to perform, and decides that the promise is unenforceable. Hence, he votes to overturn the trial court's decision. Ann, also mindful of her agreement with Arnie, is meticulous in her efforts to ensure that she decides this case purely on the law. Accordingly, she begins her analysis by asking herself why society needs contract law in the first place. She decides that the objective, nonpolitical answer is obviously that it provides an environment within which people can exercise the freedom to arrange their lives as they see fit. From this perspective, the resolution of the present case is clear. Since the FRA is essentially attempting to prevent the professor from arranging her life as she sees fit, Ann characterizes the case as one in which the parties have simultaneously rescinded an existing contract and negotiated a new one, and decides that the promise is enforceable. Hence, she votes to uphold the trial court's decision. This once again leaves the deciding vote up to Bennie, who has no idea why society needs contract law, but thinks that the professor is taking advantage of the situation in an unfair way and votes to overturn the trial court's ruling.

Both Arnie and Ann now believe that the other is an incorrigible ideologue who is destined to torment him or her throughout his or her judicial existence. Each is quite unhappy at the prospect. Each blames the other for his or her unhappiness. But, in fact, the blame lies within each. For they have never learned Professor Kingsfield's lesson that it is impossible to reach an objective decision based solely on the law. This is because the law is always open to interpretation and there is no such thing as a normatively neutral interpretation. The way one interprets the rules of law is always determined by one's underlying moral and political beliefs.

VI

I have been arguing that the law is not a body of determinate rules that can be objectively and impersonally applied by judges; that what the law prescribes is necessarily determined by the normative predispositions of the one who is interpreting it. In short, I have been arguing that law is inherently political. If you, my reader, are like most people, you are far from convinced of this. In fact, I dare say I can read your thoughts. You are thinking that even if I have shown that the present legal system is somewhat indeterminate, I certainly have not shown that the law is inherently political. Although you may agree that the law as presently constituted is too vague or contains too many contradictions, you probably believe that this state of affairs is due to the actions of the liberal judicial activists, or the Reaganite adherents of the doctrine of original intent, or the self-serving politicians, or the _____ (feel free to fill in your favorite candidate for the group that is responsible for the legal system's ills). However, you do not believe that the law must be this way, that it can never be definite and politically neutral. You believe that the law can be reformed; that to bring about an end to political strife and institute a true rule of law, we merely need to create a legal system comprised of consistent rules that are expressed in clear, definite language.

It is my sad duty to inform you that this cannot be done. Even with all the good will in the world, we could not produce such a legal code because there is simply no such thing as uninterpretable language. Now I could attempt to convince you of this by the conventional method of regaling you with myriad examples of the manipulation of legal language (e.g., an account of how the relatively straightforward language of the Commerce Clause giving Congress the power to "regulate Commerce . . . among the several States"[xx] has been interpreted to permit the regulation of both farmers growing wheat for use on their own farms[xxi] and the nature of male-female relationships in all private businesses that employ more than fifteen persons)[xxii]. However, I prefer to try a more direct approach. Accordingly, let me direct your attention to the quiz you completed at the beginning of this article. Please consider your responses.

If your response to question one was "True," you chose to interpret the word "no" as used in the First Amendment to mean "some."

If your response to question two was "False," you chose to interpret the word "Congress" to refer to the President of the United States and the word "law" to refer to an executive order.

If your response to question three was "False," you chose to interpret the words "speech" and "press" to refer to the exhibition of photographs and paintings.

If your response to question four was "True," you have underscored your belief that the word "no" really means "some."

If your response to question five was "False," you chose to interpret the words "speech" and "press" to refer to dancing to rock and roll music.

If your response to question six was "False," you chose to interpret the word "Congress" to refer to the Internal Revenue Service and the word "law" to refer to an IRS regulation.

If your response to question seven was "False," you chose to interpret the words "speech" and "press" to refer to the act of burning a flag.

Unless your responses were: 1) False, 2) True, 3) True, 4) False, 5) True, 6) True, and 7) True, you chose to interpret at least one of the words "Congress," "no," "law," "speech," and "press" in what can only be described as something other than its ordinary sense. Why did you do this? Were your responses based on the "plain meaning" of the words or on certain normative beliefs you hold about the extent to which the federal government should be allowed to interfere with citizens' expressive activities? Were your responses objective and neutral or were they influenced by your "politics"?

I chose this portion of the First Amendment for my example because it contains the clearest, most definite legal language of which I am aware. If a provision as clearly drafted as this may be subjected to political interpretation, what legal provision may not be? But this explains why the legal system cannot be reformed to consist of a body of definite rules yielding unique, objectively verifiable resolutions of cases. What a legal rule means is always determined by the political assumptions of the person applying it.[xxiii]

VII

Let us assume that I have failed to convince you of the impossibility of reforming the law into a body of definite, consistent rules that produces determinate results. Even if the law could be reformed in this way, it clearly should not be. There is nothing perverse in the fact that the law is indeterminate. Society is not the victim of some nefarious conspiracy to undermine legal certainty to further ulterior motives. As long as law remains a state monopoly, as long as it is created and enforced exclusively through governmental bodies, it must remain indeterminate if it is to serve its purpose. Its indeterminacy gives the law its flexibility. And since, as a monopoly product, the law must apply to all members of society in a one-size-fits-all manner, flexibility is its most essential feature.

It is certainly true that one of the purposes of law is to ensure a stable social environment, to provide order. But not just any order will suffice. Another purpose of the law must be to do justice. The goal of the law is to provide a social environment which is both orderly and just. Unfortunately, these two purposes are always in tension. For the more definite and rigidly-determined the rules of law become, the less the legal system is able to do justice to the individual. Thus, if the law were fully determinate, it would have no ability to consider the equities of the particular case. This is why even if we could reform the law to make it wholly definite and consistent, we should not.

Consider one of the favorite proposals of those who disagree. Those who believe that the law can and should be rendered fully determinate usually propose that contracts be rigorously enforced. Thus, they advocate a rule of law stating that in the absence of physical compulsion or explicit fraud, parties should be absolutely bound to keep their agreements. They believe that as long as no rules inconsistent with this definite, clearly-drawn provision are allowed to enter the law, politics may be eliminated from contract law and commercial transactions greatly facilitated.

Let us assume, contrary to fact, that the terms "fraud" and "physical compulsion" have a plain meaning not subject to interpretation. The question then becomes what should be done about Agnes Syester.[xxiv] Agnes was "a lonely and elderly widow who fell for the blandishments and flattery of those who" ran an Arthur Murray Dance Studio in Des Moines, Iowa.[xxv] This studio used some highly innovative sales techniques to sell this 68-year-old woman 4,057 hours of dance instruction, including three life memberships and a course in Gold Star dancing, which was "the type of dancing done by Ginger Rogers and Fred Astair only about twice as difficult,"[xxvi] for a total cost of $33,497 in 1960 dollars. Of course, Agnes did voluntarily agree to purchase that number of hours. Now, in a case such as this, one might be tempted to "interpret" the overreaching and unfair sales practices of the studio as fraudulent[xxvii] and allow Agnes to recover her money. However, this is precisely the sort of solution that our reformed, determinate contract law is designed to outlaw. Therefore, it would seem that since Agnes has voluntarily contracted for the dance lessons, she is liable to pay the full amount for them. This might seem to be a harsh result for Agnes, but from now on, vulnerable little old ladies will be on notice to be more careful in their dealings.

Or consider a proposal that is often advanced by those who wish to render probate law more determinate. They advocate a rule of law declaring a handwritten will that is signed before two witnesses to be absolutely binding. They believe that by depriving the court of the ability to "interpret" the state of mind of the testator, the judges' personal moral opinions may be eliminated from the law and most probate matters brought to a timely conclusion. Of course, the problem then becomes what to do with Elmer Palmer, a young man who murdered his grandfather to gain the inheritance due him under the old man's will a bit earlier than might otherwise have been the case.[xxviii] In a case such as this, one might be tempted to deny Elmer the fruits of his nefarious labor despite the fact that the will was validly drawn, by appealing to the legal principle that no one should profit from his or her own wrong.[xxix] However, this is precisely the sort of vaguely-expressed counter-rule that our reformers seek to purge from the legal system in order to ensure that the law remains consistent. Therefore, it would seem that although Elmer may spend a considerable amount of time behind bars, he will do so as a wealthy man. This may send a bad message to other young men of Elmer's temperament, but from now on the probate process will be considerably streamlined.

The proposed reforms certainly render the law more determinate. However, they do so by eliminating the law's ability to consider the equities of the individual case. This observation raises the following interesting question: If this is what a determinate legal system is like, who would want to live under one? The fact is that the greater the degree of certainty we build into the law, the less able the law becomes to do justice. For this reason, a monopolistic legal system composed entirely of clear, consistent rules could not function in a manner acceptable to the general public. It could not serve as a system of justice.

VIII

I have been arguing that the law is inherently indeterminate, and further, that this may not be such a bad thing. I realize, however, that you may still not be convinced. Even if you are now willing to admit that the law is somewhat indeterminate, you probably believe that I have vastly exaggerated the degree to which this is true. After all, it is obvious that the law cannot be radically indeterminate. If this were the case, the law would be completely unpredictable. Judges hearing similar cases would render wildly divergent decisions. There would be no stability or uniformity in the law. But, as imperfect as the current legal system may be, this is clearly not the case.

The observation that the legal system is highly stable is, of course, correct, but it is a mistake to believe that this is because the law is determinate. The stability of the law derives not from any feature of the law itself, but from the overwhelming uniformity of ideological background among those empowered to make legal decisions. Consider who the judges are in this country. Typically, they are people from a solid middle- to upper-class background who performed well at an appropriately prestigious undergraduate institution; demonstrated the ability to engage in the type of analytical reasoning that is measured by the standardized Law School Admissions Test; passed through the crucible of law school, complete with its methodological and political indoctrination; and went on to high-profile careers as attorneys, probably with a prestigious Wall Street-style law firm. To have been appointed to the bench, it is virtually certain that they were both politically moderate and well-connected, and, until recently, white males of the correct ethnic and religious pedigree. It should be clear that, culturally speaking, such a group will tend to be quite homogeneous, sharing a great many moral, spiritual, and political beliefs and values. Given this, it can hardly be surprising that there will be a high degree of agreement among judges as to how cases ought to be decided. But this agreement is due to the common set of normative presuppositions the judges share, not some immanent, objective meaning that exists within the rules of law.

In fact, however, the law is not truly stable, since it is continually, if slowly, evolving in response to changing social mores and conditions. This evolution occurs because each new generation of judges brings with it its own set of "progressive" normative assumptions. As the older generation passes from the scene, these assumptions come to be shared by an ever-increasing percentage of the judiciary. Eventually, they become the consensus of opinion among judicial decisionmakers, and the law changes to reflect them. Thus, a generation of judges that regarded "separate but equal" as a perfectly legitimate interpretation of the Equal Protection Clause of the Fourteenth Amendment[xxx] gave way to one which interpreted that clause as prohibiting virtually all governmental actions that classify individuals by race, which, in turn, gave way to one which interpreted the same language to permit "benign" racial classifications designed to advance the social status of minority groups. In this way, as the moral and political values conventionally accepted by society change over time, so too do those embedded in the law.

The law appears to be stable because of the slowness with which it evolves. But the slow pace of legal development is not due to any inherent characteristic of the law itself. Logically speaking, any conclusion, however radical, is derivable from the rules of law. It is simply that, even between generations, the range of ideological opinion represented on the bench is so narrow that anything more than incremental departures from conventional wisdom and morality will not be respected within the profession. Such decisions are virtually certain to be overturned on appeal, and thus, are rarely even rendered in the first instance.

Confirming evidence for this thesis can be found in our contemporary judicial history. Over the past quarter-century, the "diversity" movement has produced a bar, and concomitantly a bench, somewhat more open to people of different racial, sexual, ethnic, and socio-economic backgrounds. To some extent, this movement has produced a judiciary that represents a broader range of ideological viewpoints than has been the case in the past. Over the same time period, we have seen an accelerated rate of legal change. Today, long-standing precedents are more freely overruled, novel theories of liability are more frequently accepted by the courts, and different courts hand down different, and seemingly irreconcilable, decisions more often. In addition, it is worth noting that recently, the chief complaint about the legal system seems to concern the degree to which it has become "politicized." This suggests that as the ideological solidarity of the judiciary breaks down, so too does the predictability of legal decisionmaking, and hence, the stability of the law. Regardless of this trend, I hope it is now apparent that to assume that the law is stable because it is determinate is to reverse cause and effect. Rather, it is because the law is basically stable that it appears to be determinate. It is not rule of law that gives us a stable legal system; it is the stability of the culturally shared values of the judiciary that gives rise to and supports the myth of the rule of law.

IX

It is worth noting that there is nothing new or startling about the claim that the law is indeterminate. This has been the hallmark of the Critical Legal Studies movement since the mid-1970s. The "Crits," however, were merely reviving the earlier contention of the legal realists who made the same point in the 1920s and 30s. And the realists were themselves merely repeating the claim of earlier jurisprudential thinkers. For example, as early as 1897, Oliver Wendell Holmes had pointed out:

> *The language of judicial decision is mainly the language of logic. And the logical method and form flatter that longing for certainty and for repose which is in every human mind. But certainty generally is illusion, and repose is not the destiny of man. Behind the logical form lies a judgment as to the relative worth and importance of competing legislative grounds, often an inarticulate and unconscious judgment, it is true, and yet the very root and nerve of the whole proceeding. You can give any conclusion a logical form.*[xxxi]

This raises an interesting question. If it has been known for 100 years that the law does not consist of a body of determinate rules, why is the belief that it does still so widespread? If four generations of jurisprudential scholars have shown that the rule of law is a myth, why does the concept still command such fervent commitment? The answer is implicit in the question itself, for the question recognizes that the rule of law is a myth and like all myths, it is designed to serve an emotive, rather than cognitive, function. The purpose of a myth is not to persuade one's reason, but to enlist one's emotions in support of an idea. And this is precisely the case for the myth of the rule of law; its purpose is to enlist the emotions of the public in support of society's political power structure.

People are more willing to support the exercise of authority over themselves when they believe it to be an objective, neutral feature of the natural world. This was the idea behind the concept of the divine right of kings. By making the king appear to be an integral part of God's plan for the world rather than an ordinary human being dominating his fellows by brute force, the public could be more easily persuaded to bow to his authority. However, when the doctrine of divine right became discredited, a replacement was needed to ensure that the public did not view political authority as merely the exercise of naked power. That replacement is the concept of the rule of law.

People who believe they live under "a government of laws and not people" tend to view their nation's legal system as objective and impartial. They tend to see the rules under which they must live not as expressions of human will, but as embodiments of neutral principles of justice, i.e., as natural features of the social world. Once they believe that they are being commanded by an impersonal law rather than other human beings, they view their obedience to political authority as a public-spirited acceptance of the requirements of social life rather than mere acquiescence to superior power. In this way, the concept of the rule of law functions much like the use of the passive voice by the politician who describes a delict on his or her part with the assertion "mistakes were made." It allows people to hide the agency of power behind a facade of words; to believe that it is the law which compels their compliance, not self-aggrandizing politicians, or highly capitalized special interests, or wealthy white Anglo-Saxon Protestant males, or _____ (fill in your favorite culprit).

But the myth of the rule of law does more than render the people submissive to state authority; it also turns them into the state's accomplices in the exercise of its power. For people who would ordinarily consider it a great evil to deprive individuals of their rights or oppress politically powerless minority groups will respond with patriotic fervor when these same actions are described as upholding the rule of law.

Consider the situation in India toward the end of British colonial rule. At that time, the followers of Mohandas Gandhi engaged in nonviolent civil disobedience by manufacturing salt for their own use in contravention of the British monopoly on such manufacture. The British administration and army responded with mass imprisonments and shocking brutality. It is difficult to understand this behavior on the part of the highly moralistic, ever-so-civilized British unless one keeps in mind that they were able to view their activities not as violently repressing the indigenous population, but as upholding the rule of law.

The same is true of the violence directed against the nonviolent civil rights protestors in the American South during the civil rights movement. Although much of the white population of the southern states held racist beliefs, one cannot account for the overwhelming support given to the violent repression of these protests on the assumption that the vast majority of the white Southerners were sadistic racists devoid of moral sensibilities. The true explanation is that most of these people were able to view themselves not as perpetuating racial oppression and injustice, but as upholding the rule of law against criminals and outside agitators. Similarly, since despite the '60s rhetoric, all police officers are not "fascist pigs," some other explanation is needed for their willingness to participate in the "police riot" at the 1968 Democratic convention, or the campaign of illegal arrests and civil rights violations against those demonstrating in Washington against President Nixon's policies in Vietnam, or the effort to infiltrate and destroy the sanctuary movement that sheltered refugees from Salvadorian death squads during the Reagan era or, for that matter, the attack on and destruction of the Branch Davidian compound in Waco. It is only when these officers have fully bought into the myth that "we are a government of laws and not people," when they truly believe that their actions are commanded by some impersonal body of just rules, that they can fail to see that they are the agency used by those in power to oppress others.

The reason why the myth of the rule of law has survived for 100 years despite the knowledge of its falsity is that it is too valuable a tool to relinquish. The myth of impersonal government is simply the most effective means of social control available to the state.

X

During the past two decades, the legal scholars identified with the Critical Legal Studies movement have gained a great deal of notoriety for their unrelenting attacks on traditional, "liberal" legal theory. The modus operandi of these scholars has been to select a specific area of the law and show that because the rules and principles that comprise it are logically incoherent, legal outcomes can always be manipulated by those in power to favor their interests at the expense of the politically "subordinated" classes. The Crits then argue that the claim that the law consists of determinate, just rules which are impartially applied to all is a ruse employed by the powerful to cause these subordinated classes to view the oppressive legal rulings as the necessary outcomes of an objective system of justice. This renders the oppressed more willing to accept their socially subordinated status. Thus, the Crits maintain that the concept of the rule of law is simply a facade used to maintain the socially dominant position of white males in an oppressive and illegitimate capitalist system.

In taking this approach, the Crits recognize that the law is indeterminate, and thus, that it necessarily reflects the moral and political values of those empowered to render legal decisions. Their objection is that those who currently wield this power subscribe to the wrong set of values. They wish to change the legal system from one which embodies what they regard as the hierarchical, oppressive values of capitalism to one which embodies the more egalitarian, "democratic" values that they usually associate with socialism. The Crits accept that the law must be provided exclusively by the state, and hence, that it must impose one set of values on all members of society. Their contention is that the particular set of values currently being imposed is the wrong one.

Although they have been subjected to much derision by mainstream legal theorists,[xxxii] as long as we continue to believe that the law must be a state monopoly, there really is nothing wrong, or even particularly unique, about the Crits' line of argument. There has always been a political struggle for control of the law, and as long as all must be governed by the same law, as long as one set of values must be imposed upon everyone, there always will be. It is true that the Crits want to impose "democratic" or socialistic values on everyone through the mechanism of the law. But this does not distinguish them from anyone else. Religious fundamentalists want to impose "Christian" values on all via the law. Liberal Democrats want the law to ensure that everyone acts so as to realize a "compassionate" society, while conservative Republicans want it to ensure the realization of "family values" or "civic virtue." Even libertarians insist that all should be governed by a law that enshrines respect for individual liberty as its preeminent value.

The Crits may believe that the law should embody a different set of values than liberals, or conservatives, or libertarians, but this is the only thing that differentiates them from these other groups. Because the other groups have accepted the myth of the rule of law, they perceive what they are doing not as a struggle for political control, but as an attempt to depoliticize the law and return it to its proper form as the neutral embodiment of objective principles of justice. But the rule of law is a myth, and perception does not change reality. Although only the Crits may recognize it, all are engaged in a political struggle to impose their version of "the good" on the rest of society. And as long as the law remains the exclusive province of the state, this will always be the case.

XI

What is the significance of these observations? Are we condemned to a continual political struggle for control of the legal system? Well, yes; as long as the law remains a state monopoly, we are. But I would ask you to note that this is a conditional statement while you consider the following parable.

A long time ago in a galaxy far away, there existed a parallel Earth that contained a nation called Monosizea. Monosizea was remarkably similar to the present-day United States. It had the same level of technological development, the same social problems, and was governed by the same type of common law legal system. In fact, Monosizea had a federal constitution that was identical to that of the United States in all respects except one. However, that distinction was quite an odd one. For some reason lost to history, the Monosizean founding fathers had included a provision in the constitution that required all shoes manufactured or imported into Monosizea to be the same size. The particular size could be determined by Congress, but whatever size was selected represented the only size shoe permitted in the country.

As you may imagine, in Monosizea, shoe size was a serious political issue. Although there were a few radical fringe groups which argued for either extremely small or extremely large sizes, Monosizea was essentially a two-party system with most of the electorate divided between the Liberal Democratic party and the Conservative Republican party. The Liberal Democratic position on shoe size was that social justice demanded the legal size to be a large size such as a nine or ten. They presented the egalitarian argument that everyone should have equal access to shoes, and that this could only be achieved by legislating a large shoe size. After all, people with small feet could still use shoes that were too large (even if they did have to stuff some newspaper into them), but people with large feet would be completely disenfranchised if the legal size was a small one. Interestingly, the Liberal Democratic party contained a larger than average number of people who were tall. The Conservative Republican position on shoe size was that respect for family values and the traditional role of government required that the legal size be a small size such as a four or five. They presented the moralistic argument that society's obligation to the next generation and government's duty to protect the weak demanded that the legal size be set so that children could have adequate footwear. They contended that children needed reasonably well-fitting shoes while they were in their formative years and their feet were tender. Later, when they were adults and their feet were fully developed, they would be able to cope with the rigors of barefoot life. Interestingly, the Conservative Republican party contained a larger than average number of people who were short.

Every two years as congressional elections approached, and especially when this corresponded with a presidential election, the rhetoric over the shoe size issue heated up. The Liberal Democrats would accuse the Conservative Republicans of being under the control of the fundamentalist Christians and of intolerantly attempting to impose their religious values on society. The Conservative Republicans would accuse the Liberal Democrats of being misguided, bleeding-heart do-gooders who were either the dupes of the socialists or socialists themselves. However, after the elections, the shoe size legislation actually hammered out by the President and Congress always seemed to set the legal shoe size close to a seven, which was the average foot size in Monosizea. Further, this legislation always defined the size in broad terms so that it might encompass a size or two on either side, and authorized the manufacture of shoes made of extremely flexible materials that could stretch or contract as necessary. For this reason, most averaged-sized Monosizeans, who were predominantly politically moderate, had acceptable footwear.

This state of affairs seemed quite natural to everyone in Monosizea except a boy named Socrates. Socrates was a pensive, shy young man who, when not reading a book, was often lost in thought. His contemplative nature caused his parents to think of him as a dreamer, his schoolmates to think of him as a nerd, and everyone else to think of him as a bit odd. One day, after learning about the Monosizean Constitution in school and listening to his parents discuss the latest public opinion poll on the shoe size issue, Socrates approached his parents and said: "I have an idea. Why don't we amend the constitution to permit shoemakers to manufacture and sell more than one size shoe. Then everyone could have shoes that fit and we wouldn't have to argue about what the legal shoe size should be anymore."

Socrates' parents found his naive idealism amusing and were proud that their son was so imaginative. For this reason, they tried to show him that his idea was a silly one in a way that would not discourage him from future creative thinking. Thus, Socrates' father said: "That's a very interesting idea, son, but it's simply not practical. There's always been only one size shoe in Monosizea, so that's just the way things have to be. People are used to living this way, and you can't fight city hall. I'm afraid your idea is just too radical."

Although Socrates eventually dropped the subject with his parents, he was never satisfied with their response. During his teenage years, he became more interested in politics and decided to take his idea to the Liberal Democrats. He thought that because they believed all citizens were entitled to adequate footwear, they would surely see the value of his proposal. However, although they seemed to listen with interest and thanked him for his input, they were not impressed with his idea. As the leader of the local party explained: "Your idea is fine in theory, but it will never work in practice. If manufacturers could make whatever size shoes they wanted, consumers would be at the mercy of unscrupulous business people. Each manufacturer would set up his or her own scale of sizes and consumers would have no way of determining what their foot size truly was. In such a case, profit-hungry shoe sales people could easily trick the unwary consumer into buying the wrong size. Without the government setting the size, there would be no guarantee that any shoe was really the size it purported to be. We simply cannot abandon the public to the vicissitudes of an unregulated market in shoes."

To Socrates' protests that people didn't seem to be exploited in other clothing markets and that the shoes manufactured under the present system didn't really fit very well anyway, the party leader responded: "The shoe market is unique. Adequate shoes are absolutely essential to public welfare. Therefore, the ordinary laws of supply and demand cannot be relied upon. And even if we could somehow get around the practical problems, your idea is simply not politically feasible. To make any progress, we must focus on what can actually be accomplished in the current political climate. If we begin advocating radical constitutional changes, we'll be routed in the next election."

Disillusioned by this response, Socrates approached the Conservative Republicans with his idea, explaining that if shoes could be manufactured in any size, all children could be provided with the well-fitting shoes they needed. However, the Conservative Republicans were even less receptive than the Liberal Democrats had been. The leader of their local party responded quite contemptuously, saying: "Look, Monosizea is the greatest, freest country on the face of the planet, and it's respect for our traditional values that has made it that way. Our constitution is based on these values, and it has served us well for the past 200 years. Who are you to question the wisdom of the founding fathers? If you don't like it in this country, why don't you just leave?"

Somewhat taken aback, Socrates explained that he respected the Monosizean Constitution as much as they did, but that did not mean it could not be improved. Even the founding fathers included a process by which it could be amended. However, this did nothing to ameliorate the party leader's disdain. He responded: "It's one thing to propose amending the constitution; it's another to undermine it entirely. Doing away with the shoe size provision would rend the very fabric of our society. If people could make whatever size shoes they wanted whenever they wanted, there would be no way to maintain order in the industry. What you're proposing is not liberty, it's license. Were we to adopt your proposal, we would be abandoning the rule of law itself. Can't you see that what you are advocating is not freedom, but anarchy?"

After this experience, Socrates came to realize that there was no place for him in the political realm. As a result, he went off to college where he took up the study of philosophy. Eventually, he got a Ph.D., became a philosophy professor, and was never heard from again.

So, what is the point of this outlandish parable? I stated at the beginning of this section that as long as the law remains a state monopoly, there will always be a political struggle for its control. This sounds like a cynical conclusion because we naturally assume that the law is necessarily the province of the state. Just as the Monosizeans could not conceive of a world in which shoe size was not set by the government, we cannot conceive of one in which law is not provided exclusively by it. But what if we are wrong? What if, just as Monosizea could eliminate the politics of shoe size by allowing individuals to produce and buy whatever size shoes they pleased, we could eliminate the politics of law by allowing individuals to adopt whatever rules of behavior best fit their needs? What if law is not a unique product that must be supplied on a one-size-fits-all basis by the state, but one which could be adequately supplied by the ordinary play of market forces? What if we were to try Socrates' solution and end the monopoly of law?

XII

The problem with this suggestion is that most people are unable to understand what it could possibly mean. This is chiefly because the language necessary to express the idea clearly does not really exist. Most people have been raised to identify law with the state. They cannot even conceive of the idea of legal services apart from the government. The very notion of a free market in legal services conjures up the image of anarchic gang warfare or rule by organized crime. In our system, an advocate of free market law is treated the same way Socrates was treated in Monosizea, and is confronted with the same types of arguments.

The primary reason for this is that the public has been politically indoctrinated to fail to recognize the distinction between order and law. Order is what people need if they are to live together in peace and security. Law, on the other hand, is a particular method of producing order. As it is presently constituted, law is the production of order by requiring all members of society to live under the same set of state-generated rules; it is order produced by centralized planning. Yet, from childhood, citizens are taught to invariably link the words "law" and "order." Political discourse conditions them to hear and use the terms as though they were synonymous and to express the desire for a safer, more peaceful society as a desire for "law and order." The state nurtures this confusion because it is the public's inability to distinguish order from law that generates its fundamental support for the state. As long as the public identifies order with law, it will believe that an orderly society is impossible without the law the state provides. And as long as the public believes this, it will continue to support the state almost without regard to how oppressive it may become.

The public's identification of order with law makes it impossible for the public to ask for one without asking for the other. There is clearly a public demand for an orderly society. One of human beings' most fundamental desires is for a peaceful existence secure from violence. But because the public has been conditioned to express its desire for order as one for law, all calls for a more orderly society are interpreted as calls for more law. And since under our current political system, all law is supplied by the state, all such calls are interpreted as calls for a more active and powerful state. The identification of order with law eliminates from public consciousness the very concept of the decentralized provision of order. With regard to legal services, it renders the classical liberal idea of a market-generated, spontaneous order incomprehensible.

I began this article with a reference to Orwell's concept of doublethink. But I am now describing the most effective contemporary example we have of Orwellian "newspeak," the process by which words are redefined to render certain thoughts unthinkable.[xxxiii] Were the distinction between order and law well-understood, the question of whether a state monopoly of law is the best way to ensure an orderly society could be intelligently discussed. But this is precisely the question that the state does not wish to see raised. By collapsing the concept of order into that of law, the state can ensure that it is not, for it will have effectively eliminated the idea of a non-state generated order from the public mind. Under such circumstances, we can hardly be surprised if the advocates of a free market in law are treated like Socrates of Monosizea.

XIII

I am aware that this explanation probably appears as initially unconvincing as was my earlier contention that the law is inherently political. Even if you found my Monosizea parable entertaining, it is likely that you regard it as irrelevant. You probably believe that the analogy fails because shoes are qualitatively different from legal services. After all, law is a public good which, unlike shoes, really is crucial to public welfare. It is easy to see how the free market can adequately supply the public with shoes. But how can it possibly provide the order-generating and maintaining processes necessary for the peaceful coexistence of human beings in society? What would a free market in legal services be like?

I am always tempted to give the honest and accurate response to this challenge, which is that to ask the question is to miss the point. If human beings had the wisdom and knowledge-generating capacity to be able to describe how a free market would work, that would be the strongest possible argument for central planning. One advocates a free market not because of some moral imprimatur written across the heavens, but because it is impossible for human beings to amass the knowledge of local conditions and the predictive capacity necessary to effectively organize economic relationships among millions of individuals. It is possible to describe what a free market in shoes would be like because we have one. But such a description is merely an observation of the current state of a functioning market, not a projection of how human beings would organize themselves to supply a currently non-marketed good. To demand that an advocate of free market law (or Socrates of Monosizea, for that matter) describe in advance how markets would supply legal services (or shoes) is to issue an impossible challenge. Further, for an advocate of free market law (or Socrates) to even accept this challenge would be to engage in self-defeating activity since the more successfully he or she could describe how the law (or shoe) market would function, the more he or she would prove that it could be run by state planners. Free markets supply human wants better than state monopolies precisely because they allow an unlimited number of suppliers to attempt to do so. By patronizing those who most effectively meet their particular needs and causing those who do not to fail, consumers determine the optimal method of supply. If it were possible to specify in advance what the outcome of this process of selection would be, there would be no need for the process itself.

Although I am tempted to give this response, I never do. This is because, although true, it never persuades. Instead, it is usually interpreted as an appeal for blind faith in the free market, and the failure to provide a specific explanation as to how such a market would provide legal services is interpreted as proof that it cannot. Therefore, despite the self-defeating nature of the attempt, I usually do try to suggest how a free market in law might work.

So, what would a free market in legal services be like? As Sherlock Holmes would regularly say to the good doctor, "You see, Watson, but you do not observe." Examples of non-state law are all around us. Consider labor-management collective bargaining agreements. In addition to setting wage rates, such agreements typically determine both the work rules the parties must abide by and the grievance procedures they must follow to resolve disputes. In essence, such contracts create the substantive law of the workplace as well as the workplace judiciary. A similar situation exists with regard to homeowner agreements, which create both the rules and dispute settlement procedures within a condominium or housing development, i.e., the law and judicial procedure of the residential community. Perhaps a better example is supplied by universities. These institutions create their own codes of conduct for both students and faculty that cover everything from academic dishonesty to what constitutes acceptable speech and dating behavior. In addition, they not only devise their own elaborate judicial procedures to deal with violations of these codes, but typically supply their own campus police forces as well. A final example may be supplied by the many commercial enterprises that voluntarily opt out of the state judicial system by writing clauses in their contracts that require disputes to be settled through binding arbitration or mediation rather than through a lawsuit. In this vein, the variegated "legal" procedures that have recently been assigned the sobriquet of Alternative Dispute Resolution (ADR) do a good job of suggesting what a free market in legal service might be like.[xxxiv]

Of course, it is not merely that we fail to observe what is presently all around us. We also act as though we have no knowledge of our own cultural or legal history. Consider, for example, the situation of African-American communities in the segregated South or the immigrant communities in New York in the first quarter of the twentieth century. Because of prejudice, poverty and the language barrier, these groups were essentially cut off from the state legal system. And yet, rather than disintegrate into chaotic disorder, they were able to privately supply themselves with the rules of behavior and dispute-settlement procedures necessary to maintain peaceful, stable, and highly structured communities. Furthermore, virtually none of the law that orders our interpersonal relationships was produced by the intentional actions of central governments. Our commercial law arose almost entirely from the Law Merchant, a non-governmental set of rules and procedures developed by merchants to quickly and peacefully resolve disputes and facilitate commercial relations. Property, tort, and criminal law are all the products of common law processes by which rules of behavior evolve out of and are informed by the particular circumstances of actual human controversies. In fact, a careful study of Anglo-American legal history will demonstrate that almost all of the law which facilitates peaceful human interaction arose in this way. On the other hand, the source of the law which produces oppression and social division is almost always the state. Measures that impose religious or racial intolerance, economic exploitation, one group's idea of "fairness," or another's of "community" or "family" values virtually always originate in legislation, the law consciously made by the central government. If the purpose of the law really is to bring order to human existence, then it is fair to say that the law actually made by the state is precisely the law that does not work.

Unfortunately, no matter how suggestive these examples might be, they represent only what can develop within a state-dominated system. Since, for the reasons indicated above, it is impossible to out-think a free market, any attempt to account for what would result from a true free market in law would be pure speculation. However, if I must engage in such speculation, I will try to avoid what might be called "static thinking" in doing so. Static thinking occurs when we imagine changing one feature of a dynamic system without appreciating how doing so will alter the character of all other features of the system. For example, I would be engaging in static thinking were I to ask how, if the state did not provide the law and courts, the free market could provide them in their present form. It is this type of thinking that is responsible for the conventional assumption that free market legal services would be "competing governments" which would be the equivalent of organized gang warfare. Once this static thinking is rejected, it becomes apparent that if the state did not provide the law and courts, they simply would not exist in their present form. This, however, only highlights the difficulty of describing free market order-generating services and reinforces the speculative nature of all attempts to do so.

One thing it seems safe to assume is that there would not be any universally binding, society-wide set of "legal" rules. In a free market, the law would not come in one-size-fits-all. Although the rules necessary to the maintenance of a minimal level of order, such as prohibitions against murder, assault, and theft, would be common to most systems, different communities of interest would assuredly adopt those rules and dispute-settlement procedures that would best fit their needs. For example, it seems extremely unlikely that there would be anything resembling a uniform body of contract law. Consider, as just one illustration, the differences between commercial and consumer contracts. Commercial contracts are usually between corporate entities with specialized knowledge of industrial practices and a financial interest in minimizing the interruption of business. On the other hand, consumer contracts are those in which one or both parties lack commercial sophistication and large sums do not rest upon a speedy resolution of any dispute that might arise. In a free market for legal services, the rules that govern these types of contracts would necessarily be radically different.

This example can also illustrate the different types of dispute-settlement procedures that would be likely to arise. In disputes over consumer contracts, the parties might well be satisfied with the current system of litigation in which the parties present their cases to an impartial judge or jury who renders a verdict for one side or the other. However, in commercial disputes, the parties might prefer a mediational process with a negotiated settlement in order to preserve an ongoing commercial relationship or a quick and informal arbitration in order to avoid the losses associated with excessive delay. Further, it is virtually certain that they would want mediators, arbitrators, or judges who are highly knowledgeable about commercial practice, rather than the typical generalist judge or a jury of lay people.

The problem with trying to specify the individuated "legal systems" which would develop is that there is no limit to the number of dimensions along which individuals may choose to order their lives, and hence no limit to the number of overlapping sets of rules and dispute resolution procedures to which they may subscribe. An individual might settle his or her disputes with neighbors according to voluntarily adopted homeowner association rules and procedures, with co-workers according to the rules and procedures described in a collective bargaining agreement, with members of his or her religious congregation according to scriptural law and tribunal, with other drivers according to the processes agreed to in his or her automobile insurance contract, and with total strangers by selecting a dispute resolution company from the yellow pages of the phone book. Given the current thinking about racial and sexual identity, it seems likely that many disputes among members of the same minority group or among women would be brought to "niche" dispute resolution companies composed predominantly of members of the relevant group, who would use their specialized knowledge of group "culture" to devise superior rules and procedures for intra-group dispute resolution.[xxxv]

I suspect that in many ways a free market in law would resemble the situation in Medieval Europe before the rise of strong central governments in which disputants could select among several fora. Depending upon the nature of the dispute, its geographical location, the parties' status, and what was convenient, the parties could bring their case in either village, shire, urban, merchant, manorial, ecclesiastical, or royal courts. Even with the limited mobility and communications of the time, this restricted market for dispute-settlement services was able to generate the order necessary for both the commercial and civil advancement of society. Consider how much more effectively such a market could function given the current level of travel and telecommunication technology. Under contemporary conditions, there would be an explosion of alternative order-providing organizations. I would expect that, late at night, wedged between commercials for Veg-o-matic and Slim Whitman albums, we would find television ads with messages such as, "Upset with your neighbor for playing rock and roll music all night long? Is his dog digging up your flower beds? Come to Acme Arbitration Company's grand opening two for one sale."

I should point out that, despite my earlier disclaimer, even these suggestions embody static thinking since they assume that a free market would produce a choice among confrontational systems of justice similar to the one we are most familiar with. In fact, I strongly believe that this would not be the case. The current state-supplied legal system is adversarial in nature, pitting the plaintiff or prosecution against the defendant in a winner-take-all, loser-get-nothing contest. The reason for this arrangement has absolutely nothing to do with this procedure's effectiveness in settling disputes and everything to do with the medieval English kings' desire to centralize power. For historical reasons well beyond the scope of this article, the Crown was able to extend its temporal power relative to the feudal lords as well as raise significant revenue by commanding or enticing the parties to local disputes to bring their case before the king or other royal official for decision.[xxxvi] Our current system of adversarial presentation to a third-party decisionmaker is an outgrowth of these early "public choice" considerations, not its ability to successfully provide mutually satisfactory resolutions to interpersonal disputes.

In fact, this system is a terrible one for peacefully resolving disputes and would be extremely unlikely to have many adherents in a free market. Its adversarial nature causes each party to view the other as an enemy to be defeated, and its winner-take-all character motivates each to fight as hard as he or she can to the bitter end. Since the loser gets nothing, he or she has every reason to attempt to reopen the dispute, which gives rise to frequent appeals. The incentives of the system make it in each party's interest to do whatever he or she can to wear down the opponent while being uniformly opposed to cooperation, compromise, and reconciliation. That this is not the kind of dispute-settlement procedure people are likely to employ if given a choice is evidenced by the large percentage of litigants who are turning to ADR in an effort to avoid it.

My personal belief is that under free market conditions, most people would adopt compositional, rather than confrontational, dispute settlement procedures, i.e., procedures designed to compose disputes and reconcile the parties rather than render third party judgments. This was, in fact, the essential character of the ancient "legal system" that was replaced by the extension of royal jurisdiction. Before the rise of the European nation-states, what we might anachronistically call judicial procedure was chiefly a set of complex negotiations between the parties mediated by the members of the local community in an effort to reestablish a harmonious relationship. Essentially, public pressure was brought upon the parties to settle their dispute peacefully through negotiation and compromise. The incentives of this ancient system favored cooperation and conciliation rather than defeating one's opponent.[xxxvii]

Although I have no crystal ball, I suspect that a free market in law would resemble the ancient system a great deal more than the modern one. Recent experiments with negotiated dispute-settlement have demonstrated that mediation 1) produces a higher level of participant satisfaction with regard to both process and result, 2) resolves cases more quickly and at significantly lower cost, and 3) results in a higher rate of voluntary compliance with the final decree than was the case with traditional litigation.[xxxviii] This is perhaps unsurprising, given that mediation's lack of a winner-take-all format encourages the parties to seek common ground rather than attempt to vanquish the opponent and that, since both parties must agree to any solution, there is a reduced likelihood that either will wish to reopen the dispute. Given human beings' manifest desire to retain control over their lives, I suspect that, if given a choice, few would willingly place their fate in the hands of third-party decisionmakers. Thus, I believe that a free market in law would produce a system that is essentially compositional in nature.

XIV

In this article, I have suggested that when it comes to the idea of the rule of law, the American public is in a state of deep denial. Despite being surrounded by evidence that the law is inherently political in nature, most people are nevertheless able to convince themselves that it is an embodiment of objective rules of justice which they have a moral obligation to obey. As in all cases of denial, people participate in this fiction because of the psychological comfort that can be gained by refusing to see the truth. As we saw with our friends Arnie and Ann, belief in the existence of an objective, non-ideological law enables average citizens to see those advocating legal positions inconsistent with their values as inappropriately manipulating the law for political purposes, while viewing their own position as neutrally capturing the plain meaning immanent within the law. The citizens' faith in the rule of law allows them to hide from themselves both that their position is as politically motivated as is their opponents' and that they are attempting to impose their values on their opponents as much as their opponents are attempting to impose their values on them. But, again, as in all cases of denial, the comfort gained comes at a price. For with the acceptance of the myth of the rule of law comes a blindness to the fact that laws are merely the commands of those with political power, and an increased willingness to submit oneself to the yoke of the state. Once one is truly convinced that the law is an impersonal, objective code of justice rather than an expression of the will of the powerful, one is likely to be willing not only to relinquish a large measure of one's own freedom, but to enthusiastically support the state in the suppression of others' freedom as well.

The fact is that there is no such thing as a government of law and not people. The law is an amalgam of contradictory rules and counter-rules expressed in inherently vague language that can yield a legitimate legal argument for any desired conclusion. For this reason, as long as the law remains a state monopoly, it will always reflect the political ideology of those invested with decisionmaking power. Like it or not, we are faced with only two choices. We can continue the ideological power struggle for control of the law in which the group that gains dominance is empowered to impose its will on the rest of society, or we can end the monopoly.

Our long-standing love affair with the myth of the rule of law has made us blind to the latter possibility. Like the Monosizeans, who after centuries of state control cannot imagine a society in which people can buy whatever size shoes they wish, we cannot conceive of a society in which individuals may purchase the legal services they desire. The very idea of a free market in law makes us uncomfortable. But it is time for us to overcome this discomfort and consider adopting Socrates' approach. We must recognize that our love for the rule of law is unrequited, and that, as so often happens in such cases, we have become enslaved to the object of our desire. No clearer example of this exists than the legal process by which our Constitution was transformed from a document creating a government of limited powers and guaranteed rights into one which provides the justification for the activities of the all-encompassing super-state of today. However heart-wrenching it may be, we must break off this one-sided affair. The time has come for those committed to individual liberty to realize that the establishment of a truly free society requires the abandonment of the myth of the rule of law.

i U.S. Const. amend. I.

ii George Orwell, 1984, at 32 (Commemorative 1984 ed., The New Am. Library 1983) (1949).

iii See Iain McLean, Public Choice 71-76 (1987).

iv See Herbert Weschler, Toward Neutral Principles of Constitutional Law, 73 Harv. L. Rev. 1 (1959).

v 59 N.E. 1058 (Ind. 1901).

vi 104 S.W. 164 (Ark. 1907).

vii 42 U.S.C. S 2000e-2 (1988).

viii See United Steelworkers v. Weber, 443 U.S. 193, 228 n.9 (1979) (Rehnquist, J., dissenting)

ix Id. at 201 (quoting Holy Trinity Church v. United States, 143 U.S. 457, 459 (1892)).

x Id. at 202.

xi 110 Cong. Rec. 6548 (1964).

xii 33 N.W. 919 (Mich. 1887).

xiii Id. at 923-24.

xiv 64 Wis. 265, 25 N.W. 42 (1885).

xv Id. at 45.

xvi 43 S.E. 732 (Ga. 1903).

xvii Id. at 733.

xviii 131 N.E. 887 (N.Y. 1921).

xix Id. at 890.

xx U.S. Const. art. I, § 8, cl. 3.

xxi See Wickard v. Filburn, 317 U.S. 111, 128-29 (1942).

xxii The federal government regulates sexual harassment in the workplace under Title VII of the Civil Rights Act of 1964, 42 U.S.C. § 2000e(b) (1988), which was enacted pursuant to the Commerce Clause.

xxiii On this point, it may be relevant to observe that as I write these words, the President and Congress of the United States are engaged in a vigorous debate over what percentage of the American public must have health insurance for there to be universal coverage.

xxiv The facts of the case being described are drawn from Syester v. Banta, 133 N.W.2d 666 (Iowa 1965).

xxv Id. at 668.

xxvi Id. at 671.

xxvii As the court did in the actual case. Id. at 674-75.

xxviii See Riggs v. Palmer, 22 N.E. 188 (N.Y. 1889).

xxix As the court did in the actual case. Id. at 191.

xxx U.S. Const. amend. XIV, § 1.

xxxi Oliver Wendell Holmes, The Path of the Law, 10 Harv. L. Rev. 457, 465-66 (1897).

xxxii The Crits have been accused of being intellectual nihilists and attacked for undermining the commitment to the rule of law that is necessary for the next generation of lawyers to engage in the principled, ethical practice of law. For this reason, their mainstream critics have suggested that the Crits have no business teaching in the nation's law schools. See, e.g., Paul D. Carrington, *Of Law and the River*, 34 J. Legal Educ. 222, 227 (1984).

xxxiii See Orwell, supra note 2, at 46.

xxxiv The National Law Journal has noted, "Much of corporate America is creating its own private business courts' that are far removed from the public courthouses." William H. Schroder Jr., *Private ADR May Offer Increased Confidentiality*, Nat'l L.J., July 25, 1994, at C14.

xxxv I am fairly confident that the parties to such disputes will not choose to have them resolved by a panel composed almost exclusively of White Anglo-Saxon Protestants as is the case today.

xxxvi The story of how royal jurisdiction came to supplant all others and why the adversarial system of litigation replaced the earlier methods of settling disputes is fascinating one, but one which obviously cannot be recounted here. Those interested in pursuing it may wish to consult Harold J. Berman, *Law and Revolution* (1983); Leonard W. Levy, *Origins of the Fifth Amendment* (1986).

xxxvii Once again, any extended account of the roots of our legal system is beyond the scope of this article. For a useful general description, see Berman, supra note 36, at 49-84.

xxxviii See Joshua D. Rosenberg, *Court Studies Confirm That Mandatory Mediation Works*, Nat'l L.J., Apr. 11, 1994, at C7.

Chapter 22

MICHAEL MALICE
Why I Won't Vote This Year—Or Any Year (2014)

Michael Malice is the author of Dear Reader: the Unauthorized Autobiography of Kim Jong Il *and* The New Right. *He is also the organizer of the forthcoming* The Anarchist Handbook, *currently scheduled for release sometime last year. Malice is notorious for writing about himself in such a way as to confuse and annoy the reader, for no discernable purpose whatsoever.*

I rarely tell people that I don't believe in voting. Participation in the body politic is widely considered to be both a privilege and an imperative to the enlightened urban citizen. To choose otherwise is quite literally heresy—and heretics by and large have a difficult time of it in society.

The platitudes I face as a non-voter are known to everyone, precisely because they are platitudes—*People have marched for miles!* or *Immigrants crossed oceans!* The fables are beautiful and they are compelling. But that does not make them true.

I do not agree that secretly flicking a switch once a year constitutes "making your voice heard." Nor do I think that an annual trip to a voting booth is a criterion for whether one can complain or not. My right to free speech is not contingent upon anyone else, no matter how many of them there are, whether they were elected to some office or however much they stamp their feet.

Neither do I agree that the personal is the political. I fully reject the Kantian universalizability principle that underlies so much of contemporary moral discussion. *What if everyone acted the way you did?* is not a useful means-test for one's actions.

I am a pure liberal. I choose to live in Brooklyn, and am very consciously grateful that my friends are as diverse as humanly possible. None of them think like me, none of them act like me and none of them have the background that I do. This is a source of great pleasure, and I wouldn't change it for the world. Nor could I! I'm not egotistical enough to think that "everyone will act like I do," as if those around me were my mirror images.

It is undeniably true that I don't have the practical ability to ignore the state. I have to use state roads, and if I refuse to pay taxes the consequences will be dire for me. But there is literally nowhere on Earth for me to go without some government claiming control over my person. Though democracies are increasingly common throughout the world, it is the state that is universal. These governments will continue to act regardless of any sort of popular approval—and certainly regardless of any approval of mine.

State action proceeds *independently* of any democratic justification. The purest example of this could be seen during the 2012 Democratic Convention. Los Angeles mayor Antonio Villaraigosa sought to amend the party platform to include a reference to God and to acknowledge Jerusalem as Israel's capital. He put the edit to the convention floor, seeking to approve the change via acclamation. Having failed to receive the outcome he sought, he asked for a revote. Then he tried again. Finally, he simply pretended that those in the audience—unanimously Democrats and democrats—had agreed with him.

George W. Bush did the same thing when he sought United Nations authority to invade Iraq in 2003. Having seen that the votes were not there, he simply grounded his invasion in earlier resolutions.

A party platform is a minor matter. War—solely government's purview—is far more serious. Yet in both cases the vote was a formality; an ex-post-facto justification for an organization to do whatever it intended to do anyway.

I am not someone who thinks that he is "making a difference" by voting once a year. I was born in the Soviet Union and my personal history led me to devote the last two years of my life educating the public about the horrors of north Korea. I constantly give talks about the situation in that least-free nation...where everyone votes. I'm actually doing the work, rather than choosing a (public) servant to do it for me.

Understanding the Soviet Union and north Korea gives a bit of insight into human social psychology. No matter how absurd the state line, a huge majority of the populace can be found to promulgate it. People will say with a straight face that having one choice for dear leader is tyranny—but having two is freedom. Is that second choice on the ballot *really* the qualitative difference?

Most progressives understand that human nature is basically the same anywhere on the planet. Yet they think those who rehash propaganda only exist in other, bad countries. Barring that, they believe those types are all to be found on the other side of the political spectrum. After all, the other side is where the evil, crazy people reside—those who want what's worst for everyone.

The educated aren't immune from such traps; they are merely more articulate about them. Frankly I am baffled that those of us who were nerds in high school now defer to the winners of popularity contests. There surely is a bit of the guard-dog psychology about the whole thing, barking loudly to defend the system in order to get the masters' respect and approval.

If pressed, the simplest explanation I have for refusing to vote is this: I don't vote for the same exact reasons that I don't take communion. No matter how admirable he is or how much I agree with him, the pope isn't the steward over my soul. Nor is any president the leader of my life. This does not make me ignorant or evil any more than not being a Christian makes me ignorant or evil. If I need representation, I will hire the most qualified person to do so.

Otherwise, I will smile and nod as my friends go to their places of worship, wishing them well while I simply pray to be left alone.

ABOUT THE AUTHOR

Michael Malice is the author of *Dear Reader: The Unauthorized Autobiography of Kim Jong Il* and *The New Right: A Journey to the Fringe of American Politics*, and coauthor of two *New York Times* best sellers. He is also the subject of the graphic novel *Ego & Hubris*, written by the late Harvey Pekar of American Splendor fame. He is the host of "YOUR WELCOME" with Michael Malice. Malice lives in Brooklyn for some increasingly unclear reason.

Made in the USA
Las Vegas, NV
25 June 2021